Managing Emotions
in Mergers and Acquisitions

NEW HORIZONS IN MANAGEMENT

Series Editor: Cary L. Cooper, *CBE Professor of Organizational Psychology and Health, Lancaster University Management School, Lancaster University, UK*

This important series makes a significant contribution to the development of management thought. This field has expanded dramatically in recent years and the series provides an invaluable forum for the publication of high quality work in management science, human resource management, organisational behaviour, marketing, management information systems, operations management, business ethics, strategic management and international management.

The main emphasis of the series is on the development and application of new original ideas. International in its approach, it will include some of the best theoretical and empirical work from both well-established researchers and the new generation of scholars.

Titles in the series include:

The Handbook of Human Resource Management Policies and Practices in Asia-Pacific Economies
Volume One
Michael Zanko

The Handbook of Human Resource Management Policies and Practices in Asia-Pacific Economies
Volume Two
Michael Zanko and Matt Ngui

Human Nature and Organization Theory
On the Economic Approach to Institutional Organization
Sigmund Wagner-Tsukamoto

Organizational Relationships in the Networking Age
The Dynamics of Identity Formation and Bonding
Edited by Willem Koot, Peter Leisink and Paul Verweel

Islamic Perspectives on Management and Organization
Abbas J. Ali

Supporting Women's Career Advancement
Challenges and Opportunities
Edited by Ronald J. Burke and Mary C. Mattis

Research Companion to Organizational Health Psychology
Edited by Alexander-Stamatios G. Antoniou and Cary L. Cooper

Innovation and Knowledge Management
The Cancer Information Service Research Consortium
J. David Johnson

Managing Emotions in Mergers and Acquisitions

Verena Kusstatscher

Formerly Lecturer at UMIST Manchester School of Management, UK and now consultant to organizations on M&A issues

Cary L. Cooper, CBE

Professor of Organizational Psychology and Health, Lancaster University Management School, Lancaster University, UK

NEW HORIZONS IN MANAGEMENT

Edward Elgar
Cheltenham, UK • Northampton, MA, USA

Published by
Edward Elgar Publishing Limited
Glensanda House
Montpellier Parade
Cheltenham
Glos GL50 1UA
UK

Edward Elgar Publishing, Inc.
136 West Street
Suite 202
Northampton
Massachusetts 01060
USA

A catalogue record for this book
is available from the British Library

ISBN 1 84542 081 0

Printed and bound in Great Britain by MPG Books Ltd, Bodmin, Cornwall

Contents

Figures and tables

Acknowledgments

The curiosity to comprehend people and their emotions was the driving force for this book. The desire to make organizational changes more pleasant and successful experiences brought the inspiration. And the vision to bring people together made this book happen.

Many people have helped me to grow during this period. I would like to thank all of them, but particularly those who have contributed to the development of this book, and first of all my co-author Cary, without whose enthusiasm and initiative you would not hold this book in your hands. He is one of the greatest motivators I have ever met.

My gratitude goes to Professor Hans Mühlbacher for his inspiring leadership during my time at Innsbruck University. Many of his astute questions and critical remarks contributed to this book. There are several people I acknowledge for stimulating and thought-provoking discussions, in particular my partner Rudolf Sinkovics, my friends Wolfgang Rigger and Dr Mo Yamin, Professor Pervez Ghauri and Professor Sue Cartwright. They all are embedded in this book in some shape or form.

Valuable time and support were received from the interview partners of Leitner, Schwarzkopf, Sportler and Zumtobel Staff who kindly shared their knowledge and M&A experiences. The learnings from these discussions were eye-opening and greatly appreciated. I hope that readers of this book benefit from them and are even better at leading and dealing with mergers and acquisitions in the future.

Many thanks go also to my supportive friends, and all my love to Rudolf, my parents Maria and Sepp, and Elisabeth and Iris for their emotional backing and for always believing in me.

Verena Kusstatscher

Professor Cooper would also like to thank Professor Sue Cartwright for stimulating his work in the field of mergers and acquisitions.

Manchester, November 2004

1. Introduction

1.1 WHY A BOOK ABOUT EMOTIONS IN MERGERS AND ACQUISITIONS IS NEEDED

Emotions play a crucial role in everybody's life. They are always present, they enrich experiences, challenge and make us feel alive. Over the last few decades, emotions have been studied in different disciplines. Psychologists, sociologists, anthropologists, philosophers, brain researchers, neurobiologists and neurophysiologists approached this subject from diverse perspectives and agreed that emotions strongly influence human thinking and acting.

While mainstream management literature is still on a 'rational' track that disregards emotions, some recent developments recognize the importance of addressing emotions in organizations. The same is true for merger and acquisition (M&A) literature. Day-to-day perceptions confirm that mergers and acquisitions are highly emotional life events for all those affected. But only after years of 'merger mania', combined with high failure rates (about 70 per cent of all mergers fail to reach their initial goals), has the importance of focusing on 'soft' issues been acknowledged. Nevertheless, even within the people-oriented stream of M&A literature, emotions as such are still underresearched. Emotions are mentioned in the context of the so-called 'merger syndrome', but they are almost never studied explicitly.

1.1.1 Why Should Managers Learn about Emotions?

Considering the high M&A failure rates, which are often combined with personal human tragedies, managers have to ask themselves: what can leaders do to make a merger or an acquisition a more successful and a more pleasant experience for all those affected? The present book was inspired by this highly relevant question, which has only received limited attention in current M&A literature.

1.1.2 Some Critical Questions which will be Addressed in this Book

Before providing an answer to the question how to manage emotions in order to integrate successfully two or more organizations, some other questions have to be answered:

- Why do mergers fail so often to reach their strategic and financial goals?
- Why are changes related to mergers and acquisitions such emotionally challenging events?
- What are emotions, actually?
- Which kinds of emotions are experienced in post-merger integration stages?
- How to deal with them?
- How does managerial behaviour and communication influence emotions of employees?
- Why do employees' emotions count? What impact can employees' emotions have on M&A outcomes?
- Do positive or negative emotions contribute more to an efficient and successful merger process? Can consciously 'installed' negative emotions, such as fears and feelings of uncertainty and stress, make M&As more efficient?
- Why not just ignore emotions, and behave like 'rational' grown-ups?

These and many similar questions will be answered in this book.

1.2 M&As AND MANAGEMENT CHALLENGES

Mergers and acquisitions (M&As) have dominated business headlines and the world economic scene for more than two decades (Buono *et al.*, 2002). There were five major waves of mergers and acquisitions in the 21st century (Buckley and Ghauri, 2002). The last wave began at the end of the 1990s and experienced its peak with a transaction volume of almost US$3.5 trillion worldwide in 2000. While the merger wave declined in recent years, it seems to have risen again since 2003 (ThomsonFinancial, 2004).

Strictly speaking, only a very small number of all so-called 'mergers and acquisitions' are real mergers according to the definition of 'merger' and 'acquisition'. An acquisition is usually known as the purchase of more than 50 per cent of an existing target company's stock capital, or as the complete takeover of a factory or department which is legally dependent on another company (Gerpott, 1993), while a merger is understood as a complete union or amalgamation of two or more companies in order to become a managerially interwoven, economical and legal unity (Gabler-Verlag, 1993). Therefore, even if the two partners are considered to be equal, in reality most of the cases are an acquisition in which one organization takes over the control of the other (Buckley and Ghauri, 2002; Buono *et al.*, 2002; UNCTAD, 2000). In fact, fewer than 3 per cent of cross-border mergers and acquisitions by number are mergers. Nevertheless the literature as well as colloquial language use the term 'merger' or 'M&A' to refer to what is actually an acquisition (Buckley and Ghauri, 2002). This custom is also followed in the present book.

M&As often became a high-risk form of business activity involving the collective annual financial investment and influencing the working lives of millions of employees. Most executives justify their decision to merge with economic considerations (Ivancevich *et al.*, 1987; Jansen, 2001; Marks, 1988; Oehlrich, 1999). However, in the long term it is suggested that between 50 and 80 per cent of all mergers are financially 'unsuccessful' or at least show no significant increase in terms of financial return (Buono *et al.*, 2002; Cooper and Gregory, 2003; FAZ, 2000; Marks, 1988; Wirtschaftswoche, 2002).[1] Between one-third and one half of all M&As fail owing to underestimated human factors (Cartwright and Cooper, 1993a, 2000; Dannemiller Tyson, 2000; Davy *et al.*, 1989). The literature since the late 1980s has suggested that human aspects should be considered of equal, if not of greater, importance in mergers and acquisitions, especially if the statement, 'Financial synergy is dependent upon "people synergy"' (Cartwright and Cooper 1990, p. 68) is taken seriously. But decision makers and managers still seem largely to overlook this fact. In other words, the reasons for failure often do not lie in the hard factors but in the forgotten soft factors. Managers' attitude that they are not able to manage those soft factors, the absence of simple models to apply, or simply managers' belief that human factors are not crucial for a successful M&A, lead to a neglect of essential soft factors (Schuler and Jackson, 2001).

An increasing amount of literature recognizes that steps undertaken in the pre-merger stage have a big influence on the success of the post-merger phase (Appelbaum *et al.*, 2000a, 2000b; Cartwright and Cooper, 2000; Jansen, 2001). This book, however, does not emphasize the pre-merger planning in general. It rather focuses on the conscious designing of communication and integration processes in order to approach and involve a critical mass of employees who accept the M&A decision, support the implementation and make its success possible. Just the awareness of employees' emotions, a sound knowledge of how emotions emerge and of their potential consequences for the M&A implementation can help managers to prepare individuals in leading functions to better manage the post-merger integration process.

1.3   M&As AND RESEARCH CHALLENGES

In academic as well as managerial discussions, financial, legal and strategic factors are strongly emphasized. Most M&A studies measure success in economic terms only, and therefore the greater part of literature does not even mention human factors. Most research studies and the majority of M&A decision makers follow this track. Their decisions are thus overtly motivated, evaluated and justified by economic aspects, ignoring culture and people-related issues (Ivancevich *et al.*, 1987; Marks, 1988).

For a long time the rather small amount of published psychological/behavioural research on mergers and acquisitions was widely criticized for being fragmented and limited whereas M&A reality was supposed to be a complex phenomenon. This literature was also criticized for having 'contributed little of substance to the acquisition debate' (for example, Buono *et al.*, 1985; Hunt, 1988). However it has to be pointed out that, after decades of forgotten human factors in M&As, the importance of soft factors seems to be increasingly recognized. This trend started in the late 1980s and is reflected by a rising number of studies since 1990 concerning the human factor in mergers and acquisitions. These studies typically focus on issues such as the compatibility of organizational cultures, employee expectations, the impact of uncertainty and stress on job satisfaction, psychological contract, motivation, commitment and loyalty, unproductive behaviour, absenteeism rates, lower morale and acts of sabotage (for example, Bruckman and Peters, 1987; Buono and Bowditch, 1989a; Buono *et al.*, 2002; Cartwright and Cooper, 1990, 1993b; Cooper and Finkelstein, 2004; Hall and Norburn, 1987; Hubbard and Purcell, 2001; Jemison and Sitkin, 1986; Schuler and Jackson, 2001; Siu *et al.*, 1997; Werner, 1999).

For many psychologists, sociologists, neurobiologists and brain researchers alike, it seems to be evident that emotions play an important role in human thinking and acting (for example, Ciompi, 1999; Elster, 1999; Frijda, 1986; LeDoux, 1998; Martin, 1998). Over the last few years, general management literature has also shown increasing interest in emotions.

Over the previous 60 to 70 years research of affects at the workplace had not progressed significantly. While progress had been rather slow and episodic over all those years, development seems to have been more rapid recently. 'Objectively, emotions matter because many forms of human behaviour would be unintelligible if we did not see them through the prism of emotion': with these words Elster (1999, p. 404) makes a claim for every-one in management to study emotions. Indeed, organizations are increasingly considered to be 'emotional arenas' (Fineman, 2000), and emotions develop into a kind of a subdiscipline in the study of work and organizations. An increasing movement towards a more 'passionate' management is discernible now (Krell and Weiskopf, 2001). Applied psychologists are increasingly studying the relations between emotions and motivation (Pinder, 1998), the consequences of affect and mood at work (for example, Bartel and Saavedra, 2000; Herriot, 2001; Weiss *et al.*, 1999) and emotional contagion: the 'catching' and passing on of emotions (Doherty, 1998; Verbeke, 1997). More popular management literature comes up with 'emotionalized' issues such as workplace envy, intimacy, sexual harassment and stress (Fineman, 2000). One of the most fashionable topics among organizational consultants and psychologist is 'emotional intelligence' (Abraham, 1999; Goleman, 1995; Goleman *et al.*, 2002b). Emotionally intelligent individuals are supposed to be better and more successful leaders. As emotional intelligence is believed to be a skill one can learn, for a few years now, management training has been mushrooming in the USA and in Europe. Another area of concern in the organizational context is the emotional–aesthetic experience (Wasserman *et al.*, 2000). People are influenced by the places and objects around their work place. Machines, office layouts, colours, noise, music, task activities, food and so on are sources of emotional experiences because they trigger – through all senses – 'feelings of "rightness", discord, warmth, harshness or alienation' (Fineman, 2000). Major management symposia, conferences, publications and web-based discussions are now incorporating emotions in their programmes. On bookshelves we find titles such as: 'Emotions in the Workplace' (Kluger and Rafaeli, 2000), 'Emotional Impact: Passionate Leaders and Corporate Transformation' (Channer and Hope, 2001), 'The Emotionally Intelligent Workplace' (Cherniss and Goleman, 2001), 'Applying Emotional Intelligence in the Workplace' (Cooper, 1997), 'Emotion in Organizations' (Fineman, 2000), 'Primal Leadership: Realizing the Power of Emotional Intelligence' (Goleman *et al.*, 2002b), 'Emotions at Work' (Herriot, 2001) and many more.

Though several disciplines, including recent management literature, consider emotions a crucial factor in human behaviour, it comes as a surprise that the M&A literature is still largely neglecting these issues. Only a few recently published studies incorporate emotions (Fugate *et al.*, 2002; Kiefer, 2002b). This is in sharp contrast to day-to-day perceptions and to reports which recognize that mergers and acquisitions elicit deep emotions such as irritation, anger, aggression, frustration or anxieties about losing career opportunities or even one's job. Negative M&A-related

emotions and desperation may sometimes even lead to suicides (Buono and Bowditch, 1989a).

Some managers intuitively know how to cope with such emotions of employees. Others do not either because they do not know how they could positively influence employees' emotions or because they are completely unaware of others' emotions. The impact of various styles of managerial communication and behaviour on employees' emotions during the M&A process is still unclear. Cognitive appraisal theorists assert that the central nervous system of individuals needs to be exposed to internal stimuli (that is, thoughts) and/or external stimuli (someone else's statements or behaviour) in order to evaluate those stimuli. Depending on the relevance, urgency or danger of the stimulus for the individual, the brain is more or less activated. This leads to a physiological state, called 'emotion', which is linked to a certain readiness to act. We deduce that employees' perception of managerial communication and behaviour constitutes a stimulus for employees. Therefore we suggest that managerial stimuli will have an influence on emotions of employees and on their disposition to react and contribute during phases of major organizational changes. Consequently it is imperative for managers to realize how their words and behaviour will have an impact on co-workers' emotions and employees' 'natural' way to react. With this awareness it will be easier to guide communication and integration processes towards success for all parties.

Against this background, which is determined by (a) the fact that mergers and acquisitions are highly emotional events for all those affected, (b) the suggestion from several disciplines that emotions are a crucial factor in human behaviour, (c) rather low levels of awareness regarding the role of emotions in organizations in general, and (d) an unconsolidated literature base on emotions in M&As, it is considered important to provide updated theoretical and empirical insights.

1.4   OBJECTIVES AND CONTRIBUTION

The work we have carried out focuses on employees' emotions after the announcement of the upcoming organizational changes; that is, in the post-M&A phase. Some statements regarding the 'merger syndrome' (for example, Appelbaum et al., 2000b; Marks and Mirvis, 1997b) assume that managers' behaviour and communication styles in the post-merger integration process might have an influence on employees' emotions. Therefore the intention is to examine theoretically and empirically the connections between employees' emotions, managerial behaviour and communication styles, and M&A outcomes.

Specifically the objectives and the contribution of the present book are as follows:

1. to create awareness of emotions in mergers and acquisitions;
2. to introduce emotions in M&A literature by providing a comprehensive conceptual framework that is able to explain the connections between management of emotions and M&A success;
3. to present 'toolkits' for emotions measurement in M&As which can guide managerial decision making;
4. to analyse four different M&A cases and to draw conclusions regarding which managerial behaviour and communication style triggers which kinds of emotions in employees;
5. to describe which effects these employee emotions have on certain M&A outcomes.

1.5 ORGANIZATION OF THE STUDY

In order to achieve the objectives mentioned above, the work will start with a conceptual background which helps to promote a broader understanding of current literature in the field and which ends with the development of a conceptual framework. Part I presents the empirical project with its result, followed by a discussion of the findings.

Part I provides the conceptual background on M&As and emotions (Chapters 2–4). It starts with a literature review regarding merger and acquisition processes (Chapter 2). After an introduction to the phenomenon of M&As and its crucial soft factors, the 'merger syndrome' is analysed.

The emotional turmoil of post-merger integration, mentioned in the context of the merger syndrome, stems largely from the fact that members of the merging organizations have to cope with a change of their social identities. Social identity theory helps to explain group formation processes and group identities, as well as emotions felt towards the own group (ingroup) and other groups (outgroups). Since mergers and acquisitions are highly emotional processes of group formation and changing group identities, social identity theory will be used as background for a deeper understanding of merger integrations and the role of emotions in the context of social identities. This will be the content of Chapter 3.

Chapter 4 deals with emotions in post-merger integration. The first section, on theoretical bases, defines emotions and describes how they emerge. Different perspectives on emotions will be presented by discussing their relation to rationality and by giving an overview of current emotion theories. In this context, cognitive appraisal theory of emotion will be adopted as the theoretical background for the present work. The following section analyses current M&A literature with respect to emotions. Based on cognitive appraisal theory of emotions, section 4.3 views managerial communication and behaviours in M&As as causes of employees' emotions. Section 4.4 relies on social identity theory and explains some specific M&A outcomes as a function of emotions. As a result of the literature review, a conceptual framework of the role of emotions in the M&A process will be developed in section 4.5.

Part II of the work is devoted to empirical M&A case studies. Chapters 5 and 6 present the goals, procedures, methods and the sampling frame. The findings of the qualitative study are presented in Chapters 7 to 10.

Part III of the book discusses the findings of the empirical study and its limitations. It concludes with implications for future research and for management.

NOTE

1. In these sources 'success' is always understood as the non-achievement of the initially intended M&A objectives, thus the term 'success' usually refers to financial aims.

PART I

Understanding M&As and emotions

2. The M&A process

In this chapter the M&A process will be presented to the reader. It seems appropriate to first explain the merger phenomenon, its motives, reasons for failure, and to describe the stages in the M&A process (section 2.1). After having pointed out that the often forgotten 'soft factors' are actually the 'tough' ones which are crucial for merger success (section 2.2), the merger syndrome will be discussed by analysing its causes, typical emotions and its consequences (section 2.3).

2.1 THE MERGER PHENOMENON

2.1.1 Merger Mania or Mergers in Decline?

The term 'merger mania' has dominated business headlines for a couple of years. One can hardly pick up a newspaper without reading of a proposed bid or the announcement of a takeover or merger. Indeed over the last decade, the level of M&A activities has increased substantially in size and in frequency. Mergers and acquisitions have also increasingly stimulated scientific publications over the last two decades.

However the merger phenomenon is not a new one. The 20th century was characterized by five major merger waves: at the turn of the century (1898–1902) the first merger wave witnessed an increase in horizontal mergers and gave rise to many American industrial groups. The second wave, between 1926 and 1939, affected mainly public utility companies. In the third merger wave (1966–9) 'diversification' was the main driving force for company mergers, while the fourth wave (1983–6) tried to reverse this earlier focus and propagate rationalization and efficiency instead. The fifth and biggest merger wave started around 1997 and continued until the early years of the 21st century. This fifth merger wave had 'globalization' as its motto and largely involved companies from continental Europe. The years 1997 to 2000 were all record years regarding the sums involved in mergers worldwide. In 1998, the sum doubled with respect to the preceding year, reaching US$2.1 trillion worldwide. In 1999, the US$3.3 trillion mark was exceeded, and in the peak year, 2000, a total of almost US$3.5 trillion was reached. Since 2001 this most recent merger wave has diminished

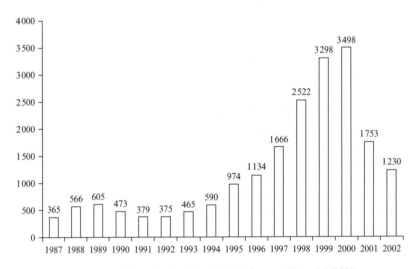

Source: Mergers&Acquisitions (2003), Picot (2002), ThomsonFinancial (2002).

Figure 2.1   Merger wave: transaction volumes worldwide, in billions US$

(see Buckley and Ghauri, 2002; Buono *et al.*, 2002; Wirtschaftspolitik, 2000), but a new increase has been noticeable since spring 2004. Figure 2.1 indicates the transaction volumes (in billions US$) involved in M&A activities worldwide since 1987. The recent merger wave is clearly visible.

2.1.2   Types of Mergers and Acquisitions

Mergers and acquisitions are often classified into four main types, depending on the extent to which the business activities of the acquired company are related to those of the acquirer: horizontal, vertical, conglomerate and concentric (Cartwright and Cooper, 1996; Nahavandi and Malekzadeh, 1993; Walter, 1985):

- *Horizontal* or *related* mergers and acquisitions combine two similar companies in a related line of business in the same industry. This can be the case of a merger between direct competitors.
- *Vertical* mergers and acquisitions unite firms from successive processes within the same industry. They refer to organizations in a supplier–customer relationship.
- *Conglomerate* mergers and acquisitions occur between companies in completely unrelated business fields. They are often a consequence of diversification strategies.

- *Concentric* mergers and acquisitions combine organizations from different but related industries. This often happens when an acquirer tries to expand into other fields of business activity.

2.1.3 Why Companies Merge and why they often Fail

Motivation for M&As

There are several motives for companies to consider a merger or an acquisition. The reasons mentioned most frequently are synergy effects or economies of scale and scope. It is widely assumed that such synergy effects would guarantee survival in an increasingly complex and dynamic environment with rising pressure from stronger competition. The unification of companies allows for centralization and rationalization of activities which lead to a better use of common resources (in production, administration, sales and so on), to cost cuttings (for example, lower purchase prices due to increased quantities) and to time saving (Buono *et al.*, 2002; Gerpott, 1993; Witt, 1998).

Other motives for M&A activities are based on managerial strategies such as the objective of product diversification, of gaining access to each other's technology or market reach and thus increasing the market share. The achievement of a dominant position in the industry and the power to manipulate the rules of competition and antitrust are also frequent reasons for M&As. Value creation for both companies (either through cost cutting or through added value due to increased scope) is a further M&A justification which is often mentioned, especially by the acquiring firm. For the selling (or acquired) company the main reasons are financial problems or succession problems (Buono *et al.*, 2002; Gerpott, 1993; Jansen, 2001; Oehlrich, 1999).

Also 'external' factors can lead to 'merger mania': market conditions that offer more companies for sale, easing regulations, increasing availability of capital, the possibility to create a monopoly or to get tax relief, the need to share risk, the existence of complex inseparable problems and increased specialization (Cartwright and Cooper, 1990; Jansen, 2001; Oehlrich, 1999).

But there are also more tacit and widely unrecognized reasons which can be put down to psychological motives. The hidden fear of obsolescence, personal interests of shareholders to maximize the value of the company (shareholder value) and management prestige, such as increasing market share and restoring market confidence, are typical examples. Furthermore bored CEOs might be looking for 'some excitement' or for the satisfaction of 'personal whims'. Egoistical needs of powerful individuals to gain collective influence, or simply the urge to follow the current fashion of empire building are additional motives which can be found in literature (Cartwright and Cooper, 1990; 2000; Cooper and Finkelstein, 2004; Halpern and Weston, 1983; Hunt, 1988; McKinsey & Associates, 1988; Napier, 1989; Rhoades, 1983).

Frequent reasons for failure
The motivations for mergers and acquisitions are manifold but many end in financial disappointment. Most M&A decisions are overtly motivated, evaluated and justified by economic considerations (Ivancevich *et al.*, 1987; Jansen, 2001; Marks, 1988; Oehlrich, 1999). Interestingly enough, precisely these goals often are the ones that cannot be reached after the merger. Existing data about merger failure rates significantly diverge from each other,[1] but there is a recognizable trend that suggests that between 50 and 80 per cent of all mergers are financially 'unsuccessful' or at least show no significant increase in terms of financial return (Buono *et al.*, 2002; Jansen and Körner, 2000; Marks, 1988; Wirtschaftswoche, 2002). In the literature the term 'success' usually refers to financial aims and the achievement is typically measured in *turnover* in relation to pre-merger times, *share price fluctuations, profit-earning ratios* or *productivity*. However the intended synergy effect is often not achieved (Appelbaum *et al.*, 2000b; Cartwright and Cooper, 1993a).

There are several assumed reasons why so many M&As fail. Under-privileged due-diligence analyses, poor selection decisions (for example, an overestimated purchase price paid), lack of pre-planning, strategic and financial mismatch or incompetence, and unpredicted changes in market conditions are only a few of the well researched merger failures related to financial and marketing issues (Cartwright and Cooper, 1990; Fairburn and Geroski, 1989; Hughes and Wolff, 1987; Rockness *et al.*, 2001).

In theory and practice, however, financial factors seem to be emphasized too heavily, and success is measured too often in financial terms only. Although human factors are supposed to be responsible for between one-third and one-half of all merger failures (Cartwright and Cooper, 1990; Dannemiller Tyson, 2000; Davy *et al.*, 1989) it is surprising that the soft factors in M&As have attracted attention only since the late 1980s. Frequently cited reasons for merger failure are poor communications, the lack of any human merger plan, absence of emotional intelligent leadership and thus an ad hoc reactive approach to human problems (Cartwright and Cooper, 1990; Fox *et al.*, 2001; Huy, 1999; Jansen and Pohlmann, 2000; Kiefer and Eicken, 2002; Kluger and Rafaeli, 2000). In these cases 'merger success' is measured in terms of *behavioural indices* like employee stress, organizational commitment and morale, job satisfaction, mental and physical well-being, sickness absence or fluctuation rates. Usually these measurable indices consist in a pre- and post-merger comparison (for example, Cartwright and Cooper, 1993a).

2.1.4 Stages in the M&A Process

The merger process can be divided into several stages. The most common classification is the categorization in 'pre-merger' (planning), 'during-the-merger' (realization) and 'post-merger (integration)' stages (Appelbaum *et al.*, 2000a, 2000b; Cartwright and Cooper, 2000; Jansen and Pohlmann, 2000; Picot, 2002).

Pre-merger stage

The pre-merger stage consists of an extensive decision-making, planning and positioning process. The decision to acquire or to merge is typically made by a few executives only, or sometimes even by a single chairman or CEO. After the decision on principle, the first step is the screening of potential targets and the drawing up of a 'hit list' of identified potential candidates, which generally comprises a maximum of five companies. The two most important criteria of selection mentioned in the literature are (a) projected earning potential and (b) strategic fit in terms of products, markets, geographical location and so on (Cartwright and Cooper, 1990; Hunt, 1988; Picot, 2002). This implies that the decision to merge is based on economic and financial considerations while the 'true' psychological reasons are often masked.

During the so called 'due-diligence process' the target is investigated in more detail, with particular emphasis on its legal and financial health and the potential strategic match. This process is highly confidential and is carried by a selected team of accountants and lawyers (Appelbaum *et al.*, 2000a, 2000b; Picot, 2002).

First impressions on the culture of the acquisition target may come up, but they are unlikely to influence the buying decision. As the companies have already invested much time and money they tend to be unwilling to pull out of a potential deal. The stage is characterized by bidding and nego-tiations between buyer and seller and, 'because the negotiation phrase is almost exclusively about bargaining, the rationale and logic of the decision to buy is never likely to be called into question' (Cartwright and Cooper, 2000, p. 10). There are of course some exceptions, with the decision to abandon the proposed merger or acquisition even after several months of negotiation, but such examples are rare.

In many cases rumours start to spread abroad in this stage of the merger and certain signs in the company indicate the changes on the horizon. For instance, the decision to 'freeze' recruitment, to run down stocks or to suspend training programmes makes people suspicious. Usually this is a very exhausting period for managers. Having completed the deal they therefore often lack the energies which are actually especially needed for the subsequent integration process (Cartwright and Cooper, 1996; Searby, 1969).

During-the-merger phase
The activities around the signing of the contracts and the official announcement are defined as the 'during-the-merger' stage: the top managers of both companies come together and negotiate the last details before signing the contracts; redundancies are defined and the merger's proclamation planned; the announcement has to be prepared thoroughly by answering questions such as who is going to announce the M&A, when, where and in which form it should take place. Finally the official (written or oral) announcement of the merger or acquisition falls within this stage (Buono *et al.*, 2002).

Post-merger phase
It is commonly accepted that the steps undertaken in the pre-merger stage have a big influence on the success of the post-merger integration phase. However, in the end, it is the integration phase that is responsible for the success or failure of the merger (Appelbaum *et al.* 2000a, 2000b; Cartwright and Cooper, 2000; Jansen, 2001).

The core assignment of the post-merger stage is the integration of the strategic capabilities of the two companies in order to realize the potential synergies and to create the expected value added. Therefore a certain atmosphere has to be generated that allows the transfer of resources and skills. Managers of different hierarchical levels have to interact with colleagues from the partner organization. The intention is to coordinate, adapt, change, reorganize and to set up common structures and processes in the different business areas (Haspeslagh and Jemison, 1991; Jansen, 2001; Picot, 2002).

Effective communication and interaction between the merging partners is an indispensable component for the creation of an atmosphere that allows for the transfer of capabilities. This transfer and integration of capabilities will only be successful under the conditions that both partners demonstrate some understanding and respect for each other's organizational structures, processes and corporate culture. Furthermore the willingness to cooperate and the availability of financial and non-financial resources are crucial to enabling integration success. This explains why managerial behaviour is crucial after the signing of the contract (Haspeslagh and Jemison, 1991).

Merger integration can happen on different levels (Jansen, 2001): the integration of two companies on a *strategic level* means coordinating their strategies, their visions, the business units and their management orientations. On the *administrative level*, common planning and control processes have to be defined, accountancy and information technologies have to get harmonized and interfaces have to be welded together. On the *operative level*, the two partners have to come to an agreement regarding their future product lines and technologies, their research projects, the geographical location of the production sites, cost-cutting options and synergy potentials. The different stakeholders' needs have to be discussed and taken into consideration on a so-called 'external integration' level. Personnel integration has to be achieved in terms of harmonization of management styles, incentives and remunerations, personnel development, conflict management, socialization, communication and decision-making structures and processes. Similar to personnel integration, cultural integration is an often forgotten but crucial factor in the integration of two companies. Cultural integration means solving the question of how far corporate cultures should be maintained or assimilated, according to which norms and values the merged organization should live and work, and which messages should be transmitted to the environment (through its corporate design, for instance). The present study focuses on these last two forms of integration, personnel and cultural integration because, as we have said, the human factor is thought to be one of the most important factors in determining success or failure of a merger or an acquisition (see, for example, Cartwright and Cooper, 1995).

2.2 THE 'TOUGH' 'SOFT FACTORS' OF MERGERS AND ACQUISITIONS

The first subsection below reviews current M&A literature with respect to people issues. Since cultural integration is one of the biggest soft factor issues discussed in the context of mergers and acquisitions, subsection 2.2.2 will address the topics of cultural compatibility and cultural integration.

2.2.1 People: the Forgotten Factor in M&As?

Although human factors have not received appropriate attention in the M&A literature for a long time, their importance has been increasingly recognized in recent years. It appears to be common knowledge that mergers and acquisitions often fail to reach the intended financial goals because of underestimated human factors. It is suggested that 'employee problems' are responsible for between one-third and one-half of all merger failures (Dannemiller Tyson, 2000; Davy *et al.*, 1989). This does not come as a surprise when considering that between 50 and 75 per cent of key managers voluntarily leave acquired companies within the first two or three years post-acquisition, and considering that the employee turnover rates are around 60 per cent. Even in friendly and (financially) successful takeovers, this extremely stressful experience is considered to have negative residual effects on employees' psychological health (Cartwright and Cooper, 2000).

The two recent merger waves are considerably different from the previous ones in terms of size, geographical spread and nature: while most of the M&As at the end of the 1960s were of the conglomerate type, now, in the last two waves of M&A activity, companies mostly merge with firms of the same kind of business (horizontal or related type). The tendency of an acquiring organization to change completely the acquired company is less strong when the two firms work in unrelated businesses. The consequences of conglomerate M&As thus remain mainly at the level of senior management and do not really affect employees. In a horizontal or related merger, however, the potential for synergies is larger, redundancies and power games are more frequent and employees are more likely to be affected by the merger or acquisition. As a result, the successful integration of people, their systems, procedures, practices and organizational cultures is more important than ever before (Cartwright and Cooper, 1995). This has become the challenge par excellence for communication and for change management.

It is suggested that good and informative communication between the merging partners is an indispensable component for the creation of an atmosphere of interaction that allows the transfer of capabilities (Haspeslagh and Jemison, 1991). This transfer and thus the use of synergies will only be successful if both partners show some understanding and respect for each other's organizational structures, processes, corporate culture and emotions. The willingness to understand, to cooperate and to create a common and better whole is considered to be as important as the availability of material resources.

Despite increasing awareness of human factors in current studies, according to Buono *et al.* (2002), understanding of the full effects of mergers on organizations and their human resources is still limited because relevant literature is largely pragmatic in nature. These studies are mostly concerned with the question either of how to survive the merger or of how to maintain organizational morale and productivity (Birch, 1983; Sinetar, 1981; Uttal and Fierman, 1983). Current literature including the human factor in mergers and acquisitions focuses on such aspects as organizational culture, whether people's expectations are met or not, the (in)compatibility of the two cultures, uncertainty and stress and their impact on job satisfaction, psychological contract, motivation, commitment and loyalty, unproductive behaviour, absenteeism rates, lower morale and on acts of sabotage (for example, Bruckman and Peters, 1987; Buono and Bowditch, 1989a; Buono *et al.*, 2002; Cartwright and Cooper, 1990, 1993b; Hall and Norburn, 1987; Hubbard and Purcell, 2001; Jemison and Sitkin, 1986; Kiefer, 2002a; Schuler and Jackson, 2001; Siu *et al.*, 1997; Werner, 1999).

Attitudes towards the job and other facets of organizational life, as well as the process through which these perceptions and attitudes are formed, are still less analysed (Buono *et al.*, 2002).

Reviewing the literature of the last two decades reveals that the human factor was often cited as the 'forgotten factor' in mergers and acquisitions. This was certainly true until the 1980s. However, considering the increasing amount of M&A literature that incorporates 'soft factors', it seems that people issues can no longer be neglected. Strategic M&A preparations require thinking about both human and financial aspects (Marks and Mirvis, 1986). In this sense it can be questioned whether it is still appropriate to call the human factor 'the forgotten factor'. Nevertheless the impression remains that people issues are still widely neglected in practice, although the human factors are receiving more and more attention in the M&A literature.[2] Indifference is also reflected in daily media releases which tend to ignore the human factor when reporting mergers or acquisitions.

2.2.2 Culture Compatibility and Cultural Integration

The discussion of cultural compatibility and cultural integration of two companies is only indirectly of interest for the study of emotions in M&As, but, since it is a crucial 'soft' issue and probably the subject of one of the most intense debates in M&A literature concerned with soft factors, it seems appropriate to give an overview. People feel certain emotions towards their own organizational culture and do not readily accept the perspective of changing this identity or adopting another one (see also the discourse regarding social identity theory in the post-merger context in section 3.2). Hence it is worthwhile to give a brief introduction to the field of organizational culture in M&As.

Organizational culture and identity
The notion of organizational culture has raised considerable interest during the last two or three decades and helped to stress the importance of the human factor for organizational success. The term 'organizational

culture' first appeared in managerial discourses under the narrower expression 'corporate culture'. It was seen as playing an important role in organizational processes, leading competitive advantage, influencing performance, knowledge transfer, the internationalization of firms and other outcomes (Irrmann, 2002).

Also M&A literature recognized the impact of organizational cultures on M&A success. Comparing organizational culture with the concept of 'personality', Cartwright and Cooper declared: 'As culture is as fundamental to an organization as personality is to the individual, the degree of culture fit that exists between the combining organizations is likely to be directly correlated to the success of the combination' (Cartwright and Cooper, 1993b, p. 60). Since culture clashes and collision of mentalities are not an exception in post-merger phases, the exploration of organizational cultures, their similarities, their compatibility and the possibilities to integrate them indeed became hot topics in M&A research (Brooks and Dawes, 1999; Buono *et al.*, 1985; Cartwright and Cooper, 1993b, 1996; Cooper and Cartwright, 1996; Gertsen and Søderberg, 1998; Nahavandi and Malekzadeh, 1993; Olie, 1990; Søderberg *et al.*, 1998; Walter, 1985).

Organizational culture has been defined in manifold ways. Most of the definitions consider organizational culture as the complex whole of explicit and implicit patterns which are transmitted by symbols. Examples of explicit patterns or 'objective culture' are visible artefacts and behaviours produced by the organization. This includes architecture and interior design of the building, configuration of the offices, dress codes, established rites and so on. Implicit or 'subjective culture' of an organization is based on common experience and determines what is perceived as 'acceptable'. Subjective culture consists of patterns of knowledge, capabilities, beliefs, assumptions, values, roles, expectation norms, characteristics of perceiving the environment, expected organizational citizenship behaviour, myths, 'language' and similar issues (Buono and Bowditch, 1989b; Hofstede, 1980; Nahavandi and Malekzadeh, 1993; Pettigrew, 1979; Schein, 1983, 1985).

It is remarkable that organizational culture is generally presented as a set of values, norms, roles, assumptions and ideas that are 'homogeneously and unanimously shared by the entire organization (. . .) as if the organization would be a closed, homogeneous and well-defined universe whose super-ordinate culture would dictate attitudes and behaviours to the individuals' (Irrmann, 2002, p. 3). In such a single-culture perspective, organizational culture is seen as something 'pre-existing' and imposed upon employees. Researchers often assume that leaders are the (main) source of organizational culture (for example, Schein, 1983, 1985). This is why followers of this monolithic view of culture tend only to approach top managers when exploring organizational cultures.

However a company does not consist of managers only. Several studies showed that organizational members bring their mentalities and their social background (such as their working-class background) into the company as well (Irrmann, 2002). The background influences people's perception of their own and others' identity (Hochschild, 1983). This explains why there are heterogeneous cultures and identities within one organization,[3] and it is in line with studies related to social identity theory: employees, for instance, tend to identify more with the group of most interaction during periods of important changes than with the company as a whole (Dahler-Larsen, 1997; Hernes, 1997; Kramer, 1991). It is hence more realistic to talk about coexisting subcultures and subidentities and not to refer to a single homogeneous culture when studying organizations (Sackmann, 1992). Since the coexistence of multiculturality is neglected in most of the M&A culture studies, in the following sections the expression 'organizational culture' refers to the culture of the company as a whole.

Types of organizational cultures and culture compatibility

Various researchers have tried to find explanations for the high failure rate of M&As in cultural differences between the two companies (Buono *et al.*, 1985). These studies follow a monolithic approach in general and rely on normative typologies of organizational cultures. Deshpande *et al.* (1993), for example, classify organizational cultures into four categories:

1. *market culture* (emphasis on competitive advantage and market superiority);
2. *clan culture* (emphasis on internal maintenance of commitment, cohesiveness, morale);
3. *hierarchical culture* (with bureaucratic structures, orders and rules);
4. *adhocracy culture* (creative, flexible, innovative, entrepreneurial culture).

Another example of classification stems from Harrison (1972) and is cited in Cartwright and Cooper (1993b). Harrison describes the following four culture types:

1. *power* culture (emphasis on power, individualism, valuing prestige, autocratic government, implicit rules; motivation through personal loyalties and fear of punishment);
2. *role* culture (bureaucratic, hierarchical, impersonal, predictable and efficient culture; emphasis on formal procedures, standardization and written rules which make employees dispensable);
3. *task/achievement* culture (emphasis on team commitment, organizational mission statements, customized products, work structures

according to task requirements; offers employees flexibility, high levels of autonomy, satisfying and creative environments that, however, can be exhausting);

4. *person/support* culture (emphasis on egalitarianism, personal growth and development; typical of communities, cooperative and non-profit organizations).

Scientists claim that culture fit (or cultural similarity) is of equal, if not of greater, importance than 'strategic fit' for a successful M&A integration (Cartwright and Cooper, 1993b). Several researchers have therefore tried to prove that higher cultural similarity would lead to fewer difficulties in the post-merger integration and thus lead to a smoother and better integration (for example, Datta and Puia, 1995).

However, when two cultures collide, they (have to) adjust to each other to a certain extent. This phenomenon is called 'acculturation'. In general, the weaker company, which is usually the acquired company, adapts its own culture more to the culture of the acquirer, which tends to be the stronger firm after the merger (Buono *et al.*, 1985; Nahavandi and Malekzadeh, 1993; Walter, 1985). The extent to which members of an organization are ready to adapt their culture to the culture of the merging partner is known as 'acculturation mode'. The acculturation mode depends on certain factors: on whether company members retain or abandon their own organizational culture, for example, or on how far they adopt or refuse the partner's culture. Nahavandi and Malekzadeh (1988) first proposed the often cited acculturation model that focuses on the adaptation and acculturation in mergers and acquisitions. The model consists of four possible forms of acculturation:

1. *assimilation*: when the partner's culture is perceived as very attractive; high willingness to relinquish one's own, old culture;
2. *integration*: the other's culture is seen as very attractive, but there is no willingness to leave one's own culture;
3. *deculturation/marginalization*: the partner's culture is not attractive, but neither is one's own, and therefore there is willingness to abandon the old culture;
4. *separation*: the other's culture is perceived as unattractive, and there is no willingness to adopt it.

Underlying this model is the assumption that, whenever two companies agree on the preferred method of acculturation for the implementation of an M&A, the integration process will go more smoothly. In contrast, when the two firms do not agree on the acculturation mode this can lead to tension and organizational resistance. Cartwright and Cooper (1993b) examine the importance of the cultural fit and compatibility for the integration of the merging companies. The authors point out that cultural fit and cultural compatibility are different things: 'cultural fit' usually defines a similarity between cultures, while 'compatibility' in the M&A context does not necessarily mean having a similar organizational culture.

Cartwright and Cooper compare M&As with marriages and assume that premarital culture type(s) influence post-merger compatibility. Comparable to a civil marriage, in the organizational 'marriage', success does not only depend on the two personalities. Similar personalities do not necessarily match better than two different but 'compatible' partners. In the same way, a successful integration of two cultures does not imply that the two cultures are similar. The congruence or 'fit' refers to the common preference for a certain acculturation mode to adopt after the M&A. The authors therefore provide an analysis of compatibility in various cultural combinations, relying on Harrison's (1972) culture types (power, role, task/achievement, person/support) and on Nahavandi and Malekzadeh's (1988) acculturation modes mentioned above.

The authors discuss the various combinations of these four types of organizational cultures in an M&A situation where one partner dominates and state that almost all M&A cases fall into the *redesign merger* type, which is comparable to traditional marriages in which one partner is more dominant and considered as superior. The *collaborative merger* type corresponds to modern marriages that aim at win–win situations. The best of both parts is unified in a new organizational culture. This is, however, a very rare form of organizational marriage. *Extension mergers* are a kind of 'open' marriage where each partner accepts the differences of the other's culture without the intention to change it. This almost never happens in practice. Cartwright and Cooper (1993b) further suggest that combinations of role and power, role and role, and task with power, role or task are potentially successful. All other combinations are potentially problematic and sometimes even potentially disastrous. This clearly shows that a well working 'organizational marriage' does not necessary require similarity of the two organizational cultures, but cultural compatibility or agreement on the same sort of 'marriage'.

Cultural integration in the post-merger stage
In order to realize the potential synergies and to create the expected value added after an M&A, the two companies' duty is to coordinate, adjust, reorganize and set up common processes and systems, like production systems, technologies, customers and sales know-how, purchase procedures

or product lines (Haspeslagh and Jemison, 1991; Jansen, 2001; Picot, 2002). Integration has to happen on various levels: for example, on a strategic, administrative, operative, external, personnel and cultural level.

The cultural integration deals with the question of how far the two organizational cultures should be maintained or assimilated. It tries to solve the question of according to which norms and values the merged organization should live and work, and which messages should be transmitted to the environment.

Integration does not necessarily mean a complete 'amalgamation' of the two companies. The degree of integration depends on various factors. One criterion is the requirement for strategic interdependence and for organizational autonomy. Accordingly we can distinguish between the three following integration approaches (Haspeslagh and Jemison, 1991; Werner, 1999): 'absorption' describes the case with high strategic interdependence and low organizational autonomy (that is, 100 per cent 'fusion'); 'preservation' is given when the two companies show a high need for organizational autonomy and for strategic interdependence. This implies a minimal adaptation to the partner; 'symbiosis' presents an intermediate integration degree between the two abovementioned forms. It is characterized by a high need of organizational autonomy and by a strong necessity for strategic interdependences. The three forms will be further explained in the empirical part of the book when discussing the analysed M&A cases (see section 9.1.1).

The degree of integration also depends on the M&A type. Related M&As, for example, require the most integration, conglomerate the least. Also the cultural fit plays a role: two very similar cultures will have fewer conflicts in agreeing on a common integration mode to adopt than two rather dissimilar cultures.

According to social identity theory, the extent of identification with their own ingroup influences people's commitment, the readiness to leave one's own culture and the willingness to adopt another identity (Doosje *et al.*, 1998; Ellemers *et al.*, 2002; Terry *et al.*, 1996; Terry *et al.*, 2001). Furthermore national culture (perceived culture distance) and the temporal dimension influence the degree of integration (Meschi, 1997).

One of the most important factors in how well two companies integrate their cultures is the way the integration is managed. Fisher (1994) asserts that those are the best mergers where the managers of both companies take the time to thoroughly understand what they are getting into. The leaders must be willing to create a new culture that makes use of the best parts from both partners. In order also to convince all company members, it is essential to be honest with employees about all aspects of the agreements and to take some time to reassure valuable workers that their jobs are safe. Companies that successfully integrate after a purchase or a merger have usually examined carefully the other's culture already in the due-diligence process. It is crucial that the two organizations follow an 'intended strategy' of cultural integration and that they are ready to spend some time on it (Meschi, 1997). Brooks and Dawes (1999) take an optimistic perspective and argue that merging institutions may gain competitive advantage if they use the cultural integration in a positive way. By extending their horizon and by matching cultural developments to the dynamics of the environment, the merging companies can achieve significant skills which are important success factors in a competitive market environment.

Risberg (1997) recognizes the necessity to stimulate cultural change too. Her suggestions focus on communication throughout the acquisition process in order to produce and negotiate a common understanding for ambiguities and cultural differences.

2.3 THE MERGER SYNDROME

The merger syndrome is a phenomenon first documented by Marks and Mirvis (1985, 1986). The term describes employees' (and managers') reactions after the announcement and in general all positive and negative effects and consequences triggered by a merger. Usually employees of the acquired company are more affected by the big changes. That is why the merger syndrome is more intensively felt in the 'weaker' organization (Appelbaum *et al.*, 2000b; Hörnig, 1985).

The merger syndrome is characterized by a change of identity, higher centralization of decision making, coping with high levels of stress, formalization of communications on the one side and starting of rumour mills on the other, moving into a crisis-management mode, power games, a loss of identity, motivation and commitment, decreased productivity, feelings of insecurity and impotence, anxiety, mistrust and by manifold similar and simultaneously occurring phenomena (Appelbaum *et al.*, 2000b; Bruckman and Peters, 1987; Dickmann, 2000; Marks, 1999; Marks and Mirvis, 1986; Schlieper-Damrich, 2000).

The literature does not clearly distinguish between causes and consequences when describing the occurrences of the merger syndrome. The phenomena rather seem to be interdependent, and the authors confine themselves to loosely describing the single events. In an attempt to structure the mentioned facts from literature, Figure 2.2 is designed to give an overview of the merger syndrome. This framework is based on cognitive appraisal theory and on the deduced propositions developed above.

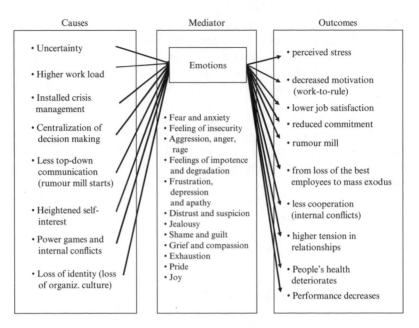

| Causes | Mediator | Outcomes |

*Figure 2.2   Structured summary of what different authors mention in the
context of the 'merger syndrome'*

2.3.1   Causes

The merger syndrome appears' in domestic as well as in international
'marriages', within and across industries, in friendly equally well as in
hostile takeovers and independently of the sizes of the involved companies
(Marks, 1997, 1999).

Post-merger integration stages are characterized by centralization of decision making and by less communication with the employees (Appelbaum
et al., 2000b; Marks, 1988). This phenomenon is presumably due to the fact
that in the pre-merger planning stage managers are expected to maintain
strict silence on the upcoming decision, and therefore they are rather cau-
tious not to reveal too much information prior to complete implementation
(Marks, 1999).

High work load and high uncertainty and expectations tend to lead
manager teams of both companies to slide into crisis management mode.
This situation is sometimes compared to states of warfare where hard
and critical decisions are made, where the other side's perspective and
priorities are misestimated or fully ignored, and where counterstrategies are
discussed (Marks, 1988, 1999; Marks and Mirvis, 1986).

Employees feel as group members of their own organization and identify with their organizational culture. With the acquisition by another
company often a loss of identity occurs (Cartwright and Cooper, 2000).
Employees' identification with their company and their commitment are
therefore likely to change after such a major intervention in organizational
life (Appelbaum *et al.*, 2000a, 2000b; Bruckman and Peters, 1987; Covin
et al., 1996; Dickmann, 2000). The challenge for people is therefore to cope
with this change of social identity.

One of the most evident signs of the merger syndrome is heightened self-
interest. People are preoccupied with what the organizational combination
might mean for themselves as individuals, for their incomes, their careers
and their families. They develop plausible stories and also figments of
imagination about possible implications of the M&A for future benefits, on
the future location of the site and headquarters, and on redundancies.
Power games become more evident: people start to fight for their positions
and privileges, for certain projects and for 'their' products (Cartwright and
Cooper, 2000; Marks, 1999).

2.3.2 Emotions

The defensive, fear-the-worst response called 'merger syndrome' is a
normal and expected human reaction to the experience of such a major
corporate change. It is also not surprising that organization members going
through a merger or an acquisition are shaken by intensive emotions
(Appelbaum *et al.*, 2000b; Dickmann, 2000; Marks and Mirvis, 1986). The
literature mentions different emotions in M&As. However these emotions
are only mentioned and never defined, poorly described, hardly ever
brought into context (causes and consequences) and never listed or
analysed completely.

The spectrum of emotions ranges from very 'negative' (or unpleasant) to
quite 'positive' (or pleasant). Most of the affected organizational members
feel irritated and *insecure*. They are not (immediately) able to see the
upcoming changes as a positive challenge. To the contrary, they see them
as a threat. There are usually not many individuals who experience *joy* and
pride after the announcement, and they are more likely to be found within
the acquiring organization. Lots of employees *fear* to lose their position,
power or even their jobs. Their *anxieties* slop over to their partners and children and become also the latter's problem (Appelbaum *et al.*, 2000a, 2000b;
Cartwright and Cooper, 1996, 2000; Marks, 1999). The reaction to uncertainty is often *aggression*. Employees feel overcome by a *sense of helpless-
ness, degradation, impotence and worthlessness* and respond with *bitterness,
anger* and *rage* against the decision makers and the acquiring organization.

These emotions, spilling over into family life, can lead to *frustration, depression* and to a sinking into *apathy* (Appelbaum *et al.*, 2000b; Cartwright and Cooper, 1993a, 2000; Dickmann, 2000). Also cases of suicide are known in situations which are perceived as frightening and hopeless (Buono and Bowditch, 1989a).

Managers tend to isolate themselves from employees in such situations. Sometimes this is because they do not know what to tell their staff or how to tell them (Gutknecht and Keys, 1993; Marks, 1999). Sometimes it is because managers are extremely stressed, or they are insecure and do not know how to deal with employees' emotions. Very often managers think erroneously that reporting all the happenings to the staff will increase their stress and so they prefer not to say anything; or they adopt a 'trust us' attitude regarding 'all those details'. The fact that managers communicate less with their employees during M&As, however, leads to *doubts* and *distrust*. This leads of course to tensions in the relationships between employees and supervisors (Marks, 1999).

In most of the M&A cases the buying company takes it for granted that they are doing business better than the 'weaker' organization. Therefore they impose their strategy, procedures and products on the acquired company. People who have to accept this feel unsuccessful and react emotionally (with aggression or frustration). This situation is similar in more 'equal' relationships when persons in a leading position meet their new colleagues in order to find potentials for future synergies. They have to check who produces the better products, uses more efficient processes, works more effectively and thus who is more 'successful'. The internal conflicts for positions, privileges and projects lead again to emotions like *jealousy, mistrust* and *suspicion*. Considering the stressful situation and people's *high involvement* and *vulnerability*, it is difficult to come to 'objective' assessments and valuations. People of the 'weaker' company often feel *disappointed* and *ashamed* of being judged 'unsuccessful' and of *feeling exhausted*.

When the first co-workers and friends have become redundant and have left the company, *grief* spreads out among the survivors and they often feel pity (*compassion*) for their colleagues and a sense of *guilt*. This phenomenon is also known as the 'survivors' syndrome' (Appelbaum *et al.*, 2000b; Davy *et al.*, 1989).

2.3.3   Consequences

The consequences of this emotional turmoil are decreased motivation, lower job satisfaction and reduced commitment towards the company. These states are expressed by reducing working input to a minimum amount and doing work-to-rule only. Another issue is the looking around on the market for job alternatives. The best employees start to leave the uncertain and exhausting situation voluntarily and take the offers of other recruiting organizations. In some cases this leads, following dismissals, to a mass exodus. In order to cope with all these challenging events people start to talk, gossip and distract each other from their work. This happens especially when top-down information is not clear or considered to be insufficient. The rumour mill starts and worst-case scenarios boom because no news is usually decoded as 'bad news'. The phone bills increase while the overall job performance goes down (Appelbaum *et al.*, 2000a; Bourantas and Nicandrou, 1998; Cartwright and Cooper, 1993a, 2000; Marks, 1999; Marks and Mirvis, 1986; McTigue Bruner and Cooper, 1991; Siu *et al.*, 1997).

Information and know-how are sometimes consciously held back as a consequence of mistrust and suspicion. In such an atmosphere cooperation becomes difficult and good teamwork almost impossible. The partner-organization and even co-workers are sometimes rather seen as competitors than partners. The tensions in relationships between people on the same hierarchical level inside and across the companies, and in superior–employee relationships are likely to increase.

Managers and employees from relatively well-prepared M&As feel an extremely high degree of stress due to the high level of uncertainty, the increased work load and high expectations of success. Stress reactions (symptoms of stress), decreased well-being and deteriorated health are the consequences which appear in the post-merger months. Executive managers are especially affected by this phenomenon (Baruch and Woodward, 1998; Marks and Mirvis, 1985, 1997b; Siu *et al.*, 1997; Warr, 1994). Among the symptoms of decreased well-being are higher blood pressure, headaches, visual problems, tingling in arms and legs, indigestion, diarrhoea or frequent urination, impotence or menstrual problems, muscle tension, sleep problems, change of eating habits, increased smoking, use of alcohol or dependence on drugs, careless driving and proneness to accidents, excessive and rapid mood swings, lack of concentration, increased irritability and anxiety. The health risk factors are high levels of stress (work demands and overloads), loneliness of command, periods of crises and risks of failure. These risk factors affect all dimensions of health, that is, physical well-being, psychological (or emotional) health, spiritual vitality and ethical health. Physical fitness, social support, stress management skills and a balanced investment in life activities are supposed to be strengths factors which influence physical and mental well-being positively and lead to positive long-term effects. For employees this means vitality, low morbidity and mortality; for companies organizational and financial health (Campbell Quick *et al.*, 2000; Cartwright and Cooper, 1993a, 1994, 2000; Cooper and Cartwright, 1994; Marks, 1999; Marks and Mirvis, 1986; Nelson *et al.*, 1995; Sparks *et al.*, 1997).

One of the main reasons why most of those affected have difficulties coping with the M&A is the fact that what they have perceived as their identity is being transformed into something new: the organizational culture of both merging partners is altering. Mergers and acquisitions can therefore be seen as a change of social identity. The following chapter will elaborate on this perspective in more detail.

NOTES

1. According to Cartwright and Cooper (1995, p. 33), 'estimates of merger failure rates vary from a pessimistic 77 per cent reported by some US studies (Marks, 1988; McKinsey & Associates, 1988) to a more optimistic 50 per cent quoted by several UK sources (British Institute of Management, 1986; Cartwright and Cooper, 1992; Hunt, 1988)'.
2. In personal conversations with human resource consultants of different international companies (for example, Mercer HR consulting, Watson Wyatt, PricewaterhouseCoopers) it was confirmed that even so-called 'HR consultancies' are more concerned with bringing together structures (that is, tax and pension schemes) instead of people. The reason is that the merging clients do not want to spend money on these soft issues (conversations, November–December 2002).
3. Organizational identity and organizational culture are sometimes implicitly, sometimes explicitly, used as synonyms (Irrmann, 2002).

3. Post-merger integration as a change of social identity

The social identity theory's focus is on identity construction and group interaction. It has been widely applied in studies of acculturation in social anthropology, in studies of inter-group relations and specifically in management studies. The social identity theory can help us to better understand what happens emotionally when two groups or identities (or organizations, in the case of M&As) come into contact with each other and are supposed to create a new common identity. While emotions in the studies of social identity have been neglected for a long time (Greenland and Brown, 2000; Johnston and Hewstone, 1990), recently the interest in this dimension of social identity theory seems to have been discovered in several authors (for example, Carr, 2001). The emergence of academic Internet discussion groups on emotions provides evidence for a growing relevance of the topic. Also conferences with titles like 'Identity and Diversity in Organizations' that call for papers regarding 'emotions in the workplace' (Lisbon, Portugal, 14–17 May 2003) are not unusual any more.

For various reasons social identity theory is of particular interest here: first, because M&A integration processes are about identity changes, group formation and inter-group relations; second, because emotions are considered as one of the components of social identity; third, because this theory implies a cognitive appraisal which leads to emotions; and fourth, because social identity theory has already been applied by some authors to the study of post-merger integration processes (Hogg and Terry, 2003; Kleppestø, 1998; Terry *et al.*, 2001).

This chapter is divided into four sections and starts with an introduction to social identity theory by presenting its fundamental concepts (3.1). The second section argues that M&As can be seen as a change of social identity. Therefore the post-merger integration process is examined from the perspective of social identity theory in section 3.2. Section 3.3 shows that emotions are connected with this process. Thus the focus will be on the affective component which has often been overlooked in social identity theory research. The final section of this chapter (3.4) aims to work out when it comes to positive and when to negative emotions.

A later chapter (section 4.4) will refer to the social identity theory discourses of this chapter when emotions will be discussed as cause of changing relationships and as reasons for employees' commitment and identification with the newly merged company.

3.1   SOCIAL IDENTITY THEORY

The social identity theory goes back to Henri Tajfel and John Turner. Their article 'An integrative theory of intergroup conflict' (Tajfel and Turner, 1979) is considered to be the classical chapter of the social identity approach (Abrams and Hogg, 1990; Tajfel, 1982). The theory plays an important role in the field of social psychology, especially within studies of inter-group interaction, group behaviour and the social self.

Identity can be seen as the way(s) an individual is or wishes to be known by certain others. It means a person's definition and description of self. Social identity theory is based on the idea that people are divided or divide themselves into groups, and that individuals define themselves according to their group membership (ingroup) and in comparison to other groups (outgroups). Social identity is hence defined as 'the individual's knowledge that he/she belongs to certain social groups together with some emotional and value[s] significance [regarding] the group membership' (Tajfel, 1972, p. 31). In other words, social identity is an individual's self-conception as a group member (Abrams and Hogg, 1990). It can therefore be seen as an individual psychological perspective and not as a social viewpoint. It is the individual who feels part of a social group. However, next to individual abilities and characteristics, also 'defining characteristics of the category' (which can be particular beliefs, behaviours or the position in the society) may become part of self-definition for the members of the category (Hogg *et al.*, 1995, p. 259).

The definition of social identity refers to the three components of group membership, postulated by Tajfel (1978a): the cognitive, evaluative and emotional components. The cognitive component points to the awareness of individuals that they are part of a specific group (ethnic group, gender, occupation, association or religion, for example). It is also responsible for one's ability to recognize similarities and differences among relevant stimuli (Hogg *et al.*, 1995). The fact that the individual is able to judge the group and its membership as positive or negative represents the evaluative component. The emotional component stems from the belief that the cognitive and evaluative aspects of a group (and its membership) are accompanied by emotions towards the ingroup as well as towards the outgroup (Tajfel, 1978a). For obvious reasons the emotional component is of special interest for this work and will thus be discussed in more detail later in the chapter.

Social identity theory relies on various concepts which will be introduced briefly in the following.

3.1.1   Fundamental Concepts of Social Identity Theory

The concept of social categorization is also known as self-categorization or social classification. It refers to the process through which people assign other people and themselves to various groups. People categorize themselves and others on the basis of perceived similarities and differences and by using abstract prototypes of member characteristics. These prototypical member characteristics, such as religion, ethnicity, political attitudes or interests, make categorization easier. People are not seen as separate distinct individuals but as carriers of specific group characteristics or prototypes. Depersonalization is one of the behavioural consequences of categorization and it is applied to both ingroup and outgroup members (Hogg and Abrams, 1988; Hogg *et al.*, 1995; Tajfel and Turner, 1986). The accentuation of differences between groups (categories) only occurs on those dimensions which are believed to be related to the categorization. This implies that effects of the categorization are more pronounced when the categories are important to the perceiver (Abrams and Hogg, 1990).

Social identity theory is also inspired by Festinger's (1954) social comparison theory. This theory states that people have an upward directional drive to compare themselves with others who are similar to or slightly better than themselves on relevant dimensions. The individual's desire for positive self-image or self-esteem builds the motivation for group comparison and evaluation (Tajfel, 1978b). Social identity theory implies that an individual's identity is influenced by his/her social identity which is achieved through social comparison. Generally the comparison is between ingroups and outgroups. The differentiation is usually based on dimensions which are of social value and on issues in which the ingroup believes itself to be better than outgroups. In this way the ingroup distinguishes itself positively from outgroups and enhances its own social identity. While social categorization stimulates the search for distinguishing features, social comparison and the need for positive identity accentuate selected differences that favour the ingroup (ingroup favouritism). The two processes act together and hence reduce perceived intra-group variation (Abrams and Hogg, 1990; Hinkle and Brown, 1990). The distinctiveness theory (see Grier and Deshpande, 2001; McGuire, 1984) goes hand in hand with the concept of social categorization and social comparison: people compare themselves with others in a social environment and use their distinct characteristics to establish that they are unique and distinctive. Each group tries to define its distinct and clear position in the social context. This happens by defining one's own group as different from other groups and one's own group members as similar to each other but different from the individuals belonging to outgroups.

These concepts can offer explanations for the frequent conflicts between members of two merging companies. As long as people feel this urge to compare their social group with outgroups, to be seen as distinctive from others and to favour their own ingroup by creating prejudices towards or by discriminating outgroups (Johnston and Hewstone, 1990), it is not surprising that the 'us versus them syndrome' (Morosini, 1998) in post-merger organizations as well as conflicts between the two 'camps' are difficult to overcome.

3.2   POST-MERGER INTEGRATION FROM A SOCIAL IDENTITY PERSPECTIVE

Against the background of social identity theory, identity construction and group interaction in M&As have to be reconsidered. The theory suggests that outgroups play a vital role in the formation of one's social identity (Abrams and Hogg, 1990; Hinkle and Brown, 1990). From an employee's perspective the original (pre-merger) organization can be seen as 'ingroup' and the new partner organization as 'outgroup'. The M&A integration process can be explained as the process of creating a common superordinate identity in the perception of the employees of both organizations. The change of identity which occurs in post-merger situations is a highly emotional process, accompanied by stress, uncertainty and big organizational changes (for example, Cartwright and Cooper, 2000). The individuals' identities (as a holder of a certain position and as a group member of one of the two prior organizations) are in danger of being transformed. As a logical consequence emotions such as fear, anxiety, frustration, depression, anger and aggression may arise.

Thus social identity theory can build an interesting background for a better understanding of post-merger integration processes. This is confirmend by several studies (Hogg and Terry, 2003; Kleppestø, 1998; Terry et al., 2001).

'Organizational identity' and 'organizational culture' are often used as synonyms, sometimes implicitly, sometimes explicitly (Irrmann, 2002). Since organizational culture is influenced by all organizational members, it will in any case change at the moment when the organization grows through a merger or an acquisition. Usually the concept of organizational identity is not referring to the individual or subgroup identity but to the group members' self-conceptualization and categorization of 'who we are' as an organization. Organizational identity is defined as comprising those characteristics of an organization that its members believe are central, distinctive and enduring (Ashforth and Mael, 1996). A large amount of the literature on organizational identity considers the existence of multiple identities within the organization as the norm and recognizes that there are many potential benefits as well as costs associated with multiple identities (Irrmann, 2002).

Organizational identities, similar to social or cultural forms of identities, radically depend on the context in which they develop. Identities are co-created in relationships with others. As Collier puts it, 'who and how we are depends on who we are with' (Collier, 1994).

In the present work, 'organizational identity', as a synonym of 'social identity', refers to the whole company after the merger. However it is suggested that social categorization and comparison are transitory phenomena (Hinkle and Brown, 1990). As each individual is a member of a number of social groups (company, subgroups such as subsidiary, department, team and so on), it will depend upon situational factors which ingroup is salient compared to other groups. Indeed employees very often identify more with their department, work team or a specific hierarchical level. The so-called 'primary group' (or group of most interaction) is often more important than the organization as a whole (Hernes, 1997; Kramer, 1991). Hence it has to be kept in mind that organizational identities are dynamic phenomena which develop through encounters. These encounters can take place between two (or more) merging companies, between subidentities of the partner organization (departments or teams) and also between the new organization as a whole and external entities.

Some authors suggest that, by becoming a member of a new group or organization, individuals surrender some of their individuality and identity (see, for example, Carr, 2001). However others (Hogg and Abrams, 1988; Hogg *et al.*, 1995; Tajfel and Turner, 1986) argue that this only corresponds to a contextual change of their identity (from one membership to another) rather than a loss of identity: prototypical characteristics of an organization (such as shared norms, emotional contagion, collective behaviour and empathy) are also assigned to the members of the organization, according to the concept of depersonalization. By changing organization, the individual only exchanges some of these specific prototypical characteristics for new ones, but they are not lost.

3.3   SOCIAL IDENTITY THEORY
AND EMOTIONS

The definition of social identity (Tajfel, 1972, 1978b)[1] implies a cognitive appraisal that leads to emotions. Tajfel explicitly included the affective or emotional significance of group membership in social identity theory. It is known that emotions towards one's own group tend to be positive, while emotions towards the outgroup are likely to be negative (Gaertner *et al.*, 2000). Nevertheless this emotional component has largely been ignored in theoretical and empirical developments of social identity theory (Hinkle and Brown, 1990). Only recent publications have suggested integrating social identity theory and research on affective processes (for example, Brown, 2000; Greenland and Brown, 2000). The argument is that, if social identity theory is to help in the resolution of social conflict, it must be able to theorize how, when and why groups display dislike, hostility and other forms of negative affect towards one another. It must be able to predict such phenomena of negative emotion and behaviour.

Among the few studies concerned with emotions in social identity theory, Wann and Branscombe (1995) researched the relationship between arousal and identification on stereotyping. They found that high 'identifiers' with the ingroup show stronger effects of arousal. Wilder and Shapiro (1989) analysed intergroup *anxiety* and *fear*. Several other studies (Greenland and Brown, 2000; Mackie *et al.*, 2000; Nehme, 1995; Smith *et al.*, 1999) followed this example. Furthermore emotions like *anger* and *contentment* (Mackie *et al.*, 2000) and *guilt* (Doosje *et al.*, 1998) became the focus of attention in studies of inter-group relations. Although the few existing pieces of research are rather speculative, they provide some starting points that invite further research (Brown, 2000).

The first to be mentioned is Smith's (1993) effort to bring social identity theory and social emotions into one framework by explaining the phenomenon of prejudice through cognitive appraisal theories. Smith explains five major emotional states: fear, jealousy, contempt, anger and disgust. Each of these emotions has its own antecedent conditions and very different consequences of inter-group behaviour. For example, *fear* and *jealousy* may be more typical of low-status groups, while *anger* and *disgust* are more likely for dominant groups. This means for M&As that fear and jealousy will be more common amongst members of the acquired company or the weaker partner, and emotions like anger and disgust more common amongst members of the stronger, acquiring company. Brown (2000) considers Smith's (1993) attempt to be a promising direction to pursue, although Smith's model still needs further specifications regarding conditions under which one emotion will change into another.

Fiske *et al.*, (1999) made a further important contribution by pointing out that not only the process but also the *content* of inter-group stereotypes should be taken into consideration (Brown, 2000). The authors suggested arranging the variety of positive and negative attributes of inter-group stereotyping along two dimensions: one representing 'competence' which leads to respect or disrespect, and the other dimension 'warmth', meaning liking or disliking. They further proposed that stereotype content is consistently related to status and interdependence: high-status groups are more likely to be seen as competent and thus respected; groups of high interdependence are more likely to consider each other as 'warm' and thus liked. For M&As this means that an acquired firm with important know-how is not necessarily in the weaker position. If its competencies are higher than in the buyer organization, the bought company might be more respected and thus in a stronger position than they would be without those competencies. Furthermore, if the members of the two merging firms realize that they are interdependent, they will consider the partner as more valuable and develop more positive emotions and higher acceptance of the M&A.

Brewer (1999) identified a number of variables which may stimulate ingroup narcissism, outgroup derogation or worse. According to Brown (2000), Brewer's analysis might help to bridge the gap between differentiation and dislike. Among the societal and social psychological variables are the following:

a. *societal complexity* (in a merger of two 'simpler' companies with fewer cross-cutting categories more inter-group hatred might be experienced than in a merger of two more complex organizations);
b. the *development of ideologies of moral superiority* (the 'legitimized' maltreatment of 'the others' is expected to be more common in large and depersonalized organizations);
c. the *presence of superordinate goals without a corresponding superordinate identity* (since in such a case groups tend to view the loss of subgroup identity aversively, it is important to create a common sense of identity immediately after the M&A);
d. the *endorsement of common values by different groups* (especially in the early post-merger stage this might enhance the desire for distinctiveness).

When two companies merge, fear of 'the others' (known as inter-group anxiety) is a frequently experienced emotion. The antecedents of inter-group anxiety, described above, can be seen as inextricably connected with various social identity processes (Wilder and Shapiro, 1978): Stephan and

Stephan (1985) define inter-group anxiety as the feeling that an individual experiences when anticipating or experiencing contact with an outgroup member. Individuals may feel inter-group anxiety because they fear that they will be discriminated against or that they might make an embarrassing mistake. Individuals might also wish to appear egalitarian and fear that they might unwittingly appear prejudiced. According to Greenland and Brown (2000) and Stephan and Stephan (1985), the antecedents of inter-group anxiety can include outgroup cognitions (stereotypes about the members of the partner company and expectations, for example), prior inter-group relations (a history of conflict or competition with only limited personal experiences, for instance) and situational or contextual factors (for example, being part of the smaller company or in situations where the roles are ambiguous).

Stereotyping, prejudices (as a consequence of negative stereotypes) and discriminating behaviour (as a consequence of prejudices) are phenomena of high interest in the research of social identity (Smith, 1993). They are common occurrences in mergers and acquisitions but hardly ever studied in this context. Therefore it is worthwhile to familiarize the reader with the findings of a few researchers of social identity theory who have tried to explain the origins of prejudice and discrimination.

Until recently inter-group prejudices and the related concepts of stereotyping and discrimination were only considered as attitudinal constructs without relation to emotions. Stereotypes of an outgroup are widely defined as the perceiver's *beliefs* about the group's attributes (for example, an outgroup can be seen as dirty, musical or lazy). These stereotypic beliefs may be positive or negative and may be attributed to the whole outgroup or to just a few members (ibid.). While there was a large consensus to define prejudice as an attitude towards an outgroup, these days the definition of prejudice triggers more disagreement (Dovidio and Gaertner, 1986).

The whole concept of prejudice and discrimination changes if we do not define prejudice as an attitude any more, but as 'a social emotion experienced with respect to one's social identity as a group member, with an outgroup as a target' (Smith, 1993, p. 304). This corresponds to Zanna and Rempel (1988), who postulated five years earlier that attitudes can be based on emotional reactions.[2] To see prejudice, not as an attitude but as a consequence of emotional reactions, allows accepting that the range of relevant appraisals goes beyond simple stereotypes. This also allows seeing prejudice as *situation-specific* and *episodic* instead of considering it as a function of general belief or attitude structures. This presents a much richer picture of inter-group relations, of social emotions and action tendencies than a pure attitudinal view of prejudice could offer. Despite the situation-specific and episodic nature of prejudice, there are relatively general and consistent attitudes concerning particular outgroups as well (Smith, 1993). One explanation is that outgroups which the perceiver never met in person are cognitively represented only in terms of the perceiver's beliefs. Such beliefs about a group's attributes are usually connected with less strong emotions. These attitudes are based on general beliefs about outgroups and exist in a relatively context-free way. They are therefore produced whenever an outgroup is mentioned. This is consistent with Fishbein and Ajzen's (1975) belief-based attitude model (attitude-driven behaviour). A second explanation for the existence of relatively consistent stereotypes about outgroups is the fact that attitudes are generated through episodic, emotional experiences over time (Frijda *et al.*, 2000). The more homogeneous the group is perceived to be and the more consistent the emotional reactions to the outgroup are, the easier it is for attitudes to become generalizations, stereotypes and prejudices (Smith and Lazarus, 1993). For the management of post-merger integrations this implies that it is obliging to generate occasions where people from the two organizations can come into contact. Once the members of the two companies meet on a personal level and see the individuals behind the (stereotyped) partner organization, the chances of experiencing more positive emotions are good.

Not only research on social identity theory reveals the connection to emotions; several M&A studies also mention emotions which arise due to the change of organizational identity. Morosini (1998), for example, suggests that, after the announcement and in the first post-merger integration process, the 'us and them syndrome' intensifies because of perceived threat to one's own organizational identity. Next to personal threats (danger of losing the personal work identity and work security) these 'us versus them' feelings are intensified by the perceived threat against one's own organizational culture (Bijlsma-Frankema, 2001; Buono and Bowditch, 1989a; Buono *et al.*, 2002; Kleppestø, 1998; Olie, 1990). These emotions seem to be more intense among members of the 'weaker' (acquired) organization who feel higher levels of stress due to uncertainties and more intense negative emotions like the fear of losing their culture and jobs, anger or frustration (Hörnig, 1985). However, members of the 'stronger' (and thus 'more valuable') company can also experience fears. Empson (2000, 2001) distinguishes between the fear of exploitation, which is the fear of not gaining anything from the cooperation, and the fear of contamination, namely the fear that one's own corporate image would be diminished through the merger with the 'lower-status' company. We suppose that negative emotions like these on both sides are responsible for the consequent desire for distinction.

3.4 CONDITIONS FOR THE CREATION OF A COMMON SOCIAL IDENTITY

If we accept the idea that M&As imply a change of social identity, the following question emerges: how to bring the two organizational identities together and how to transform them into a new, common social identity.

Numerous studies relying on contact theory have focused on ways to reduce inter-group conflicts. It has often been assumed that positive contact between members of different groups would personalize and improve inter-group relations, and in particular reduce negative outgroup stereotyping and discrimination. This simple view has been challenged by later studies which presented conflicting results (Marques, 1990): in some cases contact did reduce hostility between the groups (Caspi, 1984), but in others it had no effect or even enhanced negative feelings (Stephan and Rosenfield, 1978). Starting with the conclusion that contact per se is not sufficient to produce an improvement in the relations between the two merging companies, the question arises of which kinds of contact can help to improve the relationship.

The first sociopsychological formulation of contact theory came from Allport (1954). He suggested a number of qualifying conditions which are necessary for successful contacts in order to improve inter-group relations in the long term. Following Allport's findings, a favourable outcome of contact would be achieved if the interacting members of the two companies are of equal status, are pursuing common goals and are backed by social and organizational support. Much research has been concerned with adding to or modifying factors on Allport's list. Sherif (1967), for example, supported the assumptions; Brown and Wade (1987) added the condition that the roles of each of the groups (companies) had to be clearly defined; Brown (1984) showed that equal status of groups only improved inter-group relations in cooperative encounters. Consequently, if the two firms are in competitive situations, equal status can enhance undesired competition and animosity between the two merging partners.

Research on inter-group contact has largely been ignoring social identity theory, which proposes that outgroups can play a vital role in the formation of one's social identity (Marques, 1990). One of the main contributions of social identity theory to the contact hypothesis has been to emphasize categorization processes. There are three categorization perspectives derived from social identity theory. The first promotes interpersonal (Brewer and Miller, 1984), the second inter-group (Hewstone and Brown, 1986) and the third superordinate (Gaertner *et al.*, 1989) categorization as the optimal method for inducing positive change during inter-group contact (Gaertner *et al.*, 2000).

Brewer and Miller (1984) argue, with their decategorization model, that contact on an interpersonal level allows us to see the individuals behind the group 'cover' and to perceive outgroup members in terms of their individual qualities rather than their group memberships. Several studies support this idea (Bettencourt *et al.*, 1992, 1997; Miller *et al.*, 1985). Adapting this suggestion to M&A situations, the contact at an interpersonal level would permit the individual to see similarities, as well as differences, between their own and the partner company. Categorization and negative stereotyping would become superfluous.

Hewstone and Brown (1986), however, criticize the interpersonal contact hypothesis by arguing that group memberships must remain psychologically available if the positive effects of a beneficial contact should be attributed to the outgroup as a whole. They therefore propose intergroup categorization in which the individual's category membership (of the pre-merger organization) remains salient.[3] Under the condition that the contact is positive (as proposed by Allport, 1954), this would have the best effects on advantageous group stereotyping. Numerous studies have supported this idea by demonstrating that salient group membership is more likely to influence perceptions of the group as a whole (Desforges *et al.*, 1991, 1997; Van Oudenhoven *et al.*, 1996; Wilder, 1984). Following Greenland and Brown (2000), the members of the partner organization should ideally see each other as 'different but equal' in order to reduce conflicts between the two firms.

The third categorization model is Gaertner and his colleagues' superordinate model (Gaertner *et al.*, 1989, 1990). It can be seen as an approach in between the interpersonal and the inter-group perspectives. The superordinate model suggests that interactions lead to a recategorization of both ingroup and outgroup members into a larger superordinate category. Members of the two merging firms will be able to quickly identify with the common superordinate organization, primarily because they realize what they have in common, and because intra-group processes will increase attraction between the members of the whole post-merger organization. Gaertner and colleagues have demonstrated that superordinate categorization is associated with positive outgroup attitude (Dovidio *et al.*, 1997; Gaertner *et al.*, 1989, 1996). However it has to be noted that all the experiments have also incorporated positive inter-group interdependence (Greenland and Brown, 2000). Transposed to the post-merger context, this means that the perception of mutual dependence can be a crucial factor for successful integration.

A number of criticisms can be made of categorization literature. These include an overreliance on methodologies that have no psychological significance to the participants (such as ad hoc experimental groups) and that overemphasize the differences between the categorization models (Greenland and Brown, 2000). Gaertner *et al.* (2000) have therefore proposed that optimal categorization should simultaneously involve salient superordinate and subgroup categories. For a post-M&A situation this could be interpreted as an invitation to create a common superordinate identity, but also to establish project groups across the two companies in order to allow for subgroup categories. The most important criticism of categorization literature for the purpose of this project is the fact that affective processes in categorization are neglected (Greenland and Brown, 2000). The present study aims to make a contribution in this respect.

Early M&A literature inquires whether similar pre-merger organizational cultures, under certain conditions, provided a better fit than two very different cultures. Scholars following social identity theory presented conflicting results. According to the belief congruence theory (Rokeach *et al.*, 1960), similarity leads to attraction (Byrne, 1971). In other words, individuals prefer to socialize with individuals who are similar to themselves (rather than dissimilar) and to be part of a group with similar group members regarding social status, interests and so on (Nesdale and Flesser, 2001). Recalling the distinctiveness theory, which asserts that groups aim for a clear positioning by presenting themselves as different from others, it becomes clear that a similar partner organization might be considered as a threat to the ingroup's identity, while a dissimilar merging partner might not. Studies indeed confirm discrimination against similar but not against dissimilar outgroups (Brown and Abrams, 1986; Diehl, 1988, experiment 2). These results pose serious problems for both belief congruency theory and social identity theory. Belief congruency theory, for example, is challenged because it predicts attraction to outgroups which share similar attitudes. Social identity theory on the other hand is disputed because it predicts that dissimilar outgroups are less discriminated than similar outgroups. However similar groups are nevertheless discriminated to a certain extent because the ingroup cannot achieve positive distinctiveness by other means (Hinkle and Brown, 1990). Summing up, it appears that in intergroup contacts of two merging companies similarity does not lead to enhanced liking and attraction as is the case in interpersonal situations. Similarities within the ingroup lead to a stronger ingroup favouritism (due to the stronger homogeneity), while similarities between one's own and the partner company lead to a stronger discrimination.

Thus, following Brewer and Miller (1984) and Marques (1990), the appropriate strategy for improving inter-group relations in the post-merger context is (a) to avoid direct comparisons between the two companies, (b) to de-emphasize similarities between the two companies (that is, between the ingroup and the outgroup), and (c) to highlight dissimilarities *within* the two ingroups (companies) by focusing on their department or team levels rather on the whole (old) organization.

In order to reduce categorical responding and inter-group conflicts and extend Brewer and Miller (1984), the strategy suggested is (a) to increase differentiation (distinctiveness of individuals within the pre-merger company) and (b) to increase personalization by breaking down company boundaries and by emphasizing the treatment of individuals as individuals as opposed to pre-M&A company members. This individualization of relationships could be reached through cross-organizational projects, as well as through social events.

The underlying hypothesis is that any aspect of contact heightening group categorization will result in a negative inter-group effect. This hypothesis is supported by Miller *et al.* (1985), Wilder (1978) and Langer *et al.* (1985). Crain and Mahard (1982), however, maintain that this is not always the case. They propose another strategy to reduce inter-group conflicts, namely to make more than one overlapping category salient at the same time, so that some individuals are simultaneously members of the outgroup on one dimension and members of the ingroup on other dimensions. This is closely related to the superordinate model by Gaertner and his associates (Gaertner *et al.*, 1989, 1990), as discussed above.

Other situational factors besides perceived similarity are perceived relative position, perceived permeability of group boundaries and perceived outcome (Piontkowski *et al.*, 2000; Tajfel and Turner, 1986). Groups that perceive themselves in a disadvantaged social position relative to outgroups (perceived relative position) are more likely to feel higher degrees of discrimination by outgroups. A merging company whose individuals share low self-esteem relative to the merger partner shows more levels of insecurity, and tends to protect its identity and to discriminate against the members of the partner organization (Kleppestø, 1998). High-status partners, on the other hand, identify themselves more readily with the new organization created through a merger or an acquisition (Terry *et al.*, 2001).

This means that a company's self-image influences the perceived discrimination by the M&A partner and in consequence the readiness to contribute to a successful post-merger integration. Indeed M&A studies state that generally the dominating company (the acquirer or the organization with the higher capital involved) is more influential in shaping the newly merged organization. Van Knippenberg and his colleagues (2002) analysed two merging organizations (education and government) and concluded that a dominant position in a merger is conducive to post-merger integration because it gives a sense of continuity between pre-and post-merger identification. If the dominant position is associated with discontinuity, this is more likely to lead to a reduced organizational integration. However the complex identification processes are difficult to predict because they can lead in opposite directions (Irrmann, 2002): members of a large acquiring bank, for example, tended to accept the new superordinate culture and believed in better prospects as individuals, while the members of the acquired bank collectively resisted this view and tended to stick to their pre-acquisition identity (Anastasio *et al.*, 1997). In the example of an airline merger (Terry *et al.*, 1996), however, members of the lower-status company more readily accepted the new superordinate corporate identity because they believed it gave them better personal career opportunities. In this case it was the higher-status group members who collectively feared to lose status and resisted change.

Perceived permeability of group boundaries is defined as a group's perceived possibility of participating in the activities and life of the salient outgroup. In the case where the boundaries of the two merging companies are perceived to be permeable, employees identify more with the newly unified organization (Haslam, 2001; Terry *et al.*, 2001).

Integration of the two organizations is further facilitated when the potential outcome of the contact with the partner company is perceived, not as threatening, but as beneficial. In the case where the result is perceived to be valuable, integration attitudes are encouraged, while effects which are perceived as threatening lead to separation or discrimination attitudes (Haslam, 2001; Piontkowski *et al.*, 2000).

In conclusion we can say that mergers and acquisitions imply a change of identity which constitutes a highly emotional process for all those affected. The present study builds on the following fundamental premise: employees who demonstrate positive emotions about the merger or acquisition are more likely to abandon the previous organizational identity, to identify with the newly merged company and to show higher commitment to the new organization. This means that positive emotions like pride, joy and curiosity may lead to a stronger social identity in the new organization as a whole. On the other hand, negative emotions related to the merger or acquisition such as anxiety, anger or guilt may lead to a stronger identification with the old pre-merger organization.

NOTES

1. Social identity is defined as 'the individual's knowledge that he/she belongs to certain social groups together with some emotional and value[s] significance [regarding] the group membership' (Tajfel, 1972, p. 31).
2. Zanna and Rempel (1988) presented an attitude as an evaluation of an object (outgroup) that can stem from three types of information: from beliefs about the object (for example, beliefs about the partner organization), from the perceiver's emotional reactions (for

example, how the individual feels when meeting members of the merging partner) or from the perceiver's past behaviour. Once an attitude is formed (from any of the three mentioned bases) it is cognitively represented and retrieved separately. An attitude can therefore develop and differ from its initial state (Smith, 1993).

3. Inter-group categorization requires more than mere interaction between members of different groups. It demands, first, that the social categories be psychologically salient, second, that group homogeneity be perceived, and third, that behaviour demonstrates intra-group uniformity.

4. Emotions in post-merger integration

We have already mentioned in the context of the merger syndrome that the announcement of a merger or an acquisition can elicit deep emotions. M&As can be considered as a change of social identity. We also explained that the perception of one's identity has an emotional component. The creation or change of identity is therefore always connected with emotions. However both M&A research and research on social identity theory are still largely ignoring the emotional component. Only very recent literature in both fields considers emotions. In order to contribute to the closing of this gap, it seems necessary to discuss first some theoretical bases of emotions (section 4.1). The few noticeable exceptions of M&A studies that explicitly focus on emotions will be summarized in section 4.2. The two subsequent sections present M&As as a cause of emotions (4.3) and emotions as a reason for certain M&A outcomes (4.4). In section 4.5 a comprehensive conceptual framework will be developed which incorporates emotions. The framework is built on cognitive appraisal theory and social identity theory as well as the merger syndrome.

4.1 THEORETICAL BASES

The terms 'emotion', 'feeling', 'mood' and 'affect' are widely used in daily conversations as well as in research. It would seem fair to assume that everybody knows what these phenomena are about. However a first attempt to define these terms showed that this is not the case (Wenger *et al.*, 1962). Currently there is no unanimously accepted definition, for emotions and misunderstandings are abundant. Therefore it is useful to define what exactly is meant by 'emotions' in the present work (see section 4.1.1).

One of the barriers that makes it difficult to clearly understand emotions is the idea that an emotion, like anger or jealousy, can have an independent presence within a person through time. We commonly speak of being 'overwhelmed', 'paralysed' or 'gripped' by an emotion. In this way, the myth of some independent outside agency is used in order to describe a contrasting inner state. Or we personify an organ and speak of emotion as if it had a physical location or residence, like love in the heart and envy in the bile. In a similar way emotions are considered to have a continuous existence when we say that an emotion is 'accumulated' or when we talk about an 'old' emotion (see for example, Hochschild, 1983).

A second barrier to the understanding of emotions is the idea that, when overcome by an emotion, individuals are led to act irrationally and see reality distortedly. This may sometimes be the case but not always. When a person encounters a poisonous snake, feels afraid and runs away, for example, his/her emotion-driven action is consonant and therefore 'rational'. For sure a certain intensity of emotions can drive people to undertake actions they would not in the absence of emotional arousal. However, in colloquial language, 'acting emotionally' is often related to unwise and irrational behaviour and cited in the context of examples that prove irrationality (Hochschild, 1983). Since 'rationality' is often opposed to 'emotions' we will explain the two terms and their underlying concepts in section 4.1.2.

Many researchers from different disciplines have studied emotions. Some misunderstandings have appeared owing to the lack of awareness that researchers view emotions from different perspectives. Therefore we give below a short overview of the most influential orientations, schools and findings in emotion literature (pp. 52–8). The main focus will be on psychology because it is the discipline which showed the most intensive interest in emotions over the 20th century.

4.1.1　Terminology

Emotions have been studied within various scholarly disciplines which include psychology (see Cornelius, 1996; Frijda, 1986), sociology (see Williams, 2001), communication studies (for example, Andersen and Guerrero, 1998; Buck *et al.*, 2002; Martin, 1998), anthropology (see Darwin, 1872; Mead, 1975), biology (for example, Damasio, 1994), neurobiology and neurophysiology (LeDoux, 1996; Rolls, 1990), philosophy (for example, Freud, 2001), ethology (Kraut and Johnson, 1979), management (for example, Fineman, 2000; Herriot, 2001; Nippa, 2001) and marketing (for example, Bagozzi *et al.*, 1999; Geuens and De Pelsmacker, 1999; Hazlett and Yassky Hazlett, 1999; Luomala and Laaksonen, 2000). This multiplicity of perspectives on emotions attests to the complexity and ubiquity of the phenomenon. It complicates attempts to categorize perspectives on emotions and to find a useful definition. Only within psychology, for instance, there is a large variety of differing conceptual perspectives, overlapping with other disciplines such as cognitive sciences, physiology, anthropology and sociology (see Tomiuk, 2000).

Across the variety of disciplines which frequently offer radically different perspectives, even less consistency can be found in the use of terminology related to emotions. The lack of a consensual or classical definition of emotions is attributed to various reasons. Their characterization as unplanned, unexpected and non-rational issues makes it difficult to describe emotions in rational terms (Parkinson, 1996). Hence the complexity of the set of emotional phenomena leads to an unclear delineation between emotions and related phenomena. Against this background it becomes even more important to define some key terms which in literature are often used in vague and confusing ways. In this book *affect* will be conceived as an umbrella term, encompassing terms which describe more specific mental processes (emotion, mood). According to Bagozzi *et al.* (1999), affect is seen as a general category for mental feeling processes, rather than a particular psychological process per se.

Feeling is understood as a mental state consisting of awareness of situational meaning structure and of action readiness change at a level of mere potentiality, mere inclination and mere plan. Feelings are monitors which register the context of relevant concern (Frijda, 1986).

Many authors (for example, Bagozzi *et al.*, 1999; Frijda, 1986; Holbrook and Gardner, 2000) describe *mood* by comparing it with emotion: mood is conceived as being longer lasting and lower in intensity, as non-intentional and global. Moods describe milder, more diffuse and more general affective states than emotions. They are constantly evolving and not directly coupled with action tendencies or explicit actions.

Before presenting a definition of emotion it might be useful to look at the term from an etymological perspective. The linguistic root for what we now understand by 'emotion' is the Latin 'e' + 'movere' which means to migrate or to transfer from one place to another (Averill, 1986). Emotion can be seen in a metaphorical way as something that moves people. This movement means a change or migration within the person (Franks, 1994).

Definitions of emotions are in many cases relatively broad and open. There are researchers who even start with a vague working definition only and hope to get a clear definition of emotions as a result of their research (Meyer *et al.*, 1993). Definitions vary according to the nature attributed to emotions and according to the research question.

In this book *emotion* is defined as a mental state of (action) readiness that arises from cognitive appraisals of events, social interactions or thoughts. It has a phenomenological tone, is accompanied by physiological processes and it is often expressed physically (see Bagozzi *et al.*, 1999). The term 'emotion' has been chosen for this study, first, because it is stronger than 'feeling' and 'mood', and more specific than 'affect'. Second, the above-mentioned definition of emotion implies 'action readiness' which is based on 'inner movement' (Frijda, 1986). This is in line with the etymology of the term 'emotion'. Furthermore 'action readiness' is easier to identify and to measure compared to a 'diffuse affective state' of 'mere potentiality' and 'mere inclination'.

4.1.2   Different Perspectives on Emotions

In everyday language, as well as in managerial literature, emotions are frequently seen in contrast to (or at least in connection with) rationality. The present section will therefore present different perspectives on the emotion–rationality relationship.

Although emotions are still an underresearched topic in management literature, various views and definitions of emotions have emerged within different disciplines. In order to understand where the different definitions, attitudes towards emotions or measurement instruments stem from, a classification of emotion theories will be presented in the second part of this section. We are aware that this will be an overview rather than a complete detailed picture of the huge amount of existing emotion theories in different disciplines.

Emotions and rationality

Fineman (1999, 2000) distinguishes three possible relations between emotions and rationality: emotions disturb rationality, emotions serve rationality, and emotions and (rational) cognitions are inextricably knotted.[1] Case one (emotions disturb rationality) seems to reflect the 'common sense' in Western societies and in most current management literature. This view implies that emotions should be eliminated as far as possible. In the second case (emotions serve rationality) emotions constitute an important supplement for limited rationality, where 'supplement' could be understood in two different ways: emotions constitute an 'addition' to rationality or emotions serve as a 'substitute' for rationality. When emotions and rationality are seen as inextricably knotted, as in the third case, emotions 'cannot exist outside the thought, so the cognitive/affective distinction cannot be sustained' (Fineman, 1999, p. 550). In the following, the three perspectives will be discussed in more detail.

Emotions disturb rationality

The approach of seeing emotions as disturbing elements of rationality is deeply embedded in Western philosophical thought (Fineman, 2000). According to Ortmann (2001), in 'primitive times' emotions constituted a condition for survival. Some Greek philosophers (for example, Seneca, 1981, De Ira, I, viii, 1) and European church fathers saw emotions as something primitive and not justifiable by reason, while reason itself was seen as a divine gift (Howard, 1993). This ancient meaning of emotion as a disturbing passion, agitation and perturbation is still deeply embedded in the minds of many researchers and practitioners. Emotions are often seen in a narrow, negative meaning and as something that 'overcomes' individuals and transforms them into helpless victims (Franks, 1994). Therefore, rationality is still privileged and very often seen in the Aristotlic way, this is in opposition to emotions (Fineman, 2000; Haspeslagh and Jemison, 1991; Ortmann, 2001).

Emotions are seen as interference and as 'sand in the machinery of action' (Elster, 1999, p. 284). Supporters of this approach point out that emotions can undermine rationality through (a) belief formation (for example, wishful thinking), (b) information acquisition (for example, jumping to conclusions), (c) the tendency to act impulsively when action is triggered by perception alone rather than by reason, and (d) inducing intentional action that is reward-insensitive. However the main mechanism by which emotions undermine rationality is through their disregard of consequences and required information (Elster, 1999).

This position informed management and economic literature, such as rational choice theory, which – at least implicitly – asserts that emotions should be eliminated as far as possible (Cacioppo and Gradner, 1999). Psychoanalytic theory is particular about the 'irrational' behaviour of individuals or organizational members caused by conscious and unconscious fears, anxieties, shame or guilt. These emotions are supposed to be able to keep the actor from forming an accurate perception of a certain situation. The logical consequence is to 'channel' or 'manage' them in order to achieve or restore rationality (for example, Fineman, 2000; Hochschild, 1983; Krell and Weiskopf, 2001).

We assume that this dominating perception of emotions as a disturbing factor is one of the central reasons why emotions are still largely overlooked both in M&A research and in studies of social identity.

Emotions serve rationality

In this perspective emotions are seen as less problematic because they complement rather than harm rationality (for example, Damasio, 1994; De Sousa, 1987). Over the last decade some neurologists (Damasio, 1994; LeDoux, 1996) have studied the functions of the human brain and realized that emotions are not disturbing but essential to rational thinking. The absence of emotion can prevent rationality and make wise decision making almost impossible. In *Descartes' Error: Emotion, Reason, and the Human Brain*, Damasio (1994) describes the interconnectedness of mind and body. He found that individuals who survived brain damage without severe physical impairment experienced bizarre degradations of personality and thought processes. The patients are still able to think and argue rationally, and to consider the pros and cons of a certain alternative, but they are unable to make a decision. Damasio explains these puzzling maladies by analysing the various systems in the brain, from those associated with life support to the highest echelon of cognition. He illuminates numerous ways the body and the mind work together to process stimuli, draw upon memory, and fuel thought and judgment. He concludes that emotions are essential to our ability to reason and make decisions. Descartes' error, then, was his belief that mind and body are separate entities. On the contrary, Damasio shows convincingly that their continual collaboration is the key to consciousness and individuality.

Similar findings are expressed by De Sousa (1987) who emphasizes the role of 'values'. De Sousa argues that in cases of incommensurable alternatives people base their decisions on their links to past emotional experiences. Following De Sousa, emotions are tied to values. Emotions determine what is regarded as important, what options are considered, what relative importance is given to certain attributes and thus how the potential infinity of choices is limited.

Obviously the intensive sensation of an emotion limits the range of information and the options taken into account. On the other hand, without emotion decision makers would be unable to come to a decision. Emotions determine the salience of things and act as arbitrators among reasons by assigning values to options and so determining trade-offs. Rationality alone can proscribe but cannot prescribe (ibid.).

Emotions and rationality are inextricably knotted

Seen from this third viewpoint emotions and rationality are not distinct. They interpenetrate each other constantly. All thinking and deciding is influenced by affects. An individual may be dimly aware of this process, or emotions may intervene unconsciously. Furthermore there are different layers of thoughts and emotions: directly experienced emotions like anger, fear or love (basic emotions), and meta (and meta meta) processes where the individual reflects his/her own and others' emotions: human beings can experience emotions about emotions (for example, feeling guilt for having been angry) as well as emotions about thoughts (for instance, being proud of an idea; see Fineman, 2000).

And, on the other hand, every emotion is influenced by the cognitive mindset, by beliefs and thoughts (Frijda *et al.*, 2000; Lazarus, 1991). The cognitive appraisal school of emotions sustains the view that a belief about something or someone (for example, 'it is dangerous', 'he likes me') triggers a particular emotion (such as fear or excitement).

Incorporating one of the two latter perspectives (emotions serve rationality, or emotions and rationality are inextricably interwoven) poses serious problems to mainstream management literature. It implicates that the dominant hard-fact oriented M&A literature has to open up to encompass also emotion-related issues. For researchers and managers who are aware of the power of emotions the logical consequence is to pay more attention to employees' emotions. In order to comprehend how employees' emotions emerge, and what impact they can have on M&A outcomes, it is useful to understand the basic concepts of different schools. The following section shows how emotions emerge according to different emotion theories.

Emotion theories

Modern psychological theories of emotions can be classified according to different criteria and lead to diverse types of classifications. Hochschild (1983), for example, distinguishes between two basic models of emotion that emerged over the last 150 years: the so-called 'organismic' and 'interactional' models. The organismic model defines emotion mainly as a biological process and postulates a basic constant of emotion and a basic similarity of emotions across cultures. Supporters of the interactional model, on the other hand, recognize that there is always a biological component involved in emotion. However this part of emotion is of little theoretical interest to them. The interactionists (for example, Tomkins, Dewey, Gerth, Mills, Goffman, Ekman, Rosenthal, Izen and Lazarus) are interested in the meaning psychological processes assume.

A more detailed picture is provided if emotion theories are put into three categories: (a) somatic (or functionalist), (b) appraisal and (c) social constructivist theories (Tomiuk, 2000).

Somatic theories

The functionalist perspective on emotions, first proposed by Charles Darwin (1872) and later extended by William James (1890) and James and Lange (1922), views emotions as universal and culturally invariant. According to the somatic perspective, emotions have evolved through natural selection. They have adaptional functions which help the organism to deal with environmental demands and to survive. Expression and recognition of emotions in facial configurations are two important aspects of emotions, whereas cognitive functions are not involved in the emotional experience under this view.

Darwin's evolutionary theory and James's further development influenced many modern scientists (Tomiuk, 2000). Some researchers tend to draw heavily on their perspective, especially representatives of the so-called 'expressive motor theories'. Izard (1977) and Ekman (1982, 1984), for example, build on the biological, communicative and expressive character of emotions and study emotion recognition in facial expressions. Other streams of theories evolved from the Darwinian and Jamesian perspective are the psychoevolutionary theory of emotion (Mandler, 1980; Plutchik, 1980, 1984), which presents basic emotions as prototypical, and the related evolutionary prototype theory of emotion (Shaver *et al.*, 1987; Tomkins, 1962). Emotion is treated as a mediator between environmental stimulation and behavioural response. In this sense also the 'action readiness' in Frijda's (1986) cognitive appraisal theory is influenced by this school. Furthermore, according to the somatic perspective, each emotion is distinguishable from others and serves a particular function (Smith, 1989). Recent neurological and psychophysical studies are also influenced by this 'hardwired' perspective of emotions: Damasio (1994) and LeDoux (1996) are examples of brain researchers who show interest in how and where in the body emotions arise, and they have found that the amygdala in the middle brain plays a crucial role.

The functionalist approach basically views emotional reactions such as changes of the heart rate and skeletomuscular changes, including mimic expressions, as an inevitable response to changes in the limbic system. It is suggested that emotions serve an 'adaptional function'. In the context of mergers and acquisitions this could signify that emotions help the individual to deal with the organizational changes. The drawback of the somatic approach is that it does not take into account the individual's possibilities of coping with their own emotions. Furthermore managers' prospects of influencing or managing employees' emotions cannot be explained by adopting a somatic perspective without making too many assumptions.

Social constructivist theories

Most followers of the constructivist perspective see emotions as a socially constructed phenomenon and focus on the cultural influences on emotions. They presume that all individually experienced emotions are socially shaped. This socially constructed 'syndrome' emerges from the individual's evaluation of the situation which is influenced by the person's socialization and cultural environment (Averill, 1980, 1982). Taken to the extreme, social constructivists refuse to accept that emotions exist 'in' people, ready to be studied. In their perspective emotions are intersubjective and have to do with the social and environmental context in which they are felt. What matters is how sensations, thoughts and feelings are labelled and displayed. The meaning of a certain sensation, belief or emotion is created and negotiated between people (Parrott and Harré, 1996) but it does not exist 'per se'. More moderate social constructivist approaches acknowledge both somatic and cultural factors as predominant influences on human nature. Pure biological, 'in-the-body' explanations, however, are not able to clarify the learned, 'social', interpretive, culture-specific part of emotions (Fineman, 2000). For social constructivists, emotional responses are learned from experiences (both personal and vicarious) and emotional expressions vary between and within persons, across cultures and times. This approach posits that the number of emotions is infinite as a result of the countless social and life events that can interact and then be interpreted by those who experience them (Wasserman *et al.*, 2000).

Since every individual is always influenced by the surrounding environment it is impossible to find two identical emotions either over time within the same individual or between different persons. Therefore there is no dividing line between emotions and the number of emotions is countless. Russell (1989), for example, assumes that people are unable to experience one single emotion at a time. He argues that at any time the whole range of emotions is experienced simultaneously and that only the intensity of single emotions in this 'bundle of emotions' varies.

Although the social constructivist approach could build a suitable background to explain emotional phenomena in the post-merger process, it involves a few weaknesses for the purpose of the present study. Viewing emotions as intersubjective only would imply that people from the same pre-merger company or the same department would experience the same emotions. This might be true to a certain extend. On the other hand, this view is considered as too limiting, in the sense that individuals' belief systems, situational meaning structures and prior experiences are not taken into consideration (they are also seen as socially constructed). Here we assume that every single company member has his/her own history in the company, a different role and position, a diverse personality structure and a different personal background which influence the perception of merger-related events and thus the emotional experience. The social constructivist perspective primarily focuses on similarities between members of the same social unit, but it does not provide sufficient answers to the question why individually felt emotions emerge.

Furthermore maintaining that all emotions are shaped socially means that employees' emotions are subject to all kinds of social influences. In this study we only pay attention to the managerial impact on employees' emotions. This approach may be criticized by social constructivists.

Cognitive appraisal theories of emotions

Cognitive perspectives on emotion are the dominant orientation in modern psychology (Bagozzi *et al.*, 1999). Within that, the cognitive *appraisal* perspective is the most commonly proposed orientation (Cornelius, 1996; Parkinson, 1997). The reason why it is also the most commonly accepted in organizational studies is probably to be found in management literature which until recently 'flirted' with emotions only to the extent that they were perceived as useful and applicable in psychology. Furthermore most of the management literature follows a strongly rational approach and seems more comfortable drawing on theories that are mainly cognitive.

Schachter and Singer (1962) first proposed that the interpretation of a situation is important for the full experience of emotion. Schachter (1964) further developed this cognition-arousal or two-factor theory and suggested that only interaction between physiological and cognitive processes generates affects. The arousal itself, which is triggered by the sensation of a relevant event, is emotion-unspecific; the degree of arousal determines the intensity of the felt emotion. All subsequent cognitive appraisal theories influenced by Schachter's work agree that an emotion requires cognition in the form of appraisals (for example, Frijda, 1986; Lazarus, 1991; Lazarus *et al.*, 1970; Leventhal, 1984; Mandler, 1975, 1980, 1984; Ortony *et al.*, 1988; Roseman, 1984; Scherer, 1993; Smith and Ellsworth, 1985; Weiner, 1985). Appraisals are an individual's perceptions and interpretations of the changes in the environment and their significance to the person. The quality and intensity of an emotion does therefore depend on the relevance for the individual. Each emotion provides feedback on the individual's psychosocial inner world in relation to the environment.

All appraisal theorists recognize that some form of cognitive evaluation precedes the affective response. The central questions they ask are which cognitive assessments underlie which emotion and how do these evaluations emerge (Reisenzein *et al.*, 2003; Ulich and Mayring, 1992)? Consequently cognitive appraisal theories also involve predictions and explanations of discrete emotions. Anger and resentment, for example, are consequences of perceived attack or threatened loss which lead to the 'fight mechanism'. Fear and anxiety appear when the individual perceives himself/herself to be threatened and lead to the 'flight mechanism'. Guilt involves blaming oneself for the misfortune of others, while shame involves blaming oneself for one's own thoughts, words, emotions (for instance, for having been angry) or behaviour. Individuals experience joy and happiness when they are successful in meeting their goals and needs, or when they experience acceptance. Unhappiness, on the other hand, arises from real or threatened loss of sources of safety, satisfaction and self-esteem (Frijda, 1986, 1993; Lazarus, 1991; Lazarus and Cohen-Charash, 2001; Smith and Lazarus, 1993; Stanley and Burrows 2001).

Figure 4.1 shows the emergence of an emotion from a cognitive appraisal perspective as conceived by Frijda (1986): the individual is confronted with

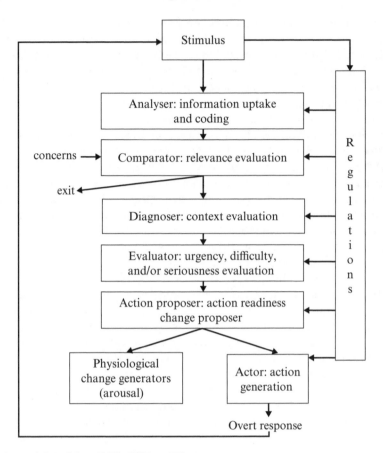

Source: Adapted from Frijda (1986, p. 454).

Figure 4.1 Cognitive appraisal approach on emotions

a stimulus which can also be an 'inner event', such as a thought. This stimulus is either received unconsciously or it is actively scanned. The so-called 'analyser' takes the information and codes it according to the individual's mind map, belief systems and prior experiences. This is a continuing and unconscious process within the individual's limbic system. Since the mind maps or belief systems change over time it is more precise to talk about 'situational meaning structure'. The evaluation of the relevance of the information (or primary appraisal) happens by comparing the individual's concerns. In the case where the result is 'irrelevant', the process stops here. Otherwise the result of this evaluation is one of four relevance signals: pleasure, pain, wonder or desire. Then the context evaluation (or secondary appraisal) starts. This diagnosing process gives information about whether or not it is possible for the individual to cope with the interpreted stimulus. The 'evaluator' checks the urgency, difficulty and seriousness of this diagnosis on the basis of previous information. In line with the result, the 'action proposer' generates an action readiness change, accompanied by physiological change. This leads to arousal which implies a physiological change and to action (readiness).

The core process of emotion described is subject to a regulatory intervention by mechanisms of outcome-controlled processes or voluntary self-control. This means that external stimuli (like stimuli announcing adverse response consequences) as well as inputs coming from the emotion process itself or from conscious interventions (that is, thoughts) are influencing the generation process of an emotion. Inputs to these regulation processes can be external stimuli (such as stimuli announcing adverse response consequences), inputs coming from the emotion process itself or conscious interventions by the individual (thoughts).

The phases of the emotion process described mostly happen unconsciously. This means that the sensation of the 'perceived' stimulus and its 'interpretation' occur in most of the cases automatically and without the support of the individual's consciousness. The threshold of consciousness is usually only exceeded when a stimulus is decoded as relevant and 'serious' for the person: the individual becomes aware of a certain emotion and often only then does he/she consciously draw attention to the stimulating event.

According to cognitive appraisal theory, no emotion emerges without 'reason' and without a 'trigger pulse'. However it is *not* essential that the 'interpretation' of the stimulus reach the level of consciousness (in the sense of a rational explanation of the causes). Nevertheless, in order to feel joy, anger, fear or grief, it is necessary that the individual 'interpret' the event as joyful, annoying, frightening or sad, based on the personal meaning structure and belief system. The individual's mind maps and thus the 'interpretation' of the stimulus are subject to continuous change. Emotions are therefore situation and context-specific.

We have said that it is not necessary for the experience of emotions that the individual cognitively understand the underlying reasons of a felt emotion. However awareness is an advantage, if not essential, for steering one's emotions in a more positive direction and for being less affected by negative emotions.[2] According to the emotional intelligence literature (for example, Bar-On and Parker, 2000; Goleman, 1995; Mayer and Salovey, 1993; Salovey and Mayer, 1990), knowing why certain emotions appear makes it easier for individuals to change their mind maps and beliefs, and to accelerate the modification of their (future) 'predispositions'. The individual cannot change or eliminate the 'trigger pulse' or the event per se. But the individual can influence his/her own 'predispositions' in order to 'interpret' the same event as irrelevant or as less negative.

There are several advantages to adopting cognitive appraisal theory for the present M&A study. First, this approach allows arguing that individuals with different prior experiences (such as prior M&A experience or prior trust/mistrust relationships between management and employees) sense certain stimuli differently, interpret them in their own way and feel other emotions than their co-workers'. Second, it helps us to state that employees are able to change their mental 'predispositions' and to cope individually with their emotions triggered by the merger or acquisition. It also makes it possible to assume that managers can purposefully contribute to this change of employees' meaning structures and thus to their emotional experience.

It must be noted that a strict appraisal theory perspective is insufficient to account for the dynamic nature of emotion in interaction. Since the individual undergoing a merger or an acquisition is always embedded in an organizational environment, the organizational group dynamics also influence the individual's emotions. Although emotions are felt and dealt with by individuals, it is argued that emotions can be initiated and altered through social interactions. Therefore it is necessary also to include the social perspective. Since the social constructivist approach presupposes that all emotions are shaped socially, it is not able to accept the abovementioned individual dimensions of experience as is possible in cognitive appraisal theory. Therefore cognitive appraisal theory will be linked with another individual psychological theory which is able to explain the highly emotional M&A integration processes. The social identity theory seems to provide a good second pillar for this purpose.

Combining cognitive appraisal theory with social identity theory   Cognitive appraisal theorists have generally looked at emotions only from an individual perspective. But the statement 'self-relevant information has affective and motivational significance' (Smith, 1993, p. 302) is also applicable to groups. People do not just know things about the self (for example, 'I just passed my final exam'), but they care about this information and may feel emotionally aroused. This is also valid for groups: when self-categorization becomes salient, all information regarding one's own group evokes an emotional experience. Individuals identify with their group's success or failure and experience similar emotions as other group members. The fact that a fan of a group who is not a team member can feel event-specific emotions (which affect the team) illustrates that emotions can be shared with a group and are not only an experience related to the individual self. The key argument is that 'to the extent a self-categorization functions as a self-aspect, appraisals of events or situations with respect to that social aspect of identity will also trigger emotions' because 'the self is not limited by the skin, neither are emotions' (ibid.). Smith calls these commonly felt emotions 'social emotions', some authors talk about 'collective emotions' (Hochschild, 1983), others use the expression 'group emotions' (Kelly and Barsade, 2001; Pescosolido, 2002).

Social identity theory suggests that individuals perceive themselves in terms of their group membership. Group-relevant beliefs and appraisals tend to be shared within the ingroup. This happens because group members are motivated to conform to group norms (Smith, 1993). In an intergroup situation like a merger or an acquisition, the individual's emotions and appraisals regarding the other company (pride, perceived threat and so on) are unlikely to be a unique phenomenon. It is more likely that several members of the same pre-merger organization feel the same way.

This means that cognitive appraisal theory is also applicable byond the individual level, that is, on a social level. Social groups influence individual mind maps and therefore the individual's emotions. Nevertheless it is still the individual who reacts to stimuli and who feels emotions in his/her individual way, depending on personality structure, beliefs and prior experiences (Lazarus, 1995).

On the other hand, it is important to note that social identity, despite relating to a social phenomenon, has its effects on an individual level: it is the *individual* who feels part of a group, and commonly experienced emotions, even though they can be triggered by a group-related event, are always felt on an individual basis. Smith would not accept this argument and would reason that social rather than individual aspects of identity are more important determinants of attitudes and actions (compare Smith, 1993). This view is similar to the social constructivist perspective. Also social constructivists focus on the social (common) background which shapes the individual's emotions. For cognitive appraisal theorists, however, it does not really matter where the 'predispositions' or mind maps come from. They are not particularly concerned with the question of whether these predispositions derive from individual experiences or whether they are shaped by the social environment. In this sense, there is no fundamental difference between the processes underlying social emotions and 'individually felt' emotions. The only exception is that the appraisals behind 'social emotions' are assumed to refer to the *social* aspects of the perceiver's identity rather than to the individual experiences and beliefs.

4.2   EMOTIONS IN M&A LITERATURE

Organizational changes, like mergers and acquisitions, are highly emotional events for all those affected. Although several authors agree on this statement (Cartwright and Cooper, 1992, 1994, 2000; Huy, 1999, 2002; Marks and Mirvis, 1985, 2001; Sinetar, 1981), emotions are hardly ever considered explicitly in research on organizational changes. It is therefore justified to argue that emotions are still a neglected factor not only in M&A literature but in change literature in general.

In the M&A literature the term 'emotion' appears in the context of the merger syndrome. General statements on emotions can be found, for example that executives are expected to be 'both strategically and emotionally prepared' in order to be able to channel merger stress 'into productive, even creative, work' (Marks and Mirvis, 1985, p. 50). Yet it is explained neither how emotions are conceptualized nor how their role in organizations is seen. The conceptualization of emotions has, however, profound effects with respect to both theory development and practical interventions (Callahan and McCollum, 2002).

Emotions are almost never defined, discussed, explicitly studied or measured in the M&A literature. The concept of emotion is usually limited to the level of stress research or viewed as resistance (Kiefer, 2002b). Since in both cases emotions are seen as an unwanted and undesirable negative reaction to change, they constitute something that has to be avoided, reduced or eliminated. Emotions are thus seen as 'dysfunctional', as 'a problem', as something 'irrational' that prevent people understanding rational arguments, and as an 'inherently difficult beast to control' (Fineman, 2000; Kiefer, 2002b; Krell and Weiskopf, 2001; Rafaeli and Worline, 2001).

Although mergers and acquisitions (like every other change) also trigger positive emotions, the focus on negative emotions and their destructive impact is in general more dominant in M&As (Fugate *et al.*, 2002; Kiefer, 2002b). The positive–negative asymmetry effect of emotions could be an explanation for this phenomenon. This means that negative experiences and unpleasant emotions are more heavily weighted and longer lasting in subjective judgment processes than positive experiences and pleasant emotions (Fiedler and Bless, 2000; Gardham and Brown, 2001; Rozin and Royzman, 2001).

4.2.1   Notable Exceptions Dealing with Emotions

Nevertheless there are a few research studies which focus on emotions in mergers and acquisitions. One of the few exceptions is Kiefer's and Eicken's qualitative project with a merger in the banking sector (Kiefer, 2002b;

Kiefer and Eicken, 1999). They are interested in the kind of emotions that are felt and reported during the first six months after the announcement. Following a constructivist approach and relying on cognitive appraisal theories of emotions the authors focus on the interpretation of circumstances that trigger certain emotions. Kiefer and Eicken propose an alternative approach to look at emotions. They view emotions as an essential and helpful part of a working experience instead of considering emotions as a disturbing factor. The outcome of the study is a framework for studying emotions which is based on four categories from organizational psychology: work tasks, personal situation, relationship with the organization, and social relationships. Their attempt to focus on emotions can be seen as a valuable achievement in M&A research. A shortcoming of the study is that only one company was involved, and that within this company only selected persons from two departments were approached. For reasons of validity and generalizability, further studies are required.

Another example of emotion research in the context of a merger or an acquisition is a quantitative study by Fugate *et al.* (2002). The main interest of their research is how employees' coping mechanisms change over time. The study has therefore four moments of data collection in which the two fundamental forms of coping strategies, according to Latack and Havlovic (1992), are analysed: problem-focused coping that relates to the actions taken by an employee to change the nature of disturbing factors of the environment (this is perceived controllability); and emotion-focused coping which refers to the individual's effort to change his/her reactions to the situation (this is wishful thinking). In order to study employees' coping mechanisms their appraisals of the situation and their negative emotions were sought. The authors rely on cognitive appraisal theories and emphasize that appraisals and emotions are not identical. Therefore they suggest studying the two concepts (appraisals and emotions) separately in future research. Interesting for the present project is their finding that employees' emotions did not change over time. The fact that emotions did not change over four stages after the announcement argues in favour of a cross-sectional study. This is in line with most of the previous research on the effects of organizational restructuring which primarily used self-report cross-sectional data (Probst, 2003). Fugate *et al.*'s (2002) article considers only negative emotions because emotions and attitudes are assumed to be largely pessimistic following mergers and acquisitions. This may be true, but it ignores parts of the empirical evidence. Every organizational change is also seen in positive ways – at least by a minority – otherwise the change would not have been initiated. Another weakness of their study is related to validity and generalizability. A drawback of the study is its limited context which consists of a single merger and involves one group of employees only. Also the low

levels of the test–retest reliabilities (of the coping variables) are not satisfying and call for future research.

Within the few M&A-related emotion studies the examination of anxiety
seems to be relatively popular. Within this literature there is a noticeable tendency to focus on fears of employees of the 'weaker' (acquired) company,
that is their fear of losing power, jobs, the company's name and their identity. Empson (2000, 2001) is an exception, studying six accounting and consulting firms in the merger process. She found that employees and managers
of the 'stronger' (acquiring) firm also experience certain anxieties which have
an impact on the success of the M&A integration. Professionals, for
example, resist knowledge transfer when they perceive that the merging firms
differ fundamentally in terms of the quality of their external image and the
form of their knowledge base. Empson identified the so-called 'twin fears' of
exploitation and contamination. The fear of exploitation becomes relevant
when the members of one company perceive their knowledge to be more
valuable than that of the partner organization. As a consequence they fear
being 'exploited' and not gaining anything from the cooperation. The fear of
contamination arises when the members of one organization fear that their
corporate image, (upmarket) brand and values could be diminished through
the merger with the 'lower-status' company. Empson opines: 'often the
reasons why individuals perceive their knowledge or image to be superior are
hard to justify by any objective criteria and individuals on both sides of the
merger found reasons to look down on each other' (Empson, 2000, p. 43).

Vaara (2002, 2003) studied post-merger integrations qualitatively by
focusing on the discourse which interviewees employ in recounting their
experiences. He distinguishes between four types of discourse: 'rationalistic', 'cultural', 'role-bound' and 'individualistic'. This distinction helps in
reframing the success or failure of a merger or acquisition, as well as the
justification or legitimization of the interviewee's actions. Vaara argues
that post-M&A integration studies have mainly focused on rationalistic
explanations for the difficulties encountered in these change processes. The
'irrational' features have largely been neglected. He therefore attempts to
bridge that gap by examining the post-merger integration process from a
sense-making perspective. The analysis suggests that success stories are
likely to lead to overly optimistic or, in the case of failure stories, overly
pessimistic views on the management's ability to control these change
processes. Vaara (2002) concludes that researchers and managers should
take the discursive elements in narrators' descriptions and explanations
seriously, and allow for more intentional (re)interpretations of post-merger
integration or other organizational change processes. Although Vaara's
studies are not directly focusing on emotions, his conclusions are interesting and valid for emotion studies as well.

In conclusion it can be argued that emotions are still a largely overlooked factor in M&A research. The few exceptions mentioned above offer a good starting point and call for further research. However one could argue that M&As are only a subarea to the study of organizational change. While it is true that, within the larger context of organizational change, notions such as emotional intelligence have recently been addressed, a comprehensive literature review confirms that even in that framework the consideration of emotions is a notable exception to the rule (for example, Axtell *et al.*, 2002; Fox *et al.*, 2001; Paterson and Cary, 2002). Consequently the argument holds that mainly rational elements are discussed in change management literature in general and in M&A literature in particular.

4.3   M&As AS CAUSE OF EMOTIONS

According to cognitive appraisal theory, emotions only appear as a response to a certain internal or external stimulus such as thoughts or experiences. In the M&A context this means that emotions only emerge after people have taken notice of the merger or acquisition, that is after the announcement. The present book aims to find out what influence managers have on employees and their emotions in the integration phase. In order to be able to develop a conceptual framework it is important first to have a closer look at these 'managerial stimuli' (managers' behaviour and communication style) which are considered as antecedents of employees' emotions.

In the 1930s Hersey (1932) studied a group of workers over the period of one year. His research is considered one of the most impressive works of the time which, unfortunately, had only a limited impact on future emotional studies (Weiss and Brief, 2001).[3] Hersey recognized the importance of some workplace factors and extra-work influences as contributors to employees' emotions and affective intensity. For example, an 'understanding and efficient supervisor' is suggested as having considerable impact on the emotions of employees. Hersey also studied how work-related emotions may influence organizational members' behaviour (Weiss and Brief, 2001). Hersey's study relates to a 'normal', non-merger situation. We suppose that managerial actions and communication style have an equally great (if not a stronger) influence on the emotions and behaviour of employees in a period of major organizational changes, such as a post-merger integration phase.

Over the last decade the literature on emotional intelligence has indicated that leaders have an impact on employees' behaviour (for example, Goleman, 1998; Goleman *et al.*, 2002a; Humphrey, 2002; Wolff *et al.*, 2002; Wong and Law, 2002). Given that human behaviour is always influenced by

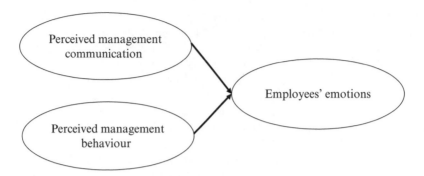

Figure 4.2   Managerial influences on employees' emotions

the individual's emotions (Damasio, 1994; LeDoux, 1996) we can argue that managers have an influence on employees' emotions, and thus on employees' behaviour. Emotional intelligence literature suggests that emotionally intelligent managers acknowledge employees' emotions because they are empathic and have an organizational and service awareness. Being aware of employees' emotions they know how to motivate, inspire and develop employees, how to manage conflicts and how to build and maintain networks. Emotionally intelligent managers are able to influence employees' emotions in a positive way through their open communication and their engaging behaviour. Because of their capability as 'change catalysts' emotionally intelligent individuals can be seen as ideal leaders to manage a post-merger integration process.

Figure 4.2 is based on cognitive appraisal theory. It illustrates schematically the connection between managerial communication and behaviour (as perceived by employees) and employees' emotions. It must be noted that employees' emotions are not influenced by what managers actually do and say. According to a cognitive appraisal approach, employees' emotions are shaped by *appraisal* of managers' behaviour and communication. It is not the 'objective facts' that matter for the generation of emotions, but the 'interpretation' and the sense which employees attribute to their sensations. Therefore it is more accurate to talk about *perceived* managerial communication and *perceived* managerial behaviour as influencing factors of emotions.

4.4   M&A OUTCOMES AS EFFECT OF EMOTIONS

M&A studies, and studies regarding organizational changes in general, analyse various outcome variables, such as the impact of uncertainty and stress on job satisfaction, psychological contract, motivation, organizational commitment and loyalty, perceptions of time pressure and of job (in)security, job stress, psychological well-being and job satisfaction, unproductive behaviour, health, absenteeism rates and turnover intentions, lower morale and acts of sabotage (for example, Bruckman and Peters, 1987; Buono and Bowditch, 1989a; Buono *et al.*, 2002; Cartwright and Cooper, 1990, 1993b; Hall and Norburn, 1987; Hubbard and Purcell, 2001; Jemison and Sitkin, 1986; Probst, 2002, 2003; Schuler and Jackson, 2001; Siu *et al.*, 1997; Werner, 1999).

The outcome factors of the present study are chosen among the non-financial M&A success factors. We aim to find out how emotions of employees influence their identification with and their commitment towards the newly merged company, their job satisfaction, their relationships (with co-workers and with superiors) and their performance evaluation of the merged organization. The conceptual framework will be based on these factors and encompass previously discussed causes of employee emotions.

Owing to the lack of emotion studies in M&A and change management literature, no prior studies could be identified to justify the link between employees' emotions and the indicated M&A outcomes. However some studies relying on social identity theory are able to explain the link between social identity and commitment, identification, job satisfaction and performance. The link of identity to relationships (in ingroups) is only partially explicable. Nevertheless social identity theory seems a good theory to adopt here. Figure 4.3 tries to express this graphically. It has already been indicated that the concept of social identity has emotions as one of its components and it has been shown that individuals feel strongly emotional about their group membership.

4.4.1 Identification

Mergers and acquisitions can have a considerable impact on the psychological bond between employees and organization. The recomposition of organizational identification after the change is not an easy process, particularly when the two organizations have perceived each other as competitors in the past (Irrmann, 2002).

Social identification is defined as a sense of belonging to a group and sharing its fate (Hogg and Abrams, 1988). This means, for example, that the individual considers group success as a personal success and group failure as an individual failure. Identification is composed of three factors: how intensely individuals identify with the group, how proud they are of the group, and whether or not they feel themselves to be typical group members.

Figure 4.3   The influence of social identity on M&A outcomes

Ingroup identification is commonly assumed to be positively related to ingroup bias (ingroup favouritism) and outgroup discrimination (Tarrant *et al.*, 2001). Terry and colleagues (Terry *et al.*, 1996, 2001) found that identification with the newly merged organization is negatively related to the levels of ingroup bias within the two previous partner organizations. This implies that, the more employees identified with their pre-merger organization, the more difficult it would be for them to identify with the new organizational culture of the merged company.

It is recommended that managers make sure that employees identify with the whole, merged company in order to achieve effective post-merger integration. The critical question is which (sub)group employees see as their 'ingroup'. Especially in the early post-merger situation, for example, employees tend to stick to their primary group or group of most inter-action (which can be a department, a team or the old company) instead of identifying with the newly merged organization as a whole (Hernes, 1997; Kramer, 1991). To confirm this, Dahler-Larsen (1997) analysed a similar situation, looking at several strikes in the Danish branch of the Scandinavian airline company SAS which is known to be a company with a strong unifying corporate culture. He showed how strikers referred alternatively to four different 'we-typifications' at different times: 'we' as flight attendants, 'we' as employees (opposed to managers), 'we' as SAS members and 'we' as Danes.

On the other hand, keeping in mind the need for positive self-esteem or self-concept, people also tend to identify with the most prestigious group (Hogg *et al.*, 1995). If we apply this finding to the post-merger situation, it is advisable to establish a new, commonly attractive ingroup as quickly as possible. The cultivation of inter-group interactions could be a means to stimulate the process of coming together. Social events, joint projects or the purposeful celebration of achieved milestones could help to reinforce interactions and achieve these integration goals. In order to enhance the attractiveness of the merged identity it appears crucial that the combined institution represents attractive values and creates a culture of more prestige compared to the culture of the two pre-merger organizations. It can also be useful to look for a new common outgroup, especially if the merger partner is a former competitor.

There is also another stream of social identity theory literature which argues that being a member of a group does not necessarily imply identification with the ingroup. One may feel oneself to be a corporate member without necessarily agreeing with and internalizing all the stereotyped values attributed to the category. Alvesson (2000) for instance argued that one can feel Italian without showing all the stereotypes of a 'typical' Italian. In a similar way employees can feel themselves to be members of an organization without identifying with all aspects of the organizational identity. Some authors go further than that in opposing the 'common sense' of social identity theory and demonstrate that not all identities are formed through inter-group comparison (Hinkle and Brown, 1990). But, since organizations involved in a merger or an acquisition are mostly comparative groups, this stream of literature will not be discussed further here.

Van Knippenberg *et al.* (2002) analysed social identity processes in M&As. The results suggest that organizational identification after a merger depends on the members' perceptions of both the pre- and the post-merger identities. Succinctly put, identification with one's company is contingent on a sense of continuity of the organizational identity. This sense of continuity is argued to be dependent on the extent to which the individual's own pre-merger organization dominates (or is dominated by) the merger partner. Two surveys of merged organizations showed that pre- and post-merger identification are more positively related for members of the dominant as opposed to the dominated organization, while perceived differences between the merger partners were more negatively related to post-merger identification for members of the dominated compared to members of the dominant organization. This means that members of the stronger organization find it easier to cope with a change of the company's identity and with organizational differences between the two merging firms.

In another study, van Knippenberg (2000) shows that organizational identification is positively related to work motivation, task performance and contextual performance. This supports the choice of 'identification' as a non-financial outcome variable for the present project.

4.4.2   Commitment

We chose commitment as one of the outcome variables in the present study because high employee commitment is assumed to have positive consequences for company performance (Morgan and Hunt, 1994). Individuals who strongly identify with the organization are supposed to be more committed than others (Doosje *et al.*, 1998; Ellemers *et al.*, 2002). Managerial activities which foster employees' identification with and their commitment to the post-merger institution are consequently desirable.

Social identity only becomes relevant when one of the categories includes oneself (Abrams and Hogg, 1990). For example, people who enthusiastically support athletes of their own nationality during the Olympic Games, may feel indifferent if their own country is not participating. This example demonstrates that concern and pride, and thus a sense of involvement and commitment, derive from one's knowledge of sharing a social category membership with others. This occurs irrespective of whether these interactions relate to acquaintances, close personal relationships, common material or personal interests between the members. For M&As this implies that a sense of involvement and commitment towards the whole merged company can only arise if the new organization is perceived as important to the members and if they feel part of the whole group.

Probst (2003) found that organizational restructuring has consistent negative effects on employees' organizational commitment. According to Doosje *et al.* (2002), it is more complex. They rely on social identity theory and show that an individual's commitment depends on the level of identification with the group. In a first stage of their study low 'identifiers' only expressed solidarity with their group to the extent that the improvement of group status constituted a likely prospect for the future, while high 'identifiers' maintained commitment even if their group faced an uncertain or bleak future. In a second stage, low and high 'identifiers' responded differently to actual changes in the structure of the inter-group status. Low 'identifiers' seemed more instrumental than high 'identifiers', in the sense that the former were only prepared to affirm identification with a low status group when status improvement was imminent, or had actually been realized. These results from Doosje *et al.* imply that employees of both organizations (especially those who identified themselves strongly with the former institution) need to experience successful project outcomes quickly after the M&A. This is imperative for them to reinforce commitment to the new company.

Using earlier research, Cartwright and Cooper (1992) distinguish between superficial compliance-based commitment and deeper commitment. Superficial commitment is linked to the size of one's salary cheque or the prestige value of the company, for example, while deeper commitment is based on identification and internalization of organizational values. The present study follows their example and focuses on deeper commitment when assessing the levels of renewed commitment.

4.4.3   Job Satisfaction

In the context of the merger syndrome (section 2.3) it has already been mentioned that the consequences of the M&A–related emotional turmoil are lower job satisfaction, decreased motivation and reduced commitment towards the company. Unsatisfied and uncommitted employees tend to reduce their working input to a minimum and to stick to a work-to-rule only. As a result, the best employees look for other jobs on the market and voluntarily leave the uncertain and exhausting situation (for example, Marks and Mirvis, 1997a; Probst, 2003).

The study of job satisfaction has been very popular in organization literature, although we have to stress that in the past satisfaction was mostly seen as an attitude and not as an affect (Weiss and Brief, 2001).[4] For most of the 20th century, the study of emotion at work was practically the study of job satisfaction. It is therefore worth mentioning some of the major contributions with respect to job satisfaction.

In 1931, Fisher and Hanna published the book, *The Dissatisfied Worker*, which at that time was considered an important contribution on a largely unexplored topic. Measured by today's standards, their position regarding job satisfaction seems extreme and strange because dissatisfaction is seen as 'non-adjustive emotional tendency', 'chronic emotional disturbances' and 'psychopathology' in the worker, rather than a consequence of an objectionable factor inherent in the work situation. Emotional maladjustment as described by Fisher and Hanna (1931) was seen as a major cause of labour problems of various types. *The Dissatisfied Worker* does not deal with job (dis)satisfaction in a later sense. Nevertheless this work, proposing the treatment of temperament, is very important because of its influence on other researchers in the 1930s. For the following 50 years affect and job satisfaction erroneously became equivalent constructs (Lazarus and Cohen-Charash, 2001).

The satisfaction–performance relationship was among the typical research topics of the 1940s and 1950s. Although later questioned, one of the remarkable works of this period is Herzberg's and his colleagues' impact on motivation literature (Herzberg _et al._, 1959). Hertzberg and his associates distinguished between factors which cause positive job attitudes (motivators) and different factors that generate negative job-related attitudes (so-called 'hygiene factors'). Subsequent research challenged this assertion (House and Wigdor, 1967; King, 1970) and this almost resulted in a complete extinction of any discussion regarding emotions or job satisfaction. A further important impact on subsequent research was made by Kunin's (1955) novel 'faces' scale which was introduced as a useful tool for measuring job satisfaction. The scale consists of a series of faces ranging from an angry frown to a pleasing grin. Respondents express their attitude or feeling by indicating the appropriate face on the scale. A few decades later Brief and Roberson (1989) proposed using this measurement more frequently because the 'face' scale seemed to capture the emotional components of job satisfaction better than other, more popular measures.

In the 1960s the main thrust of organizational psychology research continued to be the study of job satisfaction as a potential key determinant for organizational outcomes. In the same decade, key theoretical works on job satisfaction (Katzell, 1964; Locke, 1969; Porter, 1961; Vroom, 1964) were written and theory-driven measures developed. The Job Descriptive Index of Smith _et al._ (1969) and the Minnesota Satisfaction Questionnaire of Lofquist and Dawis (1969) are two examples. Discrepancy theories of satisfaction remained the top explanatory models until the 1980s. The 1960s could therefore be called the 'golden age' in satisfaction research, at least in terms of attention given to the topic. Furthermore the impact of job satisfaction on society was studied for the first time (Weiss and Brief, 2001).

In the 1980s some much earlier upcoming ideas started to grow and to mature, and new ideas regarding job satisfaction arose that would have an impact on the following decade as well. Work consequences of mood states or the discovery of dispositional influences on job satisfaction became hot topics. According to Weiss and Brief (2001), two of the most important papers of the last 20 years were written by Staw and his colleagues (Staw _et al._, 1986; Staw and Ross, 1985). They reintroduced the 'dispositional approach' to job satisfaction. In the 1930s various dimensions of personality had already been shown to be predictive of workers' emotions and thus job satisfaction. This was only rediscovered in the 1980s. It is important to note that, until the 1970s, job satisfaction was seen as an attitude and as something completely separate from emotion at work; only in the 1980s was job satisfaction recognized to have an emotional component. Standard measures of job satisfaction reflected this view too. It was not until the 1980s that emotional and cognitive components of job satisfaction were explicitly recognized.

The 1990s can be considered as an extension and elaboration of trends that began in the 1980s. The age-old problem of the relationship between job satisfaction and performance continued to be the object of studies (Lazarus and Cohen-Charash, 2001). However, in these two decades, emotions in organizations were not restricted to the study of job satisfaction any more.[5] Weiss and Cropanzano (1996) tried to distinguish clearly between emotion and satisfaction in their 'Affective Events Theory' (AET), which is more a framework than a theory to study emotions in organizations. AET defines satisfaction not as an affective reaction to a job, but as an evaluative judgment one makes about one's job. Affect and beliefs jointly influence this evaluation judgment, that is job satisfaction (see also Weiss *et al.*, Nicholas, and Daus 1999). The AET discusses the way emotion is experienced, its causes (based on basic mood and emotion literature) and its consequences (including both performance and satisfaction). Nevertheless the usefulness of the theory remains to be evaluated.

Nowadays job satisfaction, attitude and emotion can be seen as related constructs in the sense that job satisfaction (the attitudes about one's job) is suggested to have an emotional component (Brief, 1998) and/or emotional causes (Weiss and Brief, 2001). Covin *et al.* (1996) studied job satisfaction in the M&A context, without, however, explicitly mentioning emotions. The level of individual satisfaction with a merger was found to be strongly associated with several key attitudinal and demographic variables, including satisfaction with supervision, satisfaction with career future and company identification, communication with top management, agreement with the acquiring company's mission statement, turnover intent and union status.

Only a very few studies relied on social identity theory when studying job satisfaction. Salk and Shenkar (2001) is one such exception. The authors investigated job satisfaction in an international joint venture with shared management. Results of the longitudinal study showed that social entities were the dominant sense-making vehicle used by team members, although multiple sources of social identification were possible and present in this British–Italian joint venture. The dominant use of nationality-based identities did not change over time. The findings suggest that the enaction of social identity by team members, using particular boundaries to define primary social identities, mediated the relationship of environmental and structural variables with outcomes like job satisfaction. This means that employees' feeling of being part of a social identity is linked to job satisfaction.

4.4.4 Relationships

Several authors mentioning the merger syndrome (for example, Appelbaum *et al.*, 2000b; Cartwright and Cooper, 2000; Marks, 1988, 1999) talk about changes in relationships among members of the same pre-merger company: the post-merger integration stage is characterized by less top-down communication, by power games and internal conflicts, by less cooperation and higher tensions.

Numerous studies that rely on social identity theory have analysed relationships as well. However most of the studies focused on inter-group relationships, and many of them investigated the change of these inter-group relationships through contact. Although the phenomenon of ingroup favouritism is described extensively (for example, Abrams and Hogg, 1990; Hinkle and Brown, 1990), there are hardly any studies available which describe the changes of relationships between members of the same ingroup.

Dahler-Larsen's (1997) work is among the few projects that might help us to understand intra-group changes in post-M&As from the perspective of social identity theory. Dahler-Larsen found, in his SAS analysis mentioned above, that there are several subgroups and 'we'-typifications within one organization. The identification with a subgroup becomes salient at different times and according to certain events or contexts. Consequently, 'ingroup' members of one category (for instance, 'we' as employees opposed to managers) might become outgroup members when another category is salient (for example, 'we' as flight attendants or 'we' as Danes). This leads to the assumption that, with the change of a salient social identity, also the relationships between members of the same company, but members of a different subcategory, will change.

Literature which is not related to social identity theory offers certain hints which allow the presumption that emotions of employees, triggered by a merger or an acquisition, lead to a change in relationships between co-workers, as well as between superiors and employees. Burkitt (1997), for example, presents the theory that emotions are modes of communication within relationships and interdependencies. Following this idea a change of emotions (due to the organizational restructuring) leads to a change of relationships between the organizational members. Also the opposite will be true: explicitly changed relational structures and process will lead to a different sort of communication and thus to a change of emotions.

Dasborough and Ashkanasy (2002) look at the leader–member relationship in organizations from an employees' perspective. They argue that leadership is a process of social interaction and intrinsically an emotional process where leaders display emotions and attempt to evoke emotions in their members. They state that employees' emotions are influenced by the way the members evaluate, interpret and eventually label the leader's intentions (as 'true' or 'pseudo' transformational leadership). It is assumed that, when employees consider a manager's behaviour as superficial or dishonest and pretentious, employees' emotions (for example, disillusion or anger) will be affected, as will, consequently the leader–member relationships.

4.4.5 Perception of Success

The attempt to define the relationship between job satisfaction and performance is an age-old problem which was the object of studies over decades, without any significant progress being made. Research undertaken in the 1980s, however, gives reason to consider that job satisfaction and emotions might influence people's perception of their work environments (Weiss and Brief, 2001). Indeed Hersey (1932) had discovered a clear relationship between daily emotion levels and daily performance levels as early as the 1930s. He found out that negative emotional states had a more pronounced impact on negative outcomes than positive emotions on positive effects. The understanding that emotion can be shared by a group of individuals also led to some papers that studied the emotion–performance relationship at the unit level (George, 1990; Ostroff, 1992; Ryan *et al.*, 1996).

Van Knippenberg (2000) explored work motivation and performance from the perspective of social identity theory and self-categorization theory. He analysed the relation between organizational identification and motivation to exert effort on behalf of the collective. A theoretical analysis as well as a review of empirical studies led to the conclusion that organizational identification is positively related to work motivation and to performance, under the conditions that (a) social identity is salient and (b) high performance is perceived to be in the group's (or organization's) interest.

The second condition is also supported by other researchers. Recent studies documented that performance in a domain is hindered when individuals feel that their social group is negatively stereotyped in that domain (Schmader, 2002; Shih *et al.*, 1999). These studies demonstrate that implicit activation of a social identity can facilitate as well as impede performance on a quantitative task. Results showed that, when a particular social identity was made salient at an implicit level, performance was altered in the direction predicted by the stereotype associated with the identity. For example, common cultural stereotypes hold that Asians have superior quantitative skills compared with other ethnic groups (Shih *et al.*, 1999) and that women have inferior quantitative skills compared with men (Schmader, 2002). It was found that Asian–American women performed better on a mathematics test when their ethnic identity was activated, but worse when their gender identity was activated, compared with a control group who had neither identity activated. To be precise, it was not the identity per se that influenced performance (as cross-cultural investigations showed), but the stereotype with which the members identified (Shih *et al.*, 1999). Social identification (and the beliefs and emotions about it) thus have an influence on performance. This means in the M&A context that a company that is perceived positively (for example, as competent) will have better chances to perform well than a company which is perceived less positively (less competent). Therefore it is recommended that negative stereotyping against the partner company be avoided and that a superordinate organizational identity be created as soon as possible. We mentioned that negative stereotyping does not occur against the ingroup (due to ingroup favouritism). So, once members of the superordinate organizational identity perceive each other as members of the same 'ingroup', positive stereotyping and good performance are relatively easy to achieve.

Similar results derive from Pilegge and Holtz (1997) who found that, with social identity, the worker's self-esteem also counts. Strengthening social identity increases perceived similarity between ingroup members, regardless of their self-esteem. Individuals with high self-esteem and with a strong social identification set higher goals for themselves and achieve better performance than individuals with high self-esteem but a weak sense of social identity compared to members with low self-esteem and in either condition of identification. This again supports the idea that managers of post-M&As should try to create a common superordinate identity and to provide a positive image of the whole organization for all members in order to create a sense of self-esteem. This is supposed to facilitate good performance.

Some authors studied perceived performance. Planes *et al.* (2002), for example, found that not only the performance per se depends on the social identification. Performance *assessment* is also biased by identification with the self-perceived role. Frijda *et al.* (2000) argue that not only are emotions influenced by the individuals' mind maps, but emotions also influence beliefs. In line with this, Fiedler and Bless (2000) found that positive emotional states facilitate active generation of beliefs, whereas negative emotional states support the conservation of the status quo. Lindsley *et al.* (1995) explain the influence of emotion on perceived efficacy and performance through upward (overconfidence) and downward (lack of confidence) efficacy–performance spirals.

For the post-merger integration this implies that positive emotions about the merger are likely to lead to perceived success, while negative emotions about the change will lead to a poor performance assessment and to an overvaluation of the old pre-merger successes.

4.5 DEVELOPMENT OF A CONCEPTUAL FRAMEWORK

In the two previous sections employees' emotions were presented as cause and as effect. Following a cognitive appraisal approach, employees' emotions can be seen as the effect of perceived managerial behaviour and communication (see 4.3). By relying on social identity theory and on other studies, employees' feelings of being part of a social identity were shown to influence certain M&A outcomes (see 4.4). A comprehensive conceptual framework will be developed which builds on the structure of Figure 2.2 (structured summary of what different authors mention in the context of the 'merger syndrome') and on the two previously discussed approaches (emotions as a cause and as an effect). In order to make the development of the framework comprehensible, the two previous concepts will be integrated. Figure 4.4 presents this graphically by bringing together Figures 4.2 and 4.3.

The concept of social identity implies that individuals experience certain emotions towards their own ingroup as well as towards outgroups. Consequently the notion 'social identity' in Figure 4.3 (in the right-hand part of Figure 4.4) can be combined with 'employees' emotions'. Emotions are supposed to influence employees' identification with and their commitment towards the whole merged company, their job satisfaction, relationships among co-workers and between employees and superiors, as well as perceived M&A performance. The resulting and fully integrated framework is presented in Figure 4.5.

This framework builds the theoretical basis for the empirical investigation of four M&A cases, which will be presented in Part II of the book.

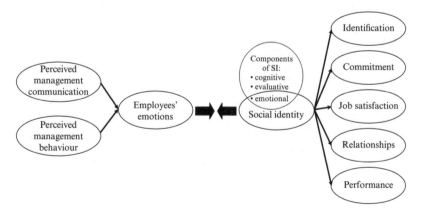

Figure 4.4   Development of a conceptual framework

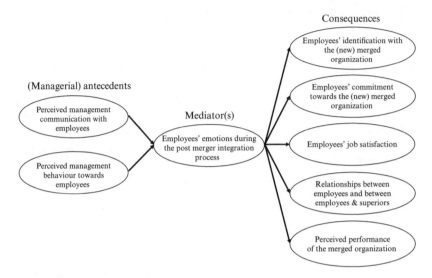

Figure 4.5   Conceptual framework

NOTES

1. It has to be noted that the two terms, 'cognition' and 'rationality', are often used as synonyms (Fineman, 2000; Ortmann, 2001). The problem with this assumption is that it may cause a neglect of emotions as a source for cognition – a view that a cognitive approach would not accept. In the cognitive approach, cognitions are based both on rational thoughts and on emotions, as we will see later (see pp. 54–8).
2. It is common sense to talk about 'positive' and 'negative' emotions instead of talking about 'pleasant' and 'unpleasant' emotions. However, considering that emotions have signalling functions (Hochschild, 1983), all emotions ('negative' emotions included) are actually 'positive'.
3. Hersey's (1932) work is remarkable for its ideas and methods used as well as for its prescience and currency. Four times a day, in blocks of 10–13 weeks, employees were given an 'emotional checklist'. Hersey observed that the individual daily affect level, while varying considerably over time, showed definite cycles. These cycles were distinct over time and different for each employee (Weiss and Brief, 2001).
4. In general, Hersey (1932) was one of the few researchers who studied emotions and not attitudes by that time (Weiss and Brief, 2001).
5. Emotions started to be studied in a broader context. For example, a general theory of emotions at work was developed (Weiss and Cropanzano, 1996), the concept of 'emotional intelligence' was extended to the work environment (Cooper, 1997; Goleman, 1998b), the attention to the role of mood increased (Isen and Bar-On, 1991), and the general theories of dispositional effects followed (Judge and Larsen, 2001; Judge *et al.*, 1998).

PART II

Case studies on emotions in M&As

5. Purpose

The main focus of this book is to develop a deeper understanding of human aspects in the M&A process, which goes beyond the information gained from current literature. The first aim of the empirical study is as follows:

- to reveal how managers behave and communicate with employees during a period of major organizational changes, such as a merger or an acquisition;
- to discover what kinds of emotions employees feel;
- to evaluate how far these emotions influence employees' commitment towards and identification with the newly merged company, their job satisfaction, the development of their relationships and their perception of M&A success.

In the M&A literature, emotions have only been investigated as a spin-off, and never accurately. To explore themes, discover patterns and better understand processes and situations within the M&A process, a qualitative methods approach is most suitable. Indeed qualitative research is considered appropriate for theory creation because it allows us to explore a new phenomenon, while quantitative research is better suited for theory testing (see Denzin, 1978; Strauss and Corbin, 1994). Qualitative techniques are less structured than questionnaires and follow an exploratory design (which corresponds to a constructivist or phenomenological approach[1]). Therefore our empirical study follows a qualitative methods approach: it consists of four M&A case studies, in which different qualitative methods and techniques were applied.

The qualitative process helps us to find out whether our conceptual framework, which was deduced from literature, makes sense or how far it has to be adapted in order to become a testable framework. This is the second aim of the empirical study: to provide a basis for the development of testable hypotheses for future projects.

Thirdly, the study aims to conduct interviews with individuals from different levels of the hierarchy (top management, middle management and employees). Following this route will contribute to a comprehensive understanding of methodological prerequisites for future research: should future quantitative studies involve multiple hierarchical layers (multi-level analysis) or is it possible to generate representative results by focusing on one hierarchical level?

NOTE

1. According to the constructivist perspective, reality is ambiguous and cannot objectively be determined. Therefore, constructivist research places less emphasis on predetermined research strategies and methods, well-formulated hypotheses or structured interview schedules. They follow a path of discovery (Denzin and Lincoln, 1994b, pp. 200–202).

6. Information gathering and how to measure emotions

Before presenting the qualitative methods and techniques applied in the empirical project, it is useful to provide an overview of frequently applied emotion measurement methods and their limitations regarding this study. Given the paucity of emotion research in mergers and acquisitions, appropriate measurement tools are not readily available. A qualitative tool was therefore developed to capture emotions in this work. This allowed summarizing and comparing the emotional experiences of respondents.

6.1 WHICH APPROACHES TO EMOTION MEASUREMENT HAVE BEEN USED IN PAST STUDIES?

Emotions are complex phenoma which are not easy to measure. They take place inside the individual, but they can trigger signals that are visible from outside. Debate is continuing among emotion researchers about how far these signals can be interpreted pursuing an outsider perspective and in which particular way this could be done.

Emotions have a physiological, an expressive and an individual experience component (Öhman, 1986).[1] Measurement methods correspondingly concentrate on techniques which (a) are able to quantify corporeal reactions, (b) help to analyse displayed emotions of others or (c) support the collecting of self-reports from the individual.

6.1.1 Measurement of Corporeal Reactions

The attempt to find 'uninfluenced' and 'reliable' indicators of emotions led researchers to focus on the physiological component of emotions and to analyse corporeal reactions. The heart rate, the activity of certain brain regions, activation of the abdominal viscera and/or skeletomuscular changes (facial expressive responses included) were considered sufficient indicators for an increase in the emotional experience of the test subject. Polygraph-based technologies (for example, Levenson *et al.*, 1992), electroencephalographic (EEG) recordings of particular brain areas (for example, Dawson, 1994), facial electromyographic (EMG) instruments (for example, Dimberg, 1988; Tassinary and Cacioppo, 1992) and simple alterations in attention, judgment or memory are used for drawing inferences on emotional activity.

Since the abovementioned measurement methods are rather complicated and costly to apply, they are more suitable for experiments than for field studies. This is one of the reasons why the measurement of corporeal reactions was not chosen for the present study. A second reason for their poor applicability in this project is the fact that these methods can only measure emotions experienced at the moment of measurement. This study, however, focuses on emotions felt over time and is therefore interested in finding an approach suitable to measuring emotions in retrospect. A further reason why these measurement methods are not suitable for the present study is the fact that a distinction among different emotions is not possible with them. They are not able to define whether an increased brain activity means anger or fear, for example. The indicated instruments only allow identifying connections between physiological arousal and emotional experience.

6.1.2 Measurement of Displayed Emotions

Measuring the expressive component of emotions represents a second approach. The attempt to determine displayed emotions is based on the categorical perspective on emotions. The underlying assumption is that every emotion experienced inside an individual is also visible from outside. Body language and mimic expressions should allow drawing conclusions about the inner states of a person. The aim of this approach therefore is to interpret body language and especially facial expressions (of others) on photographs, on videorecords or in direct observations. The test individuals have to observe, interpret and assign one of the basic emotions to the correspondent picture (Ekman and Friesen, 1971, 1975; Izard, 1971). The question of how far emotions can be suppressed and the question of the intercultural independence of emotions and facial expressions, however, represent clear limitations of these techniques.

Emotion measurement instruments based on anatomic systems for coding observable facial behaviour facilitate the study of covert expressions. They help at least to solve the 'problem' regarding the suppression of emotions. Even if a test person tries to hide an emotional expression, small, invisible changes in facial movements can nevertheless be detected by instruments such as electromyography (EMG), facial action coding systems (FACS) and facial expression coding systems (FACES). The validity of these measurement techniques was demonstrated by means of correlating the results with self-reports (for example, Grossman and Wood, 1993; Izard, 1990).

Unfortunately these methods are overly complex for certain empirical contexts, expensive and mostly restricted to controlled laboratory settings. Consequently their use is not applicable for this real-world study. Similar to the measurement methods of corporeal reaction, it is difficult to use measurement methods of displayed emotions in field studies, and it is impossible to apply them for the analysis of emotional situations in retrospect.

6.1.3 Self-report Measurement

Since emotions are considered as an individually felt experience, it seems obvious that the best way to explore emotions is to ask the individual him/herself. Leventhal (1984) considers verbal self-reports and related response methods (rating scales, checklists, bipolar scales and so on) to be the best method for the study of emotions in adults. They allow us to assess the multiple facets of emotional and perceptual experience, and are thus the easiest way but also the most difficult to verify.

By the use of different scales self-report measures try to get information about the emotional state of an individual. The difficulty lies in the assignment of words to emotional states. Also the risk of false statements is very high. Regarding the issue of verifiability, Scherer and Wallbott (1994) believe, however, that it is better to accept biased answers than not to study emotions at all. In the case of delicate topics, anonymous questionnaires can further help to reduce the interviewer and/or environmental bias (for example, demand characteristics and social desirability).

A weakness of self-report measurements is that fast emotion changes cannot be measured with this method. The response is therefore limited to a basic or final affective state. Furthermore researchers have to be aware that everyone feels in different ways and has a different ability to recognize, define and express emotions in words. In the case of retrospective self-reports it is also questionable how far people recall emotional experiences from the past. Owing to the individual's coping mechanisms researchers might only get present *perceptions* of emotions experienced in the past, instead of really felt emotions at that time. This phenomenon is also known as 'sense making' (Herriot, 2001; Weick, 1995).

But it is not only the respondent's ability, predisposition and sense making which determine the outcomes. The research question itself and the scientist's understanding of emotions also influence the measurement methods he or she applies. If, for example, emotions are seen as a person's characteristic, a description of the respondent's personality will be part of the survey. Diener and his colleagues (Diener *et al.*, 1999), for instance, describe a happy person as

> blessed with a positive temperament, tends to look on the bright side of things, does not ruminate excessively about bad events, is living in an economically developed society, has social confidants, and possesses adequate resources for making progress towards valued goals. (Ibid., p. 295)

In this case, the positive emotional state of happiness is a characteristic of the individual rather than an emotional state itself. Researchers following this approach will use a number of questions related to personal traits in order to get information regarding a particular emotion.

We mentioned that in the present project emotions are seen as a mental state of (action) readiness that arises from cognitive appraisals of events, social interactions or thoughts (according to Bagozzi *et al.*, 1999). Therefore the measurement of emotions focuses on employees' self-reports regarding their own mental, emotional and physiological state, and their (planned or undertaken) actions during the M&A integration phase. Respondents' personal characteristics will *not* play a crucial role in this study.

Despite the mentioned limitations, self-reports are a popular method for studying the effects of emotion-eliciting situations (for example, Smith and Ellsworth, 1987) and for recalling past emotional experiences or episodes (Ellsworth and Smith, 1988; Scherer, 1988). Self-reports are especially suitable as a method when the conscious aspects of emotions are to be assessed, when the circumstances under which an emotion was felt play a role and when it is not satisfying to recognize only the subject's emotions (Tomiuk, 2000).

There are several techniques which can be applied in self-reports: structured or formless diaries, for example, are an approach for investigating naturalistic settings and the development of emotions over a longer period (see, for example, Averill, 1982). The development of scales helps to further capture the test person's past or present emotional states. Again it is important to be aware of the implications of such an approach: the use of a one-dimensional measurement scale assumes that emotions are explainable mainly through arousal. Indeed they focus on single emotions and analyse their intensity. Multidimensional approaches assume that emotions are distinguishable from each other. This is in opposition to Russell's (1989) statement that individuals experience all emotions as a bundle at the same time, and that only the intensity of single emotions varies.

In retrospective investigations of emotions, the time prospect has to be considered carefully when deciding which scale to apply or to develop. If individuals are asked to rate their immediate emotions at a certain moment, usually bipolar scales do not pose a problem because a person feels either happy or sad, excited or bored. He or she is unlikely to feel both opposite emotional states at the same time. The difficulties with bipolar scales rise when the individual has to indicate the emotional states over an extended period. Under normal life circumstances it is likely that an individual has positive and negative emotional experiences, even if neither state reaches its extreme (Payne, 2001). In such a case, it is recommended to use unipolar scales because they allow the expression of both opposites (positive and negative).

There is another, more fundamental, limitation to bipolar scales: some emotions are commonly viewed as opposites, such as *joy* and *sorrow*, *fear* and *anger*. Smith and Ellsworth (1985, p. 813) pose an important question in this context and give interesting answers: 'Are joy and sorrow opposite in the same way as fear and anger? Clearly not, because joy is pleasant, but fear and anger are both unpleasant.' The authors argue that, in order to explain what 'opposite' means, it is necessary to establish dimensions to which they are referred. The most common dimensions that are used in emotion measurement and categorization are activation or arousal (high versus low intensity), valence or quality, and duration. However, everything considered, it depends on the scope of the research question and on the researcher's perception of emotion as to which scales are adopted.

6.2   METHODS AND TECHNIQUES TO STUDY EMOTIONS IN M&As

In this project, both primary and secondary methods were adopted. Hochschild (1983) assumes that emotions are best understood in relation to the social context. This argument supported the idea of choosing in-depth interviews with those affected, a method that allows us to learn more about the circumstances and to broach the topic again in case the answer has not been full enough. In order to provide a broader picture on the topic, the dyadic approach (which would imply in-depth interviews with both management and workforce) was further extended. Three hierarchy levels were sampled: in-depth interviews with top managers or company owners, middle managers and employees without leading function were conducted. The content of the interviews will be explained in section 6.3.

Various different interview techniques (projective techniques and critical incident technique) were used in the in-depth interviews and will be described below. They were combined with observations (regarding inter-view behaviour and cultural indicators) and secondary data (newsletters, newspapers). The use of different techniques, methods and target groups is suggested to provide a clearer picture of underlying phenomena (Denzin and Lincoln, 1994a; Fetterman, 1998; Maxwell, 1998; Yin, 1998).

The traditional critical incident technique (CIT) and its variants (SOPI – sequence-oriented problem identification) have mainly been applied in service research in order to capture data on and analyse both negative and positive critical incidents (Edvardsson and Roos, 2001; Edvardsson and Strandvik, 2000; Johnson, 2002; Roos, 2002; Stauss and Mang, 1999). Here the aims of using the CIT at the beginning of the interview were to help respondents to 'warm up'. This allowed us to discover which M&A events were still at the forefront of their minds, even though some events go back several months or even years.

Projective techniques have a lengthy and vital history in ethnographic research (Fetterman, 1998, p. 486), in psychographic research (Fram and Cibotti, 1991; Piirto, 1990) and in marketing research: for example, in life style segmentation (Piirto, 1990), brand image and purchase motivation (Hussey and Duncombe, 1999). Projective techniques are also used in human resource management (for example, subordinate feedback: see Moats Kennedy, 1997) and in personality assessment (Clark, 1995). Projective techniques are popular because they deliberately stimulate a relaxed free flow of associations (Strauss and Corbin, 1990). They can uncover and identify deep, normally unacknowledged feelings to an extent which is usually not attained in standard interviews or focus groups (Hollander, 1988). As such exercises are usually viewed as fun, people express themselves more fully and openly. The techniques are especially useful in eliciting honest information about sensitive or embarrassing topics (ibid.). Furthermore they perform well in revealing real-world phenomena, are relatively cost-effective to conduct, and are a useful way to examine attitudes and behaviours (Fram and Cibotti, 1991).

It should be mentioned that projective techniques are not an infallible method as both researcher and respondent bring their own styles to discussions. This provides for subjective judgment and interpretation of results. Consequently it is practically impossible to replicate this qualitative method identically over time (Hussey and Duncombe, 1999). However studies also show that the results are quite consistent with results from other methods and that different investigators obtained similar results when the studies were conducted at comparable time periods (Fram and Cibotti, 1991). Nevertheless projective techniques should not stand alone but be combined with other methods.

The first projective technique used was the 'temperature curve'. Since nothing similar could be found in emotion literature, this technique is developed here in order to measure emotions over time. The instrument is appealing and simple to apply. It consists of drawing the intensity of emotions in a system of coordinates where the horizontal axis represents the time horizon (with pre-given intervals) and the vertical axis the intensity of emotional experiences (see Figure 6.1). The interviewees were asked to draw a diagram, a 'temperature curve', of their individual emotional arousal. The time intervals on the horizontal axis were given, while respondents were free to mark the emotional intensity without indication of distances and thus with fewer restrictions. The official announcement of the merger was considered to lie in the origin of the coordinate system.

When developing this instrument, it was also considered to capture positive (pleasant) and negative (unpleasant) emotions over time. Pre-tests showed, however, that it did not make sense to ask interviewees to draw a curve with positive–negative emotions along the time axis because pleasant and unpleasant emotions often happened simultaneously. Emotions (according to their definition) are relatively short and rather intense individual experiences. Within a very short period one can experience both positive and negative emotions. For this reason the 'temperature curve' measured the perceived emotional intensity over time. In a second step, interviewees were asked to describe and to explain the 'peaks' and 'turns' of their 'temperature curve'. They presented their 'stories' about the M&A and tried to find the appropriate emotion or emotion-related terms for each arousing event.

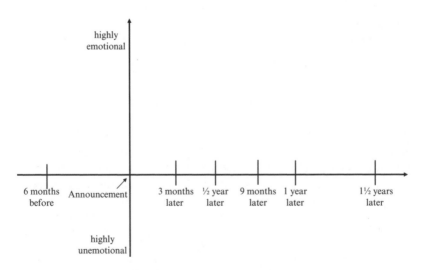

Figure 6.1   Template for the 'temperature curve'

The second projective technique consisted of the personalization of the two merging companies. The respondent had to describe the two corporate cultures as personalities, imagining personal characteristics and living circumstances of this 'personality' (hobbies, friends, favourite dish, car brand and other traits of the 'company as a person').

In addition to these different interview techniques, notes were taken during the conversation. These observations related to the respondent, his/her reaction to questions, the interview climate, the comprehensibility of questions and the interviewer's answers (for example, smiles, pauses and other non-linguistic expressions). Observations about the company itself and about sources of cultural indicators were noted as well. These comprised company culture aspects such as architecture of the buildings, the reception, behaviour and way people treated each other, dress codes, working structure, mission statement and so on. Also circulating rumours were collected, as far as these were accessible to the researcher. According to the literature (for example, Cooper and Cartwright, 1996), these methods are deemed appropriate to broaden the picture of a company's corporate culture and its communication style.

Secondary analysis consisted of analysis of documents such as employee newsletters or company magazines. Corporate web pages and public statements in newspapers were also screened. This helped to uncover information regarding the company's corporate culture and the degree of formality of communication within an organization. Indirectly, in some cases these secondary analyses also revealed managers' attitudes towards employees' emotions and towards the need to involve personnel in the M&A integration process.

Table 6.1 provides an overview of the qualitative research approach, the aims and the applied methods and techniques.

6.3   INTERVIEW GUIDELINE FOR THE CASE STUDIES

Based on suggestions from literature and on our conceptual framework, a first interview guideline was developed. All the dimensions covered in the conceptual framework were backed up by relevant questions. The interview guideline was pre-tested with two managers from different merged companies. The pre-tests were tape-recorded and transcribed. During these pre-test interviews, notes with respect to the comprehensibility of the questions were taken. These notes and a careful analysis of the transcripts of the interviews helped to improve and further develop the interview guideline: the order of some questions had to be rearranged and a few questions had

Table 6.1   Qualitative research approach and applied methods & techniques

Research stage	Techniques/methods	Purpose

Stage 1
  In-depth interviews
  with top managers
  or company owners,
  middle managers
  and employees
	CIT (critical incident
	  technique)
	SOPI (sequence-oriented
	  problem identification)
	Projective technique:
	  'temperature curve'
	  and 'company as
	  personality'
	Analysis of transcripts
	  with N*Vivo program
		Identification of . . .
		different stages in the
		  M&A process
		typical kinds/types of
		  collective emotions
		Managerial coping with
		  collective emotions
		  (how it is perceived by
		  employees and by
		  managers themselves)

	Analysis of transcripts
	  with N*Vivo program:
	  for example, 'us versus
	  them' terms indicate
	  closeness to 'the others'
	Analysis of projective
	  techniques
	Collection of current
	  mood/rumours
	  circulating
		Employees' readiness to . . .
		dismiss their own
		  organizational identity
		accept a new organizational
		  identity
		contribute to the M&A
		  success

Stage 2
  Observations of . . .
	Interview partners'(top
	  managers', middle
	  managers' and
	  employees') reactions
	  when questions are
	  asked
	Sources of cultural
	  indicators (architecture,
	  dress codes, working
	  structure, mission
	  statements . . .)	

Stage 3
  Analysis of
  documents
	Employee newsletters
	Company magazines
	Homepages of the
	  companies
	Public statements in
	  newspapers and so on
		Managers' attitude
		  (consciousness) towards
		  employees' emotions
		  and towards the need to
		  involve personnel in the
		  M&A integration
		  process
		Formality/informality of
		  communication

to be rephrased. The revisions of the interview guidelines proved to be highly meritorious. Potential interviewer biases could be reduced by making the questions neutral, and the flow of the interview conversation could be enhanced.

The 18 in-depth interviews were conducted with one person at a time, with one exception, when two colleagues did the interview together. Below we provide explanations and background information about the interview questions.

6.3.1   Introduction

Before starting the interview, the interview partner had to be introduced to the topic and its background. While interviewees needed to know what to expect, the pre-test illustrated that it was advisable not to mention words like 'emotions' or 'feelings' when explaining the purpose of the study. Interview partners seemed to feel uncomfortable when they had the impression that they had to undergo a kind of hidden psychological test or reveal personal emotions. Therefore the human side of M&As in general was stressed when introducing to the topic.

It was important to underline that no 'dangerous' question, such as strategic alignment or financial background, would be asked and that all the data would be treated in a confidential and anonymous manner. Respondents were informed that the interview would take between 45 minutes and two hours, depending on their time budget and their readiness to share their inside knowledge.

6.3.2   M&A History, Facts and Emotional Experiences

A 'warm-up' question initiated the interviews. It allowed respondents to freely express personal experiences with the merger or the acquisition and to develop an easy atmosphere for conversations and 'story-telling'. This also helped the interviewer to get an overview of the M&A situation. Respondents were encouraged to talk about the (perceived) motives for the merger or the acquisition, about their role and about the impact the organizational change had on them. They briefly illuminated key changes for the company resulting from the merger. During this more or less open talk, the focus was directed towards perceptions of group experiences during the integration process, firstly, because one of the interests was to find out whether a merger experience is seen more as an individual or as a collective experience by those affected, and secondly, because some interviewees tended to respond more openly when they were allowed to talk in the third person. Two projective techniques were used at this stage: the critical incident technique

(CIT), in order to identify the most important and outstanding events during the M&A integration process, and the 'temperature curve'.

6.3.3 Managerial Communication

This part of the interview was divided into three sections. The first section focused on the announcement of the merger or acquisition, and on how the M&A decision was presented and 'sold' to the employees: by whom it was announced, in what form and what kinds of media were used, and so on. Further questions were, for example, whether the announcement had been planned in detail before, whether all employees had been informed at the same time, and whether or not they had the opportunity to raise any pressing questions.

The second section of questions was related to the (in)formality of communication in the early post-merger integration stage. It included questions about the way news was communicated to the staff, what media were used, what kinds of rumours circulated and how management reacted to these rumours.

The third section was about the continuity and frequency of top-down communication. These questions regarded employees' perceptions of having been appropriately informed.

6.3.4 Stress

Even though stress was not a major topic to focus on in this study, interviewees were asked whether they experienced higher levels of stress than usual, who in the company was most affected by stress, which stages of the M&A process were perceived as particularly stressful, what the sources of stress were and how people coped with stress.

6.3.5 Management Behaviour

The next cluster of questions dealt with management behaviour. Respondents were asked to indicate whether the merger had concrete implications for employees. This question addressed issues such as new areas of responsibility, training on the job or whether there were new career paths emerging. Also of interest was how many job promotions occurred in relation to pre-merger times and how the fluctuation rate was affected. The focus, however, was on management's reaction and proactive behaviour towards employees in this 'turbulent' stage of the M&A. This led to questions such as how managers tried to convince the staff to accept the decision, how they motivated people, how they tried to develop a positive atmosphere in this period and whether concrete measures had been undertaken in order to integrate the two corporate cultures.

As the dismissal of employees is always a crucial part in the post-merger stage (Cartwright and Cooper, 2000; Gutknecht and Keys, 1993), it was necessary to identify whether or not people had to leave the company involuntarily, because it was supposed that this fact would have a major impact on group dynamics. And more in detail, it was important to know whether dismissals of employees were communicated right from the beginning of the merger or whether dismissals were announced gradually during the M&A integration stage. Farewell parties, as well as operational support for those dismissed, seemed to be an indication of 'responsible' management behaviour. Support included retraining, job search and financial assistance. In this context it was considered essential to find out whether employees left the company voluntarily and, if so, at what stage in the process and why.

6.3.6   Emotions

The first question was about the types of emotions that appeared in the post-merger stage, and it was asked openly. With the help of the 'temperature curve', the interview partners were invited to indicate at which stage(s) of the M&A process these emotions were predominant, and which key events had caused them. Another issue was the collectiveness of emotional experiences: it was asked whether different kinds of emotions and different levels of intensity were noticeable in different groups, departments or teams, or whether every employee experienced individual emotions.

6.3.7   Coping with Emotions

After talking about the experience of emotions, the interview tapped into coping mechanisms. It was of interest to find out how employees dealt with their own emotions. However the main focus was on managerial behaviour: whether managers coped with employees' emotions and, if so, how they reacted and whether this led to any changes in employees' emotions.

6.3.8   Corporate Culture and Identity

This cluster of questions was divided into two parts: the first was interested in the pre-merger corporate culture, the second in the post-merger corporate culture. Therefore, at the beginning, it was necessary to find out if the two company cultures differed significantly from each other prior to the merger. Respondents were invited to provide examples of differences in company cultures. For this purpose, a projective technique was helpful: interview partners were encouraged to describe both companies as personalities by indicating for each whether this 'person' would be male or female, which hobbies and friends the person would have, what his/her favourite dish would be, where he/she would live, what type of car (brand) this person would drive, what kind of clothes he/she would wear and so on. This method gives quite a good impression of the respondents' perception of the two corporate cultures.

Before continuing the interview with post-merger corporate cultures, interview partners were asked to evaluate employee commitment to the pre-merger organizations. With regard to the post-merger stage, the interview questions focused on issues like the quality of day-to-day collaboration between the two companies, the degree of noticeable changes in corporate cultures and in people's identification, and 'us versus them' feelings.

6.3.9 Job Satisfaction

In this part of the interview respondents were invited to describe their perception of employees' job satisfaction before and after the merger. As with several other interview questions, the answer was based on the interview partner's subjective interpretation of the situation. In an attempt to receive unbiased and 'objective' answers, interviewees were asked whether absenteeism rates, job fluctuation and sickness rates had changed after the merger, and how many employees had voluntarily left the company.

6.3.10 Relationships

The changes in three kinds of relationships were investigated here: what impact the merger or the acquisition had, firstly, on relationships between co-workers from the old company, secondly, on relationships between employees and their superiors, and thirdly, on the relationship between the two merged companies.

6.3.11 Perceived Performance

Since the deal with the companies was not to ask any 'delicate' questions, performance-related questions were limited to respondents' perceptions of performance. Indicators included perceived integration success, satisfaction with the integration, probability of a similar/different plan of action from ex-post perspective, and so on.

6.3.12   Final Issues

Finally interviewees were invited to comment on critical issues in the management of M&A processes. Factors were sought which, according to their perspective, had a significant impact on the outcomes of M&As. At the end of each interview, respondents filled in a form entailing demographic information.

6.4   SELECTION OF THE CASES

After two pre-test interviews, the interview guideline was revised and applied to 16 other staff members of four companies with M&A experiences. The four organizations differed in size, industry sector and M&A situation.[2] This means, some partial and some full (100 per cent) takeovers were considered, and members from acquiring as well as from acquired firms were interviewed. The M&As involved a variety of sometimes daunting organisational changes; in some cases dismissals were necessary, in others they could be avoided. All the approached companies were immediately ready to participate in this empirical study. The companies involved were the following:[3]

- *Leitner*, an Italian (South Tyrolean) producer of lifts, cableways, urban transport systems, snow groomers and snowmaking systems bought several companies in a few years. In 2000, Leitner bought Prinoth, a medium-sized South Tyrolean company, and the second biggest competitor on the global market, the French company *Poma*. Now they are the worldwide market leader in their sector. The interviews were conducted with Leitner members, and the focus of attention in the interviews was the acquisition of Poma.
- In 1995, all *Schwarzkopf* subsidiaries were sold to the Germany-based *Henkel* group. Within two years of the takeover, Henkel closed most of the Schwarzkopf subsidiaries, transferred the production of selected Schwarzkopf products to Henkel subsidiaries and extended the strong Schwarzkopf brand to a few of their own hair care products. The interviews were conducted with former Schwarzkopf staff from the Austria-based subsidiary Kematen, near Innsbruck.
- The Italian (South Tyrolean) family-owned sports article retailer *Sportler* has grown continuously over the last 25 years. The biggest expansion was experienced in 1999, when Sportler decided to buy the ten Italian outlets of the Austria-based sports article wholesaler *Hervis*.

- Staff was a medium-sized German producer of light systems that was well known for its design. Owing to the absence of descendants to run the company after the last owner's death, Staff was sold to the Austrian family business *Zumtobel*. Zumtobel is (was) also a light system producer, but with a stronger focus on engineering. In 1993, 49 per cent of Staff was bought by Zumtobel and, two years later, total takeover took place. Now the company's name is *Zumtobel Staff*. In 2000, Zumtobel Staff merged with one of its biggest competitors, the UK-based light system producer *Thorn*, which is about the same size (in terms of employees and annual turnover) as Zumtobel Staff.

Interviews were conducted with former Staff and former Zumtobel members. They were asked to comment about either of the two M&As, the Zumtobel–Staff or the Zumtobel Staff–Thorn merger, whichever they remembered better or felt more intensely about.

Table 6.2 provides an overview of the companies involved, together with some demographic data. The 'A' in Table 6.2 (for example, 'Company A', 'Employees A') refers to the company whose members were interviewed. The 'B' refers to the partner company, which could be the buying or the acquiring firm.

Unfortunately the descriptive data received from various interview partners differed significantly and did not always correspond with official communication. This is in line with research which reports that subjective measures often work better than objective measures with managers. Therefore data presented in the table represent official information from websites,[4] enriched by management input.

Eighteen interviews were conducted. The two interview partners for the pre-test were selected from a list of informal business contacts. The 16 prime respondents were identified internally after formally approaching company executives and requesting support for the study. In order to provide a broader picture on the topic, in-depth interviews were conducted on different hierarchy levels: (a) top managers or company owners, (b) middle managers (those in leading functions, but depending on at least one 'layer' above them in the hierarchy), and (c) employees (those with no leading function within the company). In addition, individuals within the companies (secretaries, support staff and workers) were approached on site, in public places of the company premises, before and after scheduled interviews.

Out of the 18 interviewees, pre-test included, six were female and 12 male. They had worked for between two and 25 years in the respective company (on average 9.9 years). Three of the respondents were top

Table 6.2 Company demographics

Company A	Leitner	Schwarzkopf	Sportler	Staff	Zumtobel Staff
M&A situation Company B	buys **Poma**	bought by **Henkel**	buys **Hervis** (10 outlets)	bought by **Zumtobel**	buys **Thorn**
Year of M&A	2000 (2002*)	1996 (according to Schwarzkopf) 1995 (according to Henkel)	1999	1993 (49%), 1995 (100%)	1999 summer or 2000 February (2000*)
Nation A	Italy	Austria	Italy (South Tyrol, German speaking)	Germany	Austria
Nation B	France	Germany/ worldwide	Austria (10 Italian outlets)	Austria	UK
Industrial sector A	Producer: (ski-) lifts, cableways, urban transport systems, mini-metro, snow groomers, snowmaking systems	Producer: body care products and cosmetics	Retailer: sports articles	Producer: light systems (design-oriented)	Producer: light systems
Industrial sector B	Producer: similar to Leitner	Producer: chemicals, cosmetics, glue, cleaners	Retailer: sports articles	Producer: light systems (technic-oriented)	Producer: light systems

Employees A	650 (717 in 2001*)	255 (145 'Handel', 110 'Friseure')	190	540/650/900 (different information)	4500 (3085*)
Employees B	650 (600*) All together (A + B + Prinoth): 1600–1700 (1500*)	47 200 (46 400 in 1996*)	145 (in the 10 outlets)	Approx. 2600 (in 1995)	4500 (over 3400*)
Turnover A	EUR 162 million (2001), 170 million francs	800 million ATS	EUR 14 million		
Turnover B	1.1 billion francs (2000)	EUR 9656 million	EUR 11.4 million (10 outlets)		EUR 566.4 million
Foundation year A	1888	1898	1977	1920s	
Foundation year B	1936	1876	1972	1950s	1928

Note: *Information according to the corresponding companies' web pages.

managers and/or company owners, eight were middle managers, and seven interview partners were employees without organizational leading functions. Half of the interviewees reported that their career was affected by the changes due to the merger, six did not experience major changes, two respondents had been dismissed, and in one case the question was not applicable.

6.5 PROCEDURE

The two pre-test interviews were conducted in July 2002. Feedback from the pre-tests was used to revise and update the interview guideline. Sixteen semi-structured interviews were conducted in September 2002. The interviews were done on the job in Italy and in Austria. During the dialogue, the interview guideline was adapted to the position, knowledge, 'language' (managers spoke another 'language' than workers and different dialects were spoken in different regions) and according to the answers of the interviewee. The duration of the one-to-one interviews (one interview was done via video conference) varied between 50 minutes and two and a half hours.

Most of the interviews (14 out of 18) were tape-recorded and transcribed, which enabled an accurate analysis and a careful interpretation of the original statements. The content of all interviews was completed by notes and observations. The transcripts were analysed with the N*Vivo program (see below). However, in some cases, respondents added some very interesting and useful information only when the recorder was already off. This information was documented in notes soon afterwards. Three of the respondents preferred their interview not to be tape-recorded.

For the sake of not losing out on those interview partners who preferred not to be recorded, taping was rejected and detailed notes were taken instead by the interviewer. The 14 transcribed interviews led to 264 pages of transcripts. The four non-transcribed interviews plus the informal 'chats' led to another 58 pages of notes and summaries.

The literature (Cartwright and Cooper, 2000; Sinkovics *et al.*, 2005) suggests taking notes regarding contextual factors of the interview situation, such as physical factors, the infrastructure of the office and the behaviour of employees within the building. Thus, during and after each interview, observation notes were taken regarding the interviewee, the company building, the reception and the notification to the interview partner, the office structure, the presence of informal spots where employees could meet and talk (for example, cafeterias, open offices), culture codes such as dress codes and formality in greeting each other.

Analyses of secondary material, such as newspaper articles, company newsletters and information from company homepages, helped to further clarify and enrich the interview data.

6.5.1   The N*Vivo Program

Qualitative research is manifold. Different qualitative methodologies serve different objectives. The use of Computer-Assisted Qualitative Data Analysis (CAQDAS) in the form of specialist software packages (for example, Ethnograph, NUD*IST, HyperQual, HyperResearch, QUALPRO, SONAR, Altas-ti, and so on) is a fairly recent development and helps to achieve various goals. These programs facilitate the management of large amounts of qualitative documents and make it possible to link them with different types of statistical analysis. Most of such analyses can be considered as intermediate steps between pure interpretations and quantitative methods because, to a certain extent, they allow treating qualitative data like quantitative data.

For this project, QSR NUD*IST Vivo (N*Vivo) was chosen as being one of the most flexible programs available at that time (Sinkovics *et al.*, 2005). N*Vivo is a further development of the NUD*IST (Non-numerical Unstructured Data * Indexing Searching and Theorizing) computer software package for qualitative research. It seeks to provide a toolkit for exploring documents, creating, developing and organizing ideas, and managing categories and patterns from previously unstructured data. Data that are particularly suitable for computer-aided qualitative research include transcripts of interviews, historical or literary documents (newspaper articles, for example), personnel records, outlines and graphs, field notes, reports, electronic papers and Internet documents, video films, tape recording and all types of documents which can be read by the computer. N*Vivo is designed to enable single or multi-user access within a networked environment. It provides audit trails and has an interface with programs such as SPSS.

N*Vivo offers the following text management capabilities:

- management of categories and codes:[5] the researcher can record new ideas, theories, definitions and memos within documents; explore and code documents (this implies combining, comparing and reviewing coded text modules); and view codes and text passages in order to examine links and issues. Relationships are displayed in 'tree structures' where the emphasis is on the conceptual relationship between codes (Richards, 1999);
- searches and reports: the user can search documents for occurrences of words or strings of characters; construct patterns for complex

searches (overlapping and intersecting themes, contexts of categories and so on); and generate reports, based on text and code searches.

To summarize, qualitative research usually has two faces: the creation and the management of complexity. The project grows in complexity while linking, coding, shaping and modelling data. The software facilitates the development and synthesis of a researcher's ideas and provides various mechanisms to arrive at answers to research questions. Nevertheless, even when using software, it is still the researcher who has to form a rich and colourful picture in his/her mind and to capture all the analytical information of the collected data.

The following chapters discuss the results of the case studies. The findings are structured according to the main topics of the interview guideline and supplemented by topics which only emerged during the analyses of the qualitative data. Chapter 7 presents empirical findings regarding emotions in M&As. Chapters 8 and 9 discuss the findings about managerial communication and managerial behaviour, respectively, and are followed by results regarding M&A outcomes, in Chapter 10. The findings presented will be substantiated by citations from the transcribed interviews.

NOTES

1. According to Lazarus (1991), emotions also have a context or environmental component. Since this context variable can be investigated through the individual experience component (through self-reports), we will not discuss this component further.
2. In the case of Zumtobel Staff, members of both former companies were interviewed, but Zumtobel Staff is only counted as one company.
3. Their support and openness in contributing to this study is gratefully acknowledged.
4. http://www.leitner-lifts.com, http://www.pomagroup.com, http://www.schwarzkopf.at, http://www.henkel.com, http://www.sportler.it, http://www.hervis.at, http://www.zumto belstaff.at, http://www.thornlighting.com/about/index.html; no corporate website available for Staff.
5. Coding is the action of assigning passages of text from a document to a node. The node is then said to be a *code* of that passage of the document. A *node* is an object in a project which is intended to represent anything that researchers may wish to refer to, such as people who are studied, concepts, places, mental states, or features of the research as a project. Nodes can be given values of *attributes* (a named generic property). According to their features, nodes can be grouped in sets, and they can code relevant passages in the documents of the project. Nodes are stored in the node system.

7. Emotions

Research has shown that organizational changes are always connected with emotional experiences (for example, Antonacopoulou and Gabriel, 2001; Carr, 2001; Cartwright and Cooper, 1994; Huy, 2002; Kiefer, 2002b; Marks and Mirvis, 2001; Mossholder *et al.*, 2000; Paterson and Cary, 2002). Most of these studies have either looked at change processes in general management contexts, focused on other dimensions than emotions, or simply analysed negative emotions.

According to Kiefer (2002b), experiences are always interwoven with emotions, certain themes and related behaviour. These constitute the parts of her analysis when studying emotional experiences. Kiefer directly asked interviewees which emotions were predominant during the previous six months, what were the causes and what were the consequences of the emotions mentioned. In the present study, however, another approach was chosen. For individuals who are not very aware of their and others' emotions and of the causes and effects of their emotions, Kiefer's approach is considered too advanced. Awareness of one's and others' emotions constitutes an important part of the concept of emotional intelligence, according to several authors (for example, Bar-On and Parker, 2000; Goleman, 1995; Humber, 2002; Mayer and Salovey, 1993; Salovey and Mayer, 1990). It might be better to acknowledge that not every interview partner is highly emotionally intelligent on this specific dimension.

The pre-test interviews further revealed that individuals do not easiliy recall emotions per se, but recall them in connection with certain events or themes. This is in line with prior research (Kiefer, 2002b; Rafaeli and Worline, 2001). Therefore interview partners were 'led through' M&A events experienced in the past in order to better activate their memories. This means the questions of the subsequent interviews focused first on typical episodes like official (and unofficial) announcements, first meeting with the members of the partner organization, integration activities and so on, before directing the conversation towards emotions.

The use of critical incident technique (CIT) and the application of the 'temperature curve', a projective technique, facilitated this exploration of emotional experiences in the M&A integration process.

7.1   THE 'TEMPERATURE CURVE'

The 'temperature curve' and the application of this technique have been discussed above. The instrument proved suitable for our context and supportive
in reporting the interviewee's emotional experience of integration processes.
The 'temperature curve' was a fundamental building block of the interview.
It set the scene for the interview, respondents developed and complemented
the figure in the course of the interview, and whenever a new perspective came
into their mind it was added. Hence this technique was also very helpful
for understanding the chronological order of the 'stories'. Some respondents mentioned differences between collective and personal experiences.
If this was not mentioned spontaneously, we asked whether divergences
would exist between a 'collective' and an 'individual temperature curve'.

Figure 7.1 presents an example of a respondent's perceived emotions over
time. Having drawn this 'temperature curve', the interview partner was asked
to explain which kind of emotions emerged over time and whether these
emotions were considered as positive or as negative. Of special interest were
those stages which were perceived as 'highly emotional'. Furthermore the
interviewee was asked to tell 'the story' underlying the curve and to indicate
by which events or management interventions the emotions mentioned were
triggered. In this case, the announcement of the M&A was considered as
the most emotional moment. It was perceived as a shocking and euphoric
event at the same time. Afterwards the situation became calmer with a small

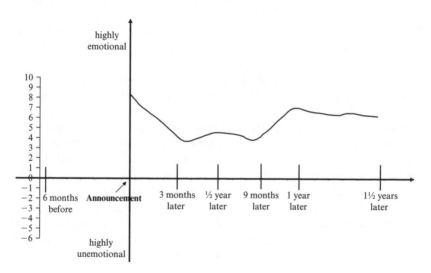

Figure 7.1   'Temperature curve': a respondent's longitudinal perspective

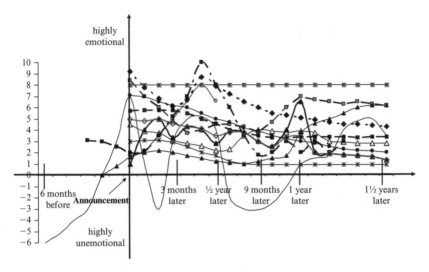

Figure 7.2   Combined 'temperature curves'

increase in emotional intensity about half a year after the announcement
(first conflicts with 'the others') and a steeper incline about one year after
when the 'disillusion' emerged. Since then the emotional intensity has more
or less kept its high level, but it has never again reached the emotional intensity of the M&A announcement.

Figure 7.2 combines the 'temperature curves' which were drawn by
interviewees. This tangle of all 'temperature curves' makes interpretation
difficult. Therefore it is better to combine them differently: first, according
to the interviewee's hierarchical level within their companies, and second,
according to company membership. These combinations are presented in
the following figures, and they illustrate some interesting patterns for each
subgroup of the sample.

Figure 7.3 presents the 'temperature curves' of top managers and/or
company owners. In contrast to interviewees who have at least one hierarchy
layer above them (that is, all employees and middle managers), top-managers
were not asked about their own emotions. They were asked how employees
(irrespective of their position) have experienced the merger or the acquisition. Although there are only three curves available, it is interesting to note
that for this group of respondents the emotional intensity does not vary as
much over time compared to middle managers' and employees' curves. What
is also remarkable is that the announcement was seen as the most (or at
least among the most) emotional events. Interestingly, emotions prior to the
merger or acquisition were not considered at all by top managers, although

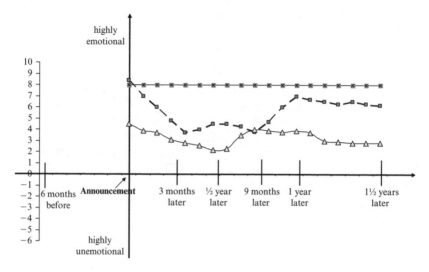

Figure 7.3   Top managers' perception of employees' 'temperature curves'

some dependants (for example, middle managers and some secretaries) were involved in the merger already before the final M&A decision was taken. It is surprising also because the interview instructions were the same for all interviewees, and the template provided a grid which allowed inclusion of a curve for the time prior to the official announcement as well.

Figure 7.4 shows middle managers' emotional experience of the M&A. It is notable that the 'temperature curves' present a wider spectrum of emotional intensity: from highly emotional to (partially) highly unemotional. The negative range of the vertical axis has only been used by one interview partner. One may deduce that middle managers encounter comparatively numerous arousing events during a merger. They are subject to both top-down and bottom-up concerns. Periods in which 'nothing special' happens in relation to other merger-related issues are thus perceived as 'unemotional' stages.

Also remarkable is that some middle managers also considered the pre-announcement period in their evaluation because they were informed about the M&A before the rest of the employees. Some middle managers had to prepare the relevant documents for the due-diligence process. Even though their M&A-related emotions started earlier, the official announcement is still considered as relatively intensive compared to the pre-merger emotional experience.

Employees' emotions regarding the M&A only emerge after the announcement. As expected, their 'temperature curves' only started with

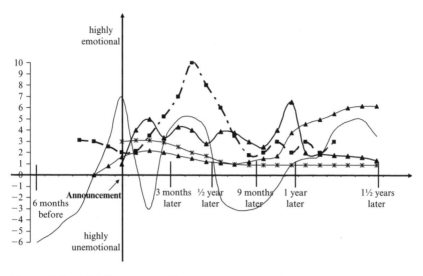

Figure 7.4   Middle managers' 'temperature curves'

the information about the upcoming changes. In most of the cases, the announcement (sometimes also a short period afterwards) is considered as the emotionally most intensive moment. No point along the time horizon is considered as 'unemotional' (see Figure 7.5). In cases where the M&A process went relatively smoothly, employees found it easier to cope and to accept the changes. The emotional intensity decreased over time.

In one case the 'temperature curve' rises sharply after the announcement. In this particular case, the individual heard about the acquisition via the direct line manager, together with a small group of colleagues from the same department. The announcement increased insecurity, but it still left some space for hopes among employees. However, in the following months, uncertainty increased, more and more rumours spread, some of the employees knew already that they would be dismissed by the end of the calendar year, and emotions became more and more intense (mistrust, anger, grief, anxieties). The emotional intensity culminated during the official announcement which was made by the general director of the buying company. This moment was perceived as particularly intense in a negative way (rage, aggression, defiance) because the way it was announced was perceived as false and misleading. For instance, a secure workplace was promised to everybody, while several employees already knew that they had to leave the company within the following few months. Therefore the official M&A announcement was considered to be the emotionally most intensive moment for employees.

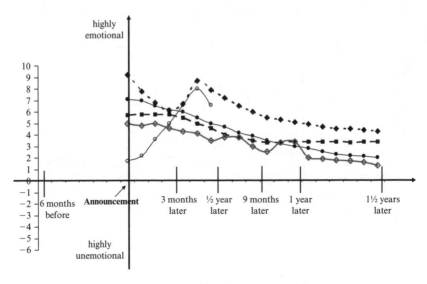

Figure 7.5   Employees' 'temperature curves'

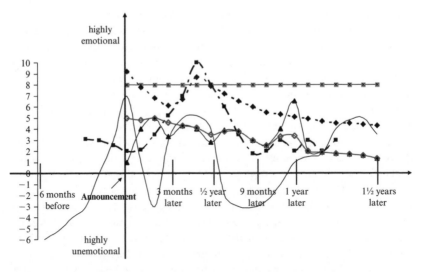

Figure 7.6   Combined 'temperature curves' from respondents of company X

The following two figures illustrate the emotional experiences of different members within two selected companies in order to find out to what extent emotional experiences are collective or individual phenomena. In the first case (Figure 7.6), members of company X seem to have experienced the

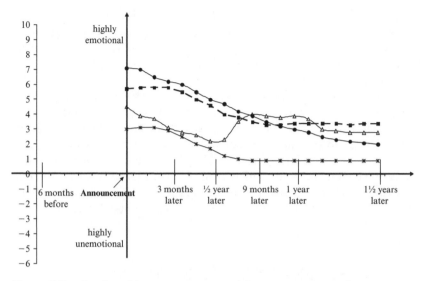

Figure 7.7   Combined 'temperature curves' from respondents of company Y

M&A process in a relatively individual way. The 'temperature curves' do not have much in common. The only trend one could identify is a tendency of increased emotional intensity about three months after the announcement and after the ninth month. Text analyses of the interviews confirm that the members of company X perceived the whole merger process as stressful and difficult.

Figure 7.7 presents a different picture. The members of company Y experienced the post-merger integration more homogeneously. The transcrips confirm that this company managed the merger in a better way, used better coping mechanisms and achieving higher acceptance.

7.2   COLLECTIVE VERSUS INDIVIDUAL EMOTIONS

Looking at Figure 7.6 and Figure 7.7, and analysing the differences between the two organizations, one can deduce that emotions are only partially a social phenomenon. Emotions are not necessarily felt in a similar way throughout an organization. On the other hand – as we will see later, when discussing the content of the interviews – it seems that emotions are relatively homogeneous among team (or department) members from the same 'hierarchical level'. They often share the same top-down information, experience similar challenges and therefore experience similar fears, motivational changes, jealousy and so on. Nevertheless, to a certain extent, every single member experiences M&As and interprets managerial communication and actions in a rather individual way. This confirms Lazarus's view that, while emotions express social relationships, they are still created by individuals and their minds (Lazarus, 1995).

Also the coping mechanisms with stressful M&A-related events differ from individual to individual. While some managers and employees cope with their emotions by sharing the experience with their family or friends, others prefer to keep these issues away from their private life and prefer to chat with their working colleagues. Also the spreading of rumours can be seen as a coping mechanism. However, as section 8.4 will explain, rumours are not the most effective way of dealing with negative emotions. Some interview partners also mentioned sport as a possibility for giving vent to their negative emotions.

7.3 DIFFERENT KINDS OF EMOTIONS

The interviewer did not mention specific emotions during the interview. The questions were open. This was a means to generate unaided response and to tone down emotional experiences. This grounded theorizing approach is well suited to the study of processual experiences in organizational life in general (see Harlos and Pinder, 2000; Martin and Turner, 1986). Here its advantage was that it allowed going beyond typical M&A studies: there was space for interviewees to talk also about positive emotions, for example. Although negative or unpleasant emotions appeared about twice as often as positive emotions (see the following section), we think that positive emotions cannot be neglected when studying organizational change processes.

Either the interview partner listed specific emotions in the context of his/her individual 'temperature curve', or specific emotions were attributed to the corresponding statements by the interviewer during the coding process. The voicing and the story (for example, perceived injustice in favour of 'the others') helped the interviewer to deduce the emotion 'jealousy'.

Table 7.1 presents an overview of the mentioned emotions and cognition-related affect terms that were reported in the interviews. Frequency counts of codes identified those emotions which were commonly and frequently shared. This provides a rough indication of which emotions were felt predominately during the post-merger processes in the companies analysed.

Table 7.1   Emotions and cognition-related affect terms reported in the empirical study

Categorization	Emotions and emotion-loaded terms	Number of statements/ paragraphs	Subtotals
Statements regarding emotions (generally)	emotion awareness (attitudes towards emotions)	73	335
	collective v. individual emotions	89	
	coping with emotions	80	
	emotional intensity	93	
'Positive'/ pleasant affects	positive attitude/mood	33	366
	feelings of certainty, safety	44	
	pride	39	
	attraction, positive challenge, looking forward	22	
	curiosity	4	
	joy, satisfaction	61	
	trust, confidence, belief	49	
	hope, expectations	32	
	motivation	61	
	enthusiasm, euphoria	21	
'Negative'/ unpleasant emotions	negative atmosphere	33	786
	incomprehension, lack of understanding/appreciation	43	
	feelings of uncertainty amongst employees	99	
	feelings of uncertainty amongst managers	59	
	anxiety, fear (existential), dread, terror	83	
	anger,[1] rage, aggression, fury; reproach, accusation	66	
	distrust	58	
	feeling tired, demotivation	35	
	impotence/powerlessness, despair/ desperation	21	
	frustration	35	
	resignation	25	
	disappointment/disillusionment	37	
	shock	11	
	lethargy, bluntness, obtuseness, being reserved	13	
	indifference, apathy	9	

Table 7.1   (continued)

Categorization	Emotions and emotion-loaded terms	Number of statements/ paragraphs	Subtotals
	envy	22	
	jealousy	22	
	arrogance	23	
	feelings of inferiority	5	
	grief, sorrow	19	
	pain	17	
	shyness, timidity	4	
	surprise (negative connotation)	3	
	compassion, sympathy, feel pity for someone	6	
	opposition, resistance	33	
	others	6	
Total sum of statements coded with an emotion-loaded term		1 487	1 487

7.4   POSITIVE AND NEGATIVE EMOTIONS

Table 7.1 demonstrates that more negative than positive emotions emerged in the cases analysed. One reason for this could be that negative experiences are more heavily weighted and longer lasting in subjective judgment processes than positive experiences. A scientific explanation for this phenomenon comes from Fiedler and Bless (2000): according to Piaget's distinction between 'assimilation' and 'accommodation', the authors argue that the 'top-down' process of assimilation is characteristic of positive, appetitive situations, while the 'bottom-up' process of accommodation is typical for negative experiences. This means that positive emotional states facilitate active generation of beliefs (change of schemas, stereotypes and scripts), whereas negative emotional states support the conservation of input data and of the 'status quo'.

An interesting finding was that interviewees tended to attribute negative emotions to others and not to themselves. For example, none of the interview partners reported their own fears while others' anxieties were merrily commented on. This is interesting considering that fear and anxiety were very frequently mentioned emotions (83 times). Similar response behaviour was observed for arrogance, feelings of superiority, jealousy or envy. We could only deduce from the reported 'stories' that the interview partners themselves had experienced such emotions too.

This comes close to Leyens and his colleagues' (2000) findings that certain emotions which are typically attributed to human beings (such as shame, resentment, love and hope) are more likely to be associated with members of the ingroup. In contrast, emotions that are not only typical (such as pain, anger, pleasure or excitement) are both consciously and unconsciously attributed to members of outgroups. This means that the ingroup is seen as more 'human' than outgroups.[2] Leyens *et al.* (2000) analysed the different emotional states attributed to ingroups and outgroups. Interestingly enough, these findings seem to be relevant on an individual level as well. From a more pragmatic perspective one could argue that negative emotions are just socially less desirable than positive ones, and that this is why negative emotions are attributed to members of outgroups.

Indeed the empirical findings imply that a few emotions are socially more accepted than others. Anger, for example, turns out to be more acceptable in these company cases than fear or jealousy. Anger and guilt were reported as emotions in their own right, although the latter was not mentioned that frequently. Furthermore guilt was only mentioned by female interview partners as their own emotion.

The following chapters address the questions which events trigger emotions, and what are the consequences of positive and negative emotions in the M&A context.

NOTES

1. German terms which respondents used to explain their anger or rage ('Ärger', 'Wut', 'Zorn', 'Aggression', 'auf den Hammer gehen', 'geht mich voll an', 'anzipfen' and so on) were categorized into one group and coded as 'anger'.
2. As a consequence, a 'dehumanization' of outgroups could justify an 'inhuman' treatment of them (Leyens *et al.*, 2000).

8. Managerial communication

8.1 IMPORTANCE OF COMMUNICATION

Regardless of their position within the organization, interviewee partners unanimously acknowledged the overarching importance of communication. Managers and employees pointed to the significance of top-down information even before communication was explicitly raised as a topic in the interviews.

Employees who were not actively involved in M&A decision-making processes but influenced by these decisions (thus including many middle managers) expected detailed and regular information updates from their superiors. If no such information was available, implicit and non-verbal cues were used to decode information. They felt that 'something is going on', but often they were not able to exactly define what it was:

> If you are sensitive, you realize that something is seething there. Signals come from different sides. (I–14, §39)[1]

> It was simply not foreseeable for employees. The upper elite, the upper management, is of course informed, but the normal worker has no information. He only feels something. Therefore, some big talks and rumours start to circulate. (I–11, §223)

8.2 THE ANNOUNCEMENT

According to the chosen categorization of the M&A stages, the post-merger phase only starts after the official announcement. Although this book mainly focuses on the post-merger stage, this section is devoted to the announcement. The reason is that the announcement was revealed to be one of the most important events. We found that the way the announcement was perceived by those affected influences all the succeeding steps in the post-merger integration process.

At the time of the official announcement, the decision makers usually have already undergone the due-diligence process and signed contracts. They have already invested significantly more time, thought and money regarding prospective organizational changes than their employees. In the case of middle managers this depended on their exact function within the company. Those who were already involved in the due-diligence process and had to prepare data for the decision making, were told in confidence months before the rest of the crew. Generally speaking, most of the middle managers were informed before the rest of the employees, but some happened to be informed only at the same moment as the rest of the staff. Therefore the moment of actual announcement differed between staff members.

Irrespective of whether or not it was possible to keep information on the upcoming M&A secret before the official announcement, the proclamation was one of the most important and emotionally intensive events for all company members. In cases where employees were completely unaware of the upcoming changes, their reactions demonstrated either shock, disappointment and anxiousness or delight, pride and optimism. The reaction depended on several factors: one aspect was the way the announcement was made. Another issue was the image of the partner company. However most important concerns in this context were related to foreseeable career changes or job losses.

In cases where rumours had spread prior to the official announcement, employees felt *tense* and *insecure* and were longing for an official explanation from superiors. *Anxieties* and *distrust* in management were typical reactions:

> You wait *trembling*, 'what will this guy now tell us?' We had read a few things in the newspapers, but nothing concrete. And most of us clung full of *hope* to the works meeting and to the CEO's words. (I–6, §33)

The announcement occurred quite differently in each of the companies analysed. Poma's condition for Leitner to be open to the sale was to keep the due-diligence process completely secret. They did not want to stir up unnecessary speculations or leak information because, should the merger not proceed, they might continue to be perceived as competitors. They were successful in their attempt, only two or three people in Leitner knew about the merger before the official announcement. The interviewees considered this a good achievement, particularly in view of the fact that the due-diligence process extended over more then ten months thanks to the complex French antitrust law. Leitner's CEO (and simultaneously main shareholder) personally announced the buying decision to the Poma board in Grenoble and to the colleagues of Leitner's French subsidiary on the same (Friday) evening.[2] In the face-to face meeting with the Poma board Leitner's CEO was subjected to many searching and detailed questions. He felt as if he was undergoing an interrogation:

> This was like a hearing of the highest degree! I remember well, the sharpest and nastiest questions came from the ladies [in the board meeting]. (. . .) The board members asked everything. They were of course looked after by the union and they asked very competent questions, also from a juridical perspective. (I–5, §§39–40, 43)

During the following weekend Leitner's CEO talked to the head of Leitner's works council, and on Monday he announced the acquisition to his own company in Italy. In a meeting he informed the departmental managers and the day after the rest of the staff through a notice on the blackboard and through the company's newsletter 'Leitner Interna'. Some employees learned about the news only casually in the corridor by chatting to colleagues. For the majority of Leitner's personnel nothing changed. This was the reason why the news was not communicated in a big way. On the contrary:

> One did not want to pompously announce it. If people [Leitner's employees] know that Leitner has bought Poma, then they tend to be arrogant towards the others, in the sense of 'we bought you, thus our opinions count more than yours'. It was intended to avoid this. (I–3, §65)

Initially they therefore let the employees believe that it was not Leitner that was buying its second biggest competitor worldwide, but the whole Seeber Group, to which Leitner belongs. This helped to prevent Leitner technicians from behaving arrogantly when they worked closely together with Poma technicians.

Leitner's board members who were informed personally by the owner felt enthusiastic about the news and proud that their company was able to buy Poma. This fact was also a big motivational boost for all, especially because they had already been reassured by the announcement that there would be no dismissals.

In the case of Schwarzkopf there were different perceptions of which event can be defined as 'the announcement'. Some considered the informal meeting in the office as 'the announcement', when their head of department informed them that Schwarzkopf would be sold and that there were several interested buyers. This moment was not considered as emotionally very intensive. It was *curiosity* rather than anything else, and lots of speculation about potential buyers dominated the scene in the following days. When Henkel was known to be the most probable buyer, people reacted differently:

> The funny thing was that we initially felt relatively *happy* about the fact that it was Henkel because we thought that nothing would change for us. Also

company X was under consideration as a potential buyer. And I remember that we said: 'Thank goodness, it is Henkel. This will be good for us.' (I–6, §18)

The [emotional] intensity increased with the question 'who could buy us?' – and then the definitive answer: 'It is Henkel! This *could be negative for us . . .*' There was a *large amount of rage and anger.* (I–6, §50)

Others, however, considered this informal information as 'rumours'. In their perception, the announcement was the official works meeting several weeks later, when Henkel's CEO came to announce the news to all employees in the canteen of the Schwarzkopf subsidiary. Again this official announcement also was experienced in completely different ways: some were only scarcely informed and felt surprised, others had a problem with the management style of Schwarzkopf and even felt delighted:

It was a surprise, yes. And for some of us, me included, [it was] quite a delight: 'Finally something is going to happen here!' because the structures [of Schwarzkopf] were partly antiquated and you did not have the chance to do anything about it. (I–8, §30)

Others again knew already that they were on the 'black list' and that their department would be closed down by the end of the same year. They felt *shocked* by the way the official announcement was made. Henkel's CEO proclaimed in front of all Schwarzkopf employees: 'never change a winning team. You are successful and we are not going to change anything here [at this Schwarzkopf subsidiary]'. Despite this official statement, some of them were well aware of redundancy plans and that they would be dismissed within the next couple of months. Hence this was not very credible. Therefore they felt *angry* and *irritated* by the official version of the news:

I was also one of those who knew already that I would be dismissed. Therefrom emerges great anger, of course. How can this guy stand up and raise the others' hope if there is no reason for hope? This was for us lots of anger and somehow also a demotivation. (I–6, §§23–4)

There was also a sort of discussion and employees could ask. (. . .) But I personally was in a kind of defiant phase and did not even want to ask him anything. (. . .) I just considered it as a cheek to raise hope in others in such a moment! I was so full of fury that I did not want to say anything. (I–6, §74)

A few asked questions, he answered professionally, but his answers were difficult to grasp and incomprehensible. People certainly know it, but they don't want to accept it. There is an *incredibly bad atmosphere*! To the point of *shock*, to the utmost *anxiety*, to the point of *desperation* . . . there were also people who had worked for the company for a long time and who had no chance of finding another job. (I–7, §§132–3)

Sportler's owner informed his employees and those of the ten Hervis outlets about the acquisition in two arranged meetings: there was a 'Meeting North' in one of the Sportler buildings and a 'Meeting South' in the rented state hall of the Sheraton hotel in Padua. The announcement itself was considered as the *'emotionally most intensive ever'* of the M&A; afterwards the intensity declined quickly. During the meeting, the Sportler management team presented its goals and programmes, and assured the former Hervis staff that nobody would be dismissed. They also tried to create awareness of new challenges.

> Of course, some employees jumped enthusiastically up, embraced us already at the end of the presentation and said: 'great that you are here!', 'finally!' and 'excellent!' And there were of course others who were more reserved. (I-9, §51)

Sportler also announced it would get in contact with each outlet in the near future and present the respective new contact people. This was described as a highly emotional moment.

The acquisition of Staff by Zumtobel and the merger between Zumtobel Staff and Thorn were announced by letter/e-mail and by the so-called 'Chairman's Letter' with a photo of the owner and his signature. Top managers had already learned about the M&A in an earlier meeting. In both cases rumours could not be avoided. Sales people, for example, had heard the news already from clients.

The four case studies show that announcements are done in different ways, and that individuals experience the same announcement differently. Interview partners explained their ideas and comments on how one could better arrange the announcement and the information process: to make clear and honest decisions is one of the most important things. After staff members have heard about the upcoming merger or acquisition for the first time, it is crucial not to leave them in uncertainty for too long. Those affected should be informed regularly. The messages should be transmitted through several 'channels' in parallel and by arranging small group conversations rather than a huge announcement event. This is in line with Krackhardt and Hanson (1993). In a second step, the official announcement could be the pro forma climax, and it could end with a social event.

> And it is important to pass on the decision with information density, not only in a huge meeting, where they say: 'Now we are here. You have to re-orientate. And we are going to inform those who will be dismissed.' There should rather be small group meetings. First, all managers should be convinced and then small group conversations should be arranged. Then you can make a big gathering as a matter of form and enjoy a glass together. But at that time everything should already be carried out. This is my opinion. (I-8, §147)

Most of the M&A literature emphasizes the importance of good top-down communication. It is suggested that the announcement of the merger or acquisition is one of the most important moments. It is argued that it has to be well prepared and, in order to avoid uncertainties and rumours, it is suggested that the merger announcement should be communicated to all staff members at the same moment. Furthermore the announcement should be made by top management or by the company owner. Some authors suggest using big company meetings which might give room for questions (for example, Appelbaum *et al.*, 2000a; Cartwright and Cooper, 2000). However the findings of the present study disconfirm this approach. During these big announcement meetings people are often overwhelmed by their feelings of excitement or shock. They frequently do not dare to ask questions and are afraid of being put on the spot.

8.3 COMMUNICATION FREQUENCY AND INTENSITY

Regular, intensive and open communication throughout the whole M&A integration process is crucial. There is a clear link between the managerial communication style such as openness or honesty and frequency of interaction, and positive/negative emotions of employees. Simply having informed knowledge about what is going on has positive effects on employees' feelings. In contrast, being uninformed generates uncertainty and demotivation:

> They did not exactly say what had happened. Therefore, the motivation immediately dropped. And rumours went around straight away. (I–7, §79)

> Information is *the* motivation factor above all. (I–3, §102)

> The communication came in with delay and was incomplete. (. . .) They only received fragments. Thus the feelings of uncertainty intensified. (I–7, §43)

> On Monday at 9 a.m. he called for the meeting and informed us about everything. This was perceived very positively by the people. (I–7, §178)

Interviewees reported that the level of information is very different from individual to individual within the organization. The amount of information depended first of all on the position held by the organization member:

> The lower you are in the hierarchy level the less information you get. This means, the really big deals are played in the upper league. The CEO knows the most, of course. The head of the business unit is second in this respect. The marketing manager, the sales manager and so on do not know as much as the head of the

business unit. The product manager only knows what he has to know anyway. The same goes for assistants . . . This means, the level of information is very different. (I–7, §27)

But the information level also depends on personal contacts with superiors: 'We got to know more because we had a better contact with the CEO' (I–7, §78).

Several interview partners also reported that they were not sure about how much their superiors knew about the merger or the acquisition. When they had the feeling of not being adequately informed they started to be *suspicious* and to *distrust* their managers:

In the beginning we were informed a lot (. . .) and then there were periods in which you did not hear anything anymore. And if you hear nothing at all, you start to be very suspicious. (I–12, §32)

Well, from our conversations I had the impression that my direct superiors were not informed either. This is at least what they told us. What and how much they really knew, I don't know. (I–12, §101)

Also a lack of information about the partner company is conspicuous. Some people seemed completely uninformed about their partner company. They reacted in the following ways on questions regarding their partner company:

Yes . . . it is a big business . . . It is big. Actually, I only know them as competitors. And I knew that their brand is very famous in Britain and in France. But actually I have the feeling that they do not belong to us. Well, we did not hear a lot [about them] . . . (I–14, §88)

Sometimes, the only contacts between members of the two companies were made at trade fairs:

We had four exhibition stands at the first trade fair. You peep at the others' exhibition stand – we didn't have a common stand. We had two and they had two. Then you have a look and you start to talk: 'What are you doing here?' So we made our first contacts through the fair. But this also took a very long time. (I–14, §95)

From a managerial perspective there were also good reasons for not passing on all the information. First, managers underwent a period of grave uncertainties too and preferred not to irritate employees 'unnecessarily': 'We realized, OK, we have to be quiet because we do not really know what is going on. We decided: "Please, let's not irritate our employees"' (I–7, §78).

The second reason for the lack of top-down communication was the fact that the informed person either felt stressed and had 'no time' to communicate or she/he just did not consider the information to be important enough to be passed on. Interestingly, all but two of the interviewees in the position of having at least one hierarchy level above them reported not having been informed 'properly' by their superior(s).

> There was simply nobody to provide us with *real* background information about the merger. We only got to know a few fragments, but no detailed background information. (I–12, §62)

> But this was only rhetoric without substantial meaning. (I–12, §121)

> All employees were invited. Just, not everything was told. He only said what a top manager had to say. (I–7, §129)

> It is important to note that there was in fact only one elitist circle which can be labelled top management. Some information was not passed on to us, simply because they sanctioned it. As a result, we were not properly informed. Certain things were going on where it was pretended they had never happened. (I–15, §38)

On the other hand, the interview partners holding a leading position (that is, top and middle managers) were convinced that they had been communicating intensively and frequently with their subordinates:

> And I have always informed the group. I told them what I planned; I presented the concept which we then would complete together. I told them which direction I had in mind and thereafter we worked together on the concept. And everybody participated. (I–8, §65)

> There were always questions. Well, for my part I said what I could communicate. But further outside, in the sales and distribution, there were of course big question marks. (I–10, §76)

This clearly demonstrates, firstly, that managers cannot overcommunicate. Just simple sentences like 'I do not know more at this moment, but I will keep you informed' can be reassuring and help to set people's mind at rest. Secondly, it demonstrates that the impression of what is 'enough' information and 'frequent' communication is only a subjective and individual perception and not an objective fact. Given that, it does not count how much, how intensively and how open superiors really communicate with their dependants. Since perceptions create realities, it only matters what is perceived by the receiver.

One thing is for sure: in such a delicate situation, people absorb every single word from managers thoroughly, irrespective of whether it is related to positive or negative news. These snatches of information will be recalled even after a long time. For example, three interview partners from the same company mentioned, independently, that a certain manager from the buying company said in front of the members of the acquired company: 'Lots of blood and water will flow' ('water' was the synonym for tears or sweat). Those words triggered a multitude of *anxieties*, resistance and rumours at that time. Even after six years those words elicited *anger* in the interviewees.

On the other hand, there are also positive examples of intense emotions caused by managerial communication.

> Mister [X from a buying company] who accompanied the merger [. . .] used to go in the factories to visit the colleagues at seven o'clock in the morning, and he asked them about their sorrows and problems. The employees loved him, although many were dismissed. Even now people are asking how this guy is doing. (I–12, §104)

The two examples show how long-lasting the emotional impact of verbal and non-verbal communication can be. Interestingly, the manager who irritated staff members with the abovementioned 'blood and water' remark and the caring manager in the latter example are one and the same person.

8.4 RUMOURS

Lack of official top-down information and lack of clearing up communication lead to rumours among employees. Such rumours are often correlated with *feelings of uncertainty* and other unpleasant emotions such as *fear, anger, frustration, demotivation and hopelessness*. Sixteen statements in the interviews clearly confirm the link between poor managerial communication, employees' uncertainty and the spreading of rumours which led to *demotivation* and to lower productivity. A few examples follow:

> (Incredibly) what ideas and rumours turned up! This is quite obvious. In a period of uncertainty someone drops something and this develops a momentum of its own. (I–8, §74)

> Such news goes of course very fast around the company. It spreads like a wildfire. Lots of negative energy grew out of this. And people talked a lot about it, instead of working productively. (I–12, §32)

> Rumours are around anyway. But the better you inform, of course, and the more security you give, the less I have to make up in order to reduce my anxieties. Mostly it is the suppression of fears that leads to fantasizing. There were of

course people who stirred these rumours up. No doubt. They disseminated even more uncertainties. But unconsciously. Driven by their own anxieties, perhaps. (I–8, §§74–5)

The following statements confirm that open and honest information is the best way to reduce rumours.

With such rumours you can only deal through facts and openness, according to my opinion. This means, coordinated top-down proceedings with background information will help to understand certain things and prevent people from inventing stories. (I–10, §85)

In the last weeks [before the announcement] a few rumours started to circulate. The manager of the selling company did the job in a clever way. He did not lie to the people. He really stood up for them. Overall, it is my view that this phase ran rather smoothly, which is quite impressive given such a complex affair. (I–9, §58)

We had an information meeting in order to reduce the circulation of rumours. (I–1, §12)

8.5 MEDIA RELEASES AND PUBLIC OPINION

Newspaper articles without a balancing internal source of information have a big influence on employees' emotions. They are a source of rumours and emotions such as irritation, anxiety and fear, aggression, rage, jealousy, demotivation, grief or arrogance. Employees do expect a managerial reaction and explanation when scary media releases appear.

Then we read those stories in the newspapers. They sounded very bad. They talked about mass dismissals and bank disasters. At that time we would have appreciated to hear something from the management floor about what really was going on. This caused a feeling of considerable uncertainty among the colleagues. You were thinking 'how are things about my job?' Lots of anxieties raised out of these articles. (I–12, §32)

Public media releases do not only affect employees. Bad news can also scare and *irritated* employees' families, potential job applicants, shareholders and clients:

At that time we experienced that even parents called in and asked: 'If we send our son as an apprentice to you, can we be sure that he can complete the apprenticeship in your company?' There were horrible reports in the press, like: 'Let the subsidiary Lemgo bleed white.' This was really dramatic. (I–12, §35)

> But I think the majority never realized what really was going on. If you ask in the public what had happened with Schwarzkopf at that time, they will talk about bankruptcy and similar staff. Well, it was wrongly communicated to the outside, and the public was never informed correctly. It would have been Schwarzkopf's job, of course, to properly inform the public. (I–8, §119)

Some managers realize that their company is embedded in a social network and that their success depends on public trust and on the company's reputation, too:

> The client must always feel secure. Through public relations you have to make sure that customers continue to have trust in the company. (I–12, §35)

> If a company is only interested in market shares and starts to dismiss employees, there is no way the acquisition is going to work! Because you get the image of a potential job killer. Competent people will leave the company voluntarily, the press is against you, and you will never increase the market share as initially planned. (I–5, §15)

8.5.1 Conclusion: Managerial Communication and Employees' Emotions

This chapter has tried to illustrate the connection between employees' emotions and managerial communication. A number of interview statements cited show that the perceived intensity, frequency, openness and honesty of managerial communication has a strong impact on how employees feel. The perceived existence or lack of top-down information determines employees' feelings of certainty or uncertainty. The creation of internal and external information and communication processes allows informing employees in time, consistently and openly about changes. Words are thus a very powerful instrument that managers can use to produce a positive (or at least a less negative) and still productive atmosphere. Nevertheless words might not be enough. Verbal messages must be consistent and should be supported by non-verbal communication and by tangible signs if they are to attain high credibility. It is not sufficient to proclaim changes if no clear sign of implementation follows. People need to see that something changes in the declared direction. This creates a sense of security, credibility and trust in management. Actions are stronger than words:

> For Poma's employees it was not that bad because right from the beginning Leitner's CEO has signalled that (. . .). He communicated this repeatedly, and by his actions he continuously confirmed it. (I–1, §22)

In this sense, the following chapter is dedicated to managerial behaviour and its links to employees' emotions.

NOTES

1. In order to maintain the interview partners' anonymity as much as possible, numbers were assigned to all interviews. The notation 'I–11, §172', for example, means that the quoted citation stems from interviewee 11, paragraph 172 in the transcribed N*Vivo version. Please note that some of the interview statements in this and the following chapters are provided to substantiate the discussion. The interview transcripts are left in the original language and therefore not necessarily polished English language.
2. Just to give an impression of how fast rumours can spread: while Leitner's CEO was driving the 80km from the Poma headquarters to the France-based Leitner subsidiary, people on the spot had already heard about the announcement meeting at Poma.

9. Managerial behaviour

Many statements in the interviews confirmed that the behaviour of leading people had a considerable impact on employees' emotions. And since emotions are the driving force for actions (according to the definition of emotion), employees' emotional states influence their readiness to contribute to merger or acquisition success.

The case of Schwarzkopf provided especially clear evidence for these connections. One department of Austrian Schwarzkopf was closed down a few months after the takeover by Henkel. One of the remaining departments had a written promise from Henkel that they would not be closed down if they performed well. Two years later, although the department had put in extra efforts and achieved good financial results, they learned that they would be closed down as well. Interviewees reported that the atmosphere in the post-acquisition stage was completely different in two diverse departments with two different managers. These managers were considered equal in terms of their professional knowledge, but different in their personalities: the first had difficulties dealing with his co-workers during the challenging period of organizational 'downsizing'. He was introverted, was perceived as 'quiet', 'distant' and difficult to approach. Employees reported that he used to show a 'poker face', and nobody really knew how to interpret it. His reserved behaviour increased employees' *uncertainties* and speculations. They felt *frustrated* and *demotivated*, started to look for other jobs and to steal office properties such as paintings from the company.

In the other case, the head of the second department was aware of the importance of being open. Personality-wise he was a more communicative individual and was able to *calm* employees and to *motivate* them by talking openly to them and by facing them with reality. Thanks to his integrating personality the team glued together even more during the tough closing down phase of their department. These group members gave their best for the company. They still cultivate their friendship today, after five years.

The two closures were perceived in two completely different ways because the managers behaved differently. In the second case he (the manager) was more open and more authentic and communicated more than the one in the first case. While during the first takeover this difficult period was characterized by uncertainty and rumour factory, for the second phase team spirit and cohesion were the characteristics. (I–7, §10)

This shows that employees' emotions and employees' willingness to contribute to a successful organizational change depend to a large degree on managers' behaviour. Therefore the following paragraphs will take a closer look at certain integration-related topics such as implementation of strategies, joint projects, social activities and dismissals.

9.1 IMPLEMENTATION OF M&A STRATEGIES

The implementation of a merger or an acquisition largely depends on the integration approach decision makers, consciously or unconsciously, have chosen. Therefore, the first part of this section will present different integration approaches by referring to the analysed M&A cases. Afterwards we will look at the effects of preparatory and accompanying training on organizational members, and conclude with an emphasis on the importance of managerial action.

9.1.1 Integration Approaches

Integration does not necessarily mean a complete 'amalgamation' of the two companies. The degree of integration depends on the requirements for strategic interdependence and for organizational autonomy (Haspeslagh and Jemison, 1991).

In cases where the need of organizational autonomy is high and the necessity for strategic interdependence is low, the focus is on 'preservation'. Organizational adaptations remain at a minimum level (ibid.; Werner, 1999). The early Zumtobel and Staff merger (49 per cent takeover), and probably also the Leitner–Poma case, fell within this category because strategies and brands were kept separate. On account of the minimal changes there are hardly huge acceptance problems among affected personnel, and negative emotions are less intense (Bourantas and Nicandrou, 1998).

Leitner and Poma profited from the merger mostly because of cost savings and marketing agreements (division of the markets). Leitner decided to maintain two separate organizations and detached brands. In most of the markets they continued to act separately, or only the one company with the stronger brand recognition appeared in the respective market. The managing committee of Poma remained French and was not changed by Leitner.

Because of that, on the one hand, we did not have the advantages of a full merger, of course. But on the other hand, we did not have all those problems which many companies usually have, that people oppose the merger and that the best individuals voluntarily leave because of identification problems. (I–5, §19)

In many M&As of this type, top management later decides to take advantage of synergy effects, to adapt the strategies and to allow less organizational autonomy. In such cases the problems emerge at that postponed moment. This was the case of Zumtobel Staff when Zumtobel bought the remaining 51 per cent of Staff. An interpretation of the 'temperature curves' confirms that.

The case of a 100 per cent 'fusion' with the desire for high strategic interdependence and low organizational autonomy is called 'absorption'. This means that original company borders disappear and that a united organizational structure is built (Haspeslagh and Jemison, 1991; Werner, 1999). Henkel's takeover of Schwarzkopf is a typical example of this integration approach, although it was more hidden than obvious over the first two years.

> We were told that Henkel worldwide decided to settle also the business unit 'Hairdresser' at the head offices in order to 'take advantage of the synergy effects' – this is how it was formulated by Henkel. (I–7, §176)

Only a few individuals had expected that it would come to a closing down of their Schwarzkopf subsidiary, and were not surprised:

> Henkel has overcapacities in its own works. It was more a political decision to give a two-years-guarantee to our small branch here. Those two years are a typical proceeding within Henkel. They have done it with many subsidiaries. And this is usual within the industrial sector. When they say 'two years of site guarantee' then you can assume that this is the end. This is somehow understandable. They are profit organizations and not politicians. You have to see it in this way. (I–8, §20)

The so-called 'symbiosis' is an intermediate degree of integration between 'preservation' and 'absorption'. The attempt here is to combine a high need of organizational autonomy with a high necessity for strategic interdependence in order to achieve a profitable interrelation. The growing-together happens through joint activities and continuous interaction over time (Haspeslagh and Jemison, 1991; Werner, 1999). The 'absorption' and 'symbiosis' approaches are the biggest challenges for an integration, because organizational members tend to offer resistance to major changes (Bourantas and Nicandrou, 1998). Zumtobel Staff has reached the 'symbiosis' stage after almost ten years of struggles. Zumtobel and Staff seem to have grown together by now and to profit from the mutual culture:

> The one company came from a more technical–informative side and the other more from an emotional glimmer–glitter world with noble-mindedness.

And they welded the complementary portfolios together. This was ideal. (I–11, §166)

I would say that the design and the way of changing the catalogues did not happen according to the former Zumtobel guidelines, but a compromise was made. A new, better brand was born. (. . .) In my opinion something really better emerged. The whole process took altogether ten years. But now we have it like we wanted it. (I–11, §§170–73)

The implementation of the M&A plan depends heavily on the integration strategy which was purposely or unconsciously chosen. In many cases, the implementation of the merger or acquisition happens very slowly and drags on for years. This delay of operation and performance extinguishes any inspirational thought, and triggers *negative affects* like *feelings of uncertainty, demotivation, frustration* and *disappointment*. This emotional letdown emerges because the *initial enthusiasm* was not harnessed. The *initial joy* at the M&A and the new challenges are not fulfilled. The consequences are diminished acceptance of the M&A decision, perceived failure, decreased employees' commitment and reduced job satisfaction which is shown by the fact that many employees and managers look and apply for jobs elsewhere (see section 9.4.3, 'voluntarily leaving the company').

9.1.2 Preparatory and Accompanying Training

Marks and Mirvis (2001) compare the M&A situation to an organ transplant, and observe that, in the case of mergers and acquisitions, the 'surgical team' as well as the 'transplantation patient' have to be prepared for the operation. The patient is not only checked physically prior to the surgery, but she/he is also accompanied psychologically in order to broaden the chances of success. In this sense, one of the analysed companies prepared their managers and employees for the M&A also regarding the 'soft' factors via internal seminars and trainings.

Leitner invited external psychologists and offered different seminars, such as communication and teamwork training, in order to prepare people for the two upcoming acquisitions (of Poma and Prinoth):

Also a psychologist came into the company and interviewed many co-workers. This happened prior to a series of seminars like communication or teamwork trainings. (I–1, §34)

A number of merging companies experience language barriers as a problem. Intense emotions and disputes are typical outcomes. In the case of Zumtobel Staff, for example, middle managers suffered from *feelings of inferiority* when they first met their new colleagues from Thorn who were native English speakers:

> The *emotions* were *very intense* at the kick-off meeting, when we first met our colleagues from the partner company, and everything was in English. There you realize that they are superior from a language point of view. Of course, they are native speakers! (I–11, §234)

In a similar way, there were a few quarrels between technicians and purchasing people from Leitner and Poma. When Leitner bought Poma they started to offer French classes twice a week for all Leitner members, in addition to English, German and Italian courses. They were aware of language barriers, and they recognized the importance of language skills in order to improve the communication with business and merger partners. Nevertheless there were some arguments between the two groups as a result of perceived injustice:

> Some people, for instance technicians and purchasing people, are steadily in contact with the French people. There are always a few quarrels going on, because our people learn French and do speak English, German and Italian as well, while lots of the French guys barely speak any English. If the conversation runs in French, then of course our technicians are disadvantaged. Psychologically, English would be the best middle course. (I–1, §34)

Overall, interview partners who had the chance to participate in pre-merger training, workshops and language courses highly appreciated such company efforts.

9.1.3 Call for Managerial Action

Although the announcement represented one of the most important steps, it was not enough to prepare people mentally and psychologically for big changes. Changes were required. People had to experience the change at a certain point, not too long after the announcement, in order to be able to appreciate its positive sides. It was important for employees to sense and perceive clear signs that showed them that the announced strategy was not an empty bundle of words, but that the decision maker(s) meant it seriously.

In cases where inactivity determined the scene for too long a period, situations became dramatic. People felt driven to *despair* and felt a *strong desire* for managerial actions:

> And if the management does not interfere, the situation becomes worse and worse. It was disastrous in the end! There were dramatic situations – it came to

a standstill. People were *not motivated* anymore and *reacted very emotionally*. People from the production, for example, said: 'So, now they are going to completely close down the business. What is happening? I started building my house two years ago, when I was fifty. What should I do?' Tragedies happened then! (I–7, §83)

There were *aggressions* and *anxieties*, obviously. This happened in the period when people took each others' projects away, which stirred up lots of *bad* blood (*feelings*). You start to realize that they do not want to cooperate with us, but you see that they [managers] send us into an arena where we tear each other apart – nobody gets anything out of this. I strongly believe that it would have been certain managers' job to interfere more strongly in that situation. (I–12, §65)

I had the feeling these would have been the two critical moments [reference to the 'temperature curve' graphic]: if you as a leader or manager notice such an *emotional downturn* then you have to steer against. But – and this is my perception – they allowed this emotional downward trend to happen. For me this would have been a call for action. (I–12, §101)

It is common sense that people tend to resist everything that is new and challenging: 'In the beginning it is like this: everything new is unwanted. People refuse it' (I–3, §50). Such resistance often culminates in interpersonal conflicts, in bullying, plotting and scheming. The call for stronger managerial interventions in highly emotional periods of big changes was very strongly supported by the interviews. Unpopular managerial decisions and actions might have been disagreeable. However, interviews showed that, in some situations, such as in cases of bullying and intrigues, immediate interventions seemed to be the best long-term solution for all those affected:

Therefore we had a relatively high personnel turnover in the first year. But this was necessary because in this subsidiary infightings were going on. And my experience is that you have to proceed radically in such situations, because intrigues are the worst for an organizational community – especially for a team-oriented philosophy as I highly appreciate it. In the case of intrigues it is just better to immediately interfere and to act uncompromisingly. (I–9, §§78, 83)

This is in line with literature that suggests aiming for fast implementations: 'fairly rapid change is preferable to that which occurs over a long period of time and so creates uncertainty' (Cartwright and Cooper, 1992, pp. 173–4).

9.2 INTEGRATION ACTIVITIES

Integration activities are a very powerful part of a successful M&A implementation. These comprise both joint projects and social events. The first section below stresses the importance of joint projects and the positive effect of quick successes, while the second tries to create awareness of the significance of social events by bearing in mind social identity theory.

9.2.1 Joint Projects and Quick Successes

> In my opinion, it is not necessarily enough to only announce the new fantastic distribution channels through the Chairman's Letter: you have to very quickly start with operative actions. It must be visible that these steps secure my future, the future of the company and the existence of the workplaces. Then you manage a lot and you manage to get psychological synergies, *motivation* and the employees will know that it is good for us all. (I–12, §38)

Interview responses illustrated that it was essential to start integration projects immediately after the announcement. Quick and small successes helped to *motivate* employees and made them *feel committed* to the newly merged company. They had to understand that the merger and all the connected painful and stressing experiences made sense. In order to direct the commitment towards the newly merged organization, it is recommended that joint cross-organizational projects be addressed. One interviewee described how 'easy' and simple this could be:

> I am still waiting for the first joint project, and it is taking a bit too long for me. I think we could do more still. We are not realising the full synergistic potential of this M&A project. It is very simple: you only have to sit together on one table and say: 'We have the project X. What could you make better and what could we do? With which capacities could you do it better, more effectively and simpler? And how can we make it better? And what could we do together?' (I–12, §23)

This implies, of course, that both companies are willing to cooperate, which might not always be a given, especially if they perceive each other as former competitors. Interview partners also emphasized the importance of concrete, visible and tangible common outcomes as soon as possible. This means that small projects can already start parallel to the development of a more detailed integration strategy.

> It does not really matter which project or product we create together. It is important that something visible and tangible has happened . . . Even if there is no strategy yet of how the two firms will be brought together in the far future, with visible and tangible things I can obtain substantially more than with a defined strategy which is only visible in three, four years. But if I realize smaller projects – which have not much to do with the strategy yet – then it goes 'click'. People understand, they are committed and say: 'Wow, it works!' And this can be done in parallel to the development of a strategy. (I–12, §§175–6)

According to social identity theory (see section 3.1), under certain conditions (such as common goals or clear role definitions), inter-group contacts reduce negative emotions and following conflicts. In cases where members of both organizations saw changes happening and when they experienced common successes, *feelings of insecurity, intergroup jealousy* and *fears* of 'the others' disappeared. It diminished *aversions*, reduced conflicts and raised *hopes*, increased *happiness* and *pride*. People were consequently more open for further challenges because they realized that changes were not necessarily connected with unpleasant emotions.

A better integration between two merging companies can also be obtained through job rotations. Leitner did this regularly by sending people abroad to another subsidiary for a couple of months. Also Zumtobel Staff had launched a so-called 'European Job-Rotation' project. This helped people to get to know new structures, to adapt organizational issues and to return with the gathered new know-how.

> The company took the risk and invested a lot of money in order to pursue this significant change, in order to get to know new structures, to adapt organizational issues, and to take the acquired know-how back home. (I–12, §148)

The positive effects were noticeable not only on an organizational level, but also language-wise and with respect to relationships between members of the two companies. The exchange can theoretically happen at all hierarchical levels, and the individuals involved would certainly come back home with a message.

> . . . and would say: 'They are not so bad at all, as we had assumed. This is really true!' There are often small human problems for which you don't have to have a university degree. You just have to bring people together. (I–12, §148)

9.2.2 Social Events

Celebrating was also a good way of bringing people together. Leitner's management team, for example, met once a month with Poma's board of management and combined the formal meeting with a social event. The CEO was convinced that good relationships paid off also on work/performance dimensions. Since they had also met regularly on a social level, the atmosphere had improved substantially.

> Ever since we established this holding-board of directory, the organizational climate has improved significantly. We meet once a month. This month we will meet in Munich and we will socialize in the evening at the 'Oktoberfest'. I believe that's why the organizational climate is functionally working quite well, now. (I–5, §51)

As indicated earlier, in one of Schwarzkopf's departments employees used to cultivate their relationship. Because of social events and the integrating personality of their line manager the team cohesion became even stronger although the problems increased.

As a result of the M&A, social activities within Sportler have changed. In its early years the Sportler team felt more like a youth group and they enjoyed their time together outside the job:

> When we started off about 25 years ago, we had a team of 20 people. Basically this was a group of young people and we also shared fun activities. We did leisure activities together and this all consolidated in a really nice team. (I–9, §134)

There was a family-like atmosphere among the Sportler members, the owner knew all his employees personally and used to make 'happy birthday' wishes in person to every single co-worker. The proprietor regrets that this has no longer been possible for a few years because of the continuous expansion, including the latest acquisition of the Hervis outlets.

Summarizing, through joint projects and social events the relationships between members of the two organizations may improve, people may experience a keener identification with 'their' project they worked on, and they may thus feel a stronger commitment towards their new 'friends', towards the new projects and towards the newly merged company. According to the sense-making approach (Weick, 1995) and according to cognitive appraisal theory, such experiences are like 'signals' that help to increase the chances that the M&A decision will be accepted and perceived as a success.

9.3   CONVINCING PEOPLE

Actions, experiences and successes seem to be superior instruments to people than words. Inconsistent managerial messages and behaviour irritate employees. For example, the use of 'war jargon' in official meetings in one company did not fit the culture values indicated in the company's mission statement. People therefore started to doubt managerial reliability. Actions, experiences and successes convince people more than words. As previously mentioned, joint projects are a powerful instrument of conviction and of creation of prospects in the future:

> I know how it went in our case [Zumtobel and Staff] and how fast we became very good through a few important projects. I am convinced that we are going to manage the integration very well also with Thorn. (I–12, §169)

Investments have a similar effect. For example, Leitner's investments in one of their subsidiaries convinced employees that the branch would not be closed down, and that they did not have to *worry* about their jobs.

> At that time we had just bought a new and bigger piece of land, on which we had built a new plant. Therefore, employees of this particular subsidiary knew that we wouldn't have built business premises if we were planning to dismiss people. Consequently, they felt very relaxed. (I–5, §46)

In a similar way, Zumtobel transferred the manufacture of certain products from the Austrian headquarters to Staff at Lemgo in Germany. Zumtobel further shifted its German distribution head office from Frankfurt to the logistically less ideal place, Lemgo. This was an important signal to demonstrate appreciation to the acquired company and to show them 'you are important to us':

> And so the 'Lemgo-ians' continuously experienced an upgrading, in the sense of 'okay, the "Zumtobels" are serious about us. They shifted production to us and they gave us cash, so we can reinvest our yields in new developments' et cetera. (I–13, §184)

Also mentioned earlier, accompanying psychological support and the preparatory training were a clear and convincing signal that the company cares about its members. Another reassuring example is Leitner announced vacancies in newspapers. This was consistent with the big speeches and helped employees to feel secure about their jobs, as we will see below.

Also very 'simple' signals can have huge effects. Leitner's CEO, for example, demonstrated to the Poma crew that he held the acquired company and its staff in high esteem. He showed this by keeping the Poma board of management as it had been before, namely completely French. The former Poma owner became the head of the supervisory board, and Leitner's CEO decided to only become his deputy. It paid off that he had not behaved arrogantly as an acquirer and that he had made an extra effort to meet the partners halfway. The following interview statement illustrates the positive effects of not feeling superior as an acquirer:

> I think that this is basically the secret behind the success. This all was mainly our CEO's strategy; a decision he made and which I *highly appreciate*. Poma maintained its autonomy. Normally, the board of management becomes reorganized; this means that someone from the parent [acquiring] company comes into the subsidiary. This did not happen here. The board of management stayed entirely French. Therefore, also the level of prepotency [of Leitner's staff] remained low. I think this is a very important point and also the reason why everything goes relatively well. (I–3, §168)

Poma members were completely *surprised* and *impressed* by the new acquirer's efforts. Leitner's CEO said:

> Previously I had hardly spoken French. I learned French. And I know exactly that I earned *huge sympathies* through this. At the first anniversary party of Poma I then made my speech in French, and they were *totally enthusiastic*. (§91)

These are shining examples. But also 'smaller' signals can create *trust, conviction* and *motivation*. In order to achieve trust, acceptance and commitment, managers had to convey similar and consistent messages, reinforced by coherent actions and body language:

> There are such small signals. If the body language and the verbal language do not build one unity then you do not achieve trustworthiness. And I think that this has an influence on whether an employee believes you, if he feels secure or insecure, and whether he stirs rumours up or whether he refutes them. (I–11, §272)

> They [the acquirer] showed them [the acquired company] 'you are important to us'. And I think this was crucial to convince them [members of the acquired company] that 'we were serious about them'. I think this changed a lot. (I–13, §184)

> And these are simple things, the smallest and most obvious things which hardly cost money and barely cost time, but with which you can create very *big effects*. In my opinion, one issue is to make sure that you notice alarm signals in time. Maybe you have to install 'sensors' that immediately tell you if something negative is happening. So you can steer against it. (I–12, §179)

9.4   DISMISSALS

The interview analysis revealed some surprising findings with respect to dismissals, in the sense that they were not mentioned in the current M&A literature. One such discovery was the fact that the exact number of dismissals seemed to be a riddle. Either interview partners were unable to answer the question at all or their answers differed quite substantially from the responses of their colleagues. One interviewee reacted in the following way when being asked how many members had to leave the company: 'Well, various statistics are available regarding this issue. It all depends on how you look at things' (I–8, §116).

Another interesting surprise was the finding that managers and employees used different 'languages' when talking about the M&A phenomenon. The literature does not pay particular attention to this, but the differences were conspicuous in the interview transcripts. Managers tended to see only the functions which were duplicated and they therefore spoke in a much more 'rational' way about job releases. They used terms like 'adaptations', 'adjustments', 'synergy effects', 'restructuring', 'clearing up', 'cost savings' or 'clean-sweeping activity' as synonyms for dismissals.

> Certainly this was also a clean-sweeping activity. Schwarzkopf had been quite social and sometimes pretty unproductive. But this was not sustainable. (I–8, §116)

> We will clearly have to split from co-workers who are not performing. (I–15, §185)

> For some of the people who were made redundant it was quite clear that this was due to cost-savings. (I–10, §97)

> Question: 'And in which form did employees get dismissed?' Response: 'Well, we just tell them that their department is no longer necessary.' (I–10, §§111–12)

Employees frequently associated 'mass redundancies' with the announcement of M&As and, for those affected, dismissals were often a synonym for *'existential fears'*.

> When employees hear about an acquisition they usually associate it with dismissals. Employees are completely *frightened* by that. (I–3, §80)

> When banking institutions jumped in, they argued something like 'You have to adapt your HR'. 'Adaptation' is a very nice term which, however, basically means 'existence' on the other side. (I–12, §74)

In many cases the dismissal was not only a personal tragedy, but it concerned the whole family. Next to *anxieties* due to the loss of income, typical psychological consequences were *feeling superfluous* and *feelings of inferiority,* up to *depressions*, findings also supported by the literature (Appelbaum *et al.*, 2000a; Cartwright and Cooper, 2000; Gutknecht and Keys, 1993). These personal emotional experiences might be the reason why employees use more emotional expressions about job removals than non-affected decision makers.

Instead of dismissing young family fathers, Zumtobel Staff and Schwarzkopf decided to retire people above a certain age earlier. From a managerial perspective the term 'early retirement' sounded less violent than announcing 'dismissals of unproductive or older employees'. But this did not necessarily mean that the hard reality behind this cosmetically upgraded term was easier to accept for those affected. Considering that retirement implies crises for many pensioners under 'normal' circumstances, it was not surprising that grief over the loss of the assignment was a common phenomenon in this context. 'One of them retired early – I think one year ahead of time. He was very saddened by this. I clearly remember this situation. It was really difficult for him'. (I–6, §159).

One of the most difficult parts to digest in the context of dismissals was the fact that the number of 'required' dismissals was usually announced to those affected only after long periods of uncertainty. In many cases this was a slow and exhausting period because the dismissals were not announced all at once but one by one. People became increasingly *frightened* by such a procedure.

> The HR department was involved in that. The practice was to make the redundancies in stages, time after time, in order to avoid sudden peaks in redundancies. (I–10, §103)

> I remember quite well that sales agents were very frightened by this. Once it was this guy, then the other who was sacked. (I–6, §159)

This led to *feelings of uncertainty, anxieties, aggression* and *rage*. People came up with worst-case scenarios, and started to *distrust* the management. They often found themselves in a trance-like state in which only the ego counted. These egocentric concerns, mentioned also by Jansen and Pohlmann (2000), led to paying less attention to day-to-day jobs. Customers and other stakeholders fell into oblivion. As a consequence productivity decreased:

> Yes, employees talk a lot about it [the dismissals] – at the coffee machine, on the phone and during the lunch. Instead of discussing 'how can we optimize the light-technique and how can we solve this problem for client X?' they talk about their *aggressions, anxieties* and *rages*. This goes throughout the company. And even if there are only a few dismissals in a department, you talk about it, you observe and look at who might be the next, who has no family, who is the oldest in the department and thus less efficient . . . And then it might happen that people say: 'You will be the next one, you are single and over fifty.' And this is very dangerous, this is deadly serious! Therefore I repeat my creed for a real open communication and for always playing with open cards. (I–12, §§117–18)

Also relationships amongst co-workers change in a period of dismissals. In most of the cases relationships deteriorate and the working climate becomes worse because those who feel underprivileged react with *jealousy* and *envy* while the 'lucky' ones *feel guilty and powerless* at the same time.

> All of a sudden people knew that they could stay with the company, at least for the next two years, while others were just about to leave. You can imagine what a devastating effect this had on the team-climate! It was very difficult . . . Suddenly

the interpersonal relationships became worse because some of the employees were forced to leave while at the same time others were allowed to stay – some of them even having quite good perspectives for their future. (I–7, §86)

In some rare cases people also melt closer together through the commonly experienced difficulties. But in such periods, usually, work relationships are dominated by rivalries and bullying. Since this will be the topic of section 10.3 it will not be further explained here.

In order to reduce this period of uncertainty with all its undesirable consequences, the literature (for example, Cartwright and Cooper, 2000) suggests exploring and deciding in advance, and announcing immediately how many in total have to be dismissed and who these individuals will be. The interviews confirmed that it was easier for employees to deal with the bad news than with uncertainty over a long period because uncertainty created unnecessary *stress* and was the most difficult thing to bear. An immediate announcement of all dismissals would therefore also reassure the remaining employees. To know that their jobs are safe and that they do not have to *worry* further about potential dismissals gives them *feelings of security* and *confidence*:

> I am sure it would have been much better to announce upfront precisely how many individuals had to leave the company. Because, obviously, undecisiveness on the part of the management and uncertainty are factors which provoke *emotional reactions*. At any rate, these things were not clear cut and nobody knew how things would turn out. (I–7, §109)

In the case of Sportler it was easier in this respect because they took over all the staff from the ten acquired Henkel outlets:

> It was our first message: 'Nobody will be dismissed. Nobody has to be *frightened*. All of you will be taken on board.' This was the reason why most of the *insecurity* disappeared. Otherwise it would have been much more difficult. (I–9, §70)

Nevertheless it has to be noted that Sportler's top-management team later *regretted* not having dismissed those non-committed at an earlier stage. They thought it would have been a better solution for all the other employees.

> Today I think we made a mistake: we should immediately have freed ourselves from a number of staff. Those who did not like what was going on would have left anyway if we had told them to go. However, at that time we wanted them to stay. It would have been far better to just accept that not all people like our decision and to let them go to look for another job. (I–9, §52)

Leitner had grown continuously over the years prior to the acquisition and had always had difficulties finding enough personnel. In order to reinforce the message that nobody had to fear being dismissed, either from Leitner or from Poma, Leitner's management further announced open job opportunities in Italian newspapers. This was consistent with the reassuring speeches and helped employees to *feel secure* about their positions.

It is evident that most of the the mergers or acquisitions are not in such a fortunate position. When duplications in positions and job assignments appear and when synergies from economies of scale are the core objective, dismissals seem to be inevitable. Such a managerial decision is not easy and unproblematic to take since it can lead to the organization's acquiring an image as a job killer, as one interview statement explicitly portrayed it in the context of public opinion (see section 8.5). Nevertheless, assuming that dismissals are the 'best' solution for a company, there are certainly better and more acceptable ways of announcing them than the following examples describe:

> I remember very well one situation, when the CEO stepped up in front of the crew and said: 'we are now merged and there will be a lot of blood and water [sweat and tears] involved', according to the motto: 'everybody's head might roll'. I felt that the way of dealing with people was terrible! They simply used war-like propaganda, which was inappropriate, excessive and unnecessary. Of course, everybody was aware of the danger of becoming redundant. However, this way of communicating it was totally inappropriate. (I–14, §22)

> It is really devastating to hear something like that (. . .). They came in and used war-like jargon. Many of us had problems with this approach. You have your problems coping with such a way, that is, people coming in and telling you bluntly that you are going to be sacked. Particularly if you are older, the chances to change over to another job have diminished and you have to look after your family. Sometimes you ask yourself, how on earth should I work together with these rough people? Many have suffered from this behaviour. This has to do with the way things were communicated. (I–14, §23)

The above-cited interview reports describe the negative atmosphere and how they suffered from managerial behaviour. Some interview statements already contained a means to improve such situations, namely to communicate the dismissals in an 'acceptable' form. The 'how' seems to be even more important than the 'what' with such delicate topics. The announcement of dismissals had its best effects when it was honest, sensitive and consistent within itself, with other messages and in line with organizational values. When managers signalled comprehension and their compassion and found the right words, this was enough to change the depressing atmosphere. Words like the following were able to open new and motivating perspectives for employees:

> I still recall the situation when the CEO said in one of the meetings: 'For everybody who is leaving now, this must clearly be a difficult situation. However, I wish you all the best for the future. Sometimes these challenges provide opportunities for renewal and new orientation. Often this new orientation leads to a clearer comprehension and perspective about things.' (I–14, §70)

9.4.1 Support for the Dismissed

Some companies had a relatively developed social plan, with redundancy payments for dismissed employees. The extent of financial compensation largely depended on government and trade union settlements in the respective country, on the power of the internal works council and/or on the company's 'goodwill'.

> Well and then a social plan was devised and coordinated with the works council because people realized that in Germany you cannot do without them. Otherwise this institution can severely hinder your work. (I–15, §195)

To come up with a good social plan, however, did not necessarily imply that the organization acted purely altruistically. Companies were also interested in keeping a good image to the public.

> We managed to develop a reasonable social plan. This was particularly helpful for people who otherwise would have found it difficult to find a job somewhere else because they were beyond 50 [years] or because of their weak educational training. Henkel managed to fund endowments to help out. However this was not a purely altruistic decision. Henkel wanted to avoid the spreading of bad news about the closing down of the plant. (I–7, §47)

In cases were employees had the feeling that the 'golden handshake' was generous, acceptance of the redundancies was higher and animosity against the employer lower or absent:

> For Zumtobel Group this involved lots of money. At any rate, this was what people did, and I believe it was the right way to go. Because in the end people who left the company were OK with it, saying 'all right they treated us well' and there were no substantial animosities involved. (I–15, §§196–7)

The analysed organizations with dismissals seem to have handled the financial compensations in a fair way. The golden handshake, however, is not always that shiny. Some companies' hypocritical way of dealing with dismissals was the topic of one of the conversations. During the biggest holiday period in July mail was sent out with the message 'we are not going to dismiss any one of our employees. But everyone who is 55 or older can take advantage of an offer and give in their notice until the end of the year, and she/he will get a certain (high) amount of money.' However one important point was not mentioned in the letter, namely that those aged over 55 who did not give notice until December would be fired anyway in the following year – at that time without special compensations. This example referred to another organization than the four analysed M&A cases, but it provides a good picture of empty offers to redundant staff members.

In addition to financial compensations, some companies offered support in the job-finding process. This was partly the case with Schwarzkopf, where managers with connections to other companies in the neighbourhood tried to find a place for their redundant employees.

> I vaguely remember that they [the management] were thinking about alternative job opportunities for people who would have to be dismissed. (I–6, §169)

> We jointly searched for jobs for our people. It was not really that large a number of dismissed staff. (I–7, §182)

People did expect support when they were dismissed, especially in cases where human values were highlighted in the organizational mission statement.

> Well, everybody got the severance pay. Further help was not available, as far as I can think of. These days, support is quite often available . . . In the end, there were also good co-workers amongst those dismissed. And they are now experiencing many private problems too. It is quite important to provide them with some support. This is what one should do. If you [as a company] talk about 'cultural standards', you should also provide support in this direction. (I–14, §73)

Some companies also offer retraining for those dismissed in order to make them more attractive to the job market (Appelbaum *et al.*, 2000b; Cartwright and Cooper, 2000; Gutknecht and Keys, 1993). However this did not occur in the companies analysed.

9.4.2 Farewell Party

The literature frequently recommends the positive effect of social events in general and farewell parties for those dismissed in particular (Cartwright and Cooper, 2000; Gutknecht and Keys, 1993). In none of the four M&A cases was there a farewell party organized for people who were leaving the company – at least none of the interviewees recalled an official party: 'Well, I can't remember a single situation or farewell party where the CEO shook hands and formally acknowledged their achievements with a "thank you"' (I–14, §70).

The main reason for missing farewell events was the fact that the dismissals happened over a period of time. Every few weeks, redundant people just 'disappeared' from the scene.

> Earlier we used to have many common parties – whenever somebody left the company. But this changed. This was one of Henkel's strategies. They always follow this pattern. The dismissal of people is fragmented over a period of time in such a way that you just cannot properly arrange for farewell parties any more. Every single co-worker left the company on a different date. (I–7, §106)

In one of the Schwarzkopf departments the atmosphere was so bad that people did not even want to keep their tradition of small informal birthday parties. In other departments and companies some particularly involved line managers arranged small parties or an away-day on their own because they felt that a 'good' goodbye was appropriate:

> The members of another division arranged for a final joint trip. In our division the work-morale and team-spirit was so low that everything just drifted apart. I do believe that this was different for every division involved. It depends on the individual person in charge. (I–6, §95)

> Finally we made a trip to Trentino with all the people. This was sort of a 'thank you' to all the people who had worked together. I believe this demonstrated how you can deal with this issue in a positive way. Well, we had learned from our previous experience. This really worked well. (I–7, §182)

However, in addition to these semi-privately organized farewell events, people would have expected an official signal of appreciation and a 'thank you':

> People expected that this guy would stand up and say: 'We have always beem working well together. What is happening now, is not in our hands, but I invite you to a big final party.' However, something like this did not happen. In my view this was neglected. (I–7, §106)

Also in the case of Sportler there was no standard farewell. Some people (mainly managers) received a present during a farewell party because the owner considered it as important and because he wanted to show them his gratitude. Since people's morale declined substantially in parallel to the expansion of the company, some employees were dismissed because of theft. In such cases, where theft was the reason for the dismissal, *disappointment* predominated and a warm farewell was difficult:

> In these days we have the huge problem of thefts committed by staff. In such cases we have very abrupt departures, without even saying 'good-bye'. You know, you are just human, you are too disappointed, and you can't look into this person's eyes anymore. You are just happy he is out of the door. (I–9, §102)

9.4.3 Voluntarily Leaving the Company

In the post-merger stage a wave of fluctuations starts and the fluctuation rate goes up to 75 per cent during the first three years post-acquisitions (Cartwright and Cooper, 1995; Unger, 1986; Walsh, 1988). Typically, between 50 and 70 per cent of key managers voluntarily leave acquired companies. Employees' turnover rate is somewhat lower but it can also reach the 60 per cent level. Usually people with the best educational background and the highest degree of know-how are the ones who get good offers from other organizations and prefer to go. This means a loss of talents and of know-how for the organization. Therefore the expected and often mentioned '2 + 2 = 5' outcome cannot be achieved in most of the cases'[1] (Cartwright and Cooper, 2000).

If the job situation and the career paths were perceived as too unstable, the atmosphere got worse and worse, and people who had the chance to get another job preferred to leave their own firm, like leaving a sinking boat. Interviews showed that companies were often unaware of their employees' negotiations with other firms, especially if the atmosphere was bad and if relationships between superiors and employees had deteriorated through the merger:

> Job negotiations with other companies were going on in parallel. But Schwarzkopf didn't know this. These are highly turbulent times in companies. A few colleagues had good connections and immediately got another job; others had more difficulties. I had also signed a job contract with an Italian company. (I–7, §§82, 85)

The motives for 'survivors' to give notice voluntarily were several. One of the most frequently mentioned reasons was the fact that many M&A integration processes were just taking too long. Many individuals were not willing to cope with unstable job situations, unpredictable career paths, no tangible progress and a deteriorating atmosphere over an extensive period:

> And there are always fears such as 'will our company be closed down? Is my position still safe in a year's time? Should I use my energies to apply for other jobs?' These are the consequences if there is no rapid progress. (I–12, §172)

I suppose that people were already looking for other jobs because the level of insecurity was so high. (I–6, §137)

The uncertainties grew, the internal working atmosphere became worse and worse. Within some small groups people worked well with each other, but nevertheless they started to look for other jobs and to leave the firm. (I–7, §80)

Owing to these *uncertainties* and to the extra amount of work which was typical of the implementation stage, some people felt high levels of *stress*. Some people were not able to cope with all the organizational changes, the new 'rules' and the new organizational culture or strategy. This was sometimes combined with *mistrust* in the success of the newly merged company. The interview statements are in line with similar findings reported in the literature (Baruch and Woodward, 1998; Cooper and Cartwright, 1994; Fotinatos-Ventouratos and Cooper, 1998; Kirkcaldy and Cooper, 1992; Marks and Mirvis, 1985; Siu *et al.*, 1997; Terry *et al.*, 1996; Widerszal-Bazyl *et al.*, 2000):

For her it was an enormous stress. It was that big that she decided to give notice within the first probationary month in the new company. (I–6, §111)

Others could not cope with the stress and they said: 'No, I can't stand this any longer! I better voluntarily leave the company.' (I–14, §67)

As many interview statements prove, some people were not able to cope with all the organizational changes, the new norms and rules, the new organizational culture and strategy. Interestingly, this lack of coping capabilities and *suspicion* was always expressed in the third person: none of the 18 interview partners talked about their own adjustment difficulties. Generally speaking, older employees especially had difficulties to adjusting. Therefore, in some cases, a new generation took over in the post-merger process:

The company was shaken up. For many persons this was very difficult, and many managers of the older generation could not take this any more and left. Within three, four years all of them were gone. In this sense, it was also a change of generation. Of course, if you are older, you are not able to adapt that easily to something new – suddenly all the offices got computers. And if you are not able to keep up with the new technology, you have your problems. (I–14, §17)

I know from one guy who left. He said: 'I can't believe this [strategy] would work out.' (. . .) He was in a leading position, and he was very good. He made it clear relatively early: 'I have a problem with this strategy.' (I–12, §§77, 80)

Also *disappointment* about the changed job circumstances was a reason for employees to give notice. Some employees who felt unappreciated preferred to leave.

> Someone from a department which was completely reorganized did not like the idea of changing to another department. He did not identify with it because he perceived his new position as 'inferior' compared to his prior post. Yes, we had such cases, and they decided to voluntarily leave the company. (I–14, §67)

Sometimes companies invited people to stay for a certain transitional phase. Henkel, for example, 'convinced' Schwarzkopf's employees who were already on the dismissal list to stay for a certain period by offering a very tempting but conditional social plan. If those affected had left earlier, they would have lost the promised extra money:

> This was of course a great incentive! On the one hand side, it was positive for us because we got a lot out of it, but on the other hand it was of course a hindrance because we had to stay until the company would give notice to us. This ensured that we would not leave earlier, because in that case we would have given away money to the company – only because of two months . . . But I have to say that the frustration was sometimes so intense that we really reflected if it wouldn't be better to just renounce and to look for another job. But the incentive was really huge, after all. (I–6, §138)

Although a few individuals were very close to giving up just a few weeks before this special contract expired, the incentives were just too tempting. In this sense, the company's semi-forced way of keeping employees worked.

NOTE

1. The performance outcomes of a merger or an acquisition are expected to be more than the sum of its parts (more than the outcomes of the two single companies). This is commonly referred to as '2 + 2 = 5'.

10. M&A outcomes

10.1 EMPLOYEES' IDENTIFICATION AND COMMITMENT

In theory, identification and commitment can be considered as two separate concepts. In the interviews, however, commitment implied identification. Most of the time, identification was expressed through commitment. Here, in the empirical part of the work, the two concepts identification and commitment will therefore be presented together.

The interviews revealed that in many cases organization members identify with their pre-merger company. It takes a long time until the employees of the two companies really feel committed to the newly merged company, and until they develop a 'we' feeling: 'We have a working colleague – it took her more than two years to say, "I am a Sportler-member", in the sense of having internalized it. Superficially she had already tried to say this earlier' (I–9, §31).

Most of the interviewees did not express 'we' identifications when talking about the whole merged organization. Zumtobel and Staff are an exception. Two interviewees estimated that more then 80 per cent of the members would identify with Zumtobel Staff as a whole. However it took them ten years to come to this common identity, and there are still a few members in both organizations who differentiate between 'we' and 'them'. Respondents also claimed that the process could have happened much faster. The dramatic interventions and the changes only happened five years after the announcement. Five years for undertaking the first big steps towards integration was considered far too long. Nevertheless in many M&As it is part of the strategy to keep a double brand for the first post-merger period in order to retain employees' identification with their familiar group and thus their commitment. Since managers are more often in contact with members of the partner organization, it is easier for them to develop a common superordinate identity. Contact theory supports this finding.

> 'We'-feelings exist more on management levels than on employee levels because the exchanges between managers and top managers of the two companies are more intense. But the 'we'-feelings amongst Leitner members are not more

intense than the 'we'-feelings amongst Poma members. The intensity is more or less the same. (I–3, §146)

Employees also identified highly with 'their' products. Interestingly members of all four companies considered their own products better than the products of the partner organization:

> The research and development department here in Sterzing (Italy) fully identi-fies with their product, and the R&D department in France fully identifies with their product. This is the problem. It is simple: people prefer their own creations and tend to stick to what they have done for the last 15 years. (I–3, §42)

When Schwarzkopf was bought by Henkel, the employees of Schwarzkopf had to hand over their brands to Henkel employees. This was not an easy shift for them because they felt so *proud* of 'their' brand and fully identified with it. In the example of the brand Glem Vital, for instance, they told Henkel members only what they had to, but they refused to tell every-thing about how to 'treat' the brand. Schwarzkopf members were *angry* and *frustrated* because they thought Henkel members, being used to rather low-price mass products, would not appreciate the value of their 'baby'. Many dismissed Schwarzkopf employees did not buy their former products under the lead of Henkel any more because they were *envious* and did not want to support Henkel's profits with 'their' (Schwarzkopf's) products. Since the emotional turmoil amongst Schwarzkopf members was experi-enced as highly intensive and the emotions as mostly negative, the iden-tification with the new company and a sense of commitment could not be developed. Indeed everybody from the former Schwarzkopf staff who had been taken over by Henkel voluntarily left within the first one or two years.

Behind the identification with the product there was often also a high identification with one's organizational culture. Where employees had strongly positive feelings towards their own pre-merger culture, it was more difficult to convert this identification to a new one. In some cases, employ-ees identified first of all with their group or department and less with the (pre-merger) company as a whole. The commitment was based on a per-sonal relationship. This corresponds to the hypothesis of social identity theorists that members often identify with the group of most interaction (Dahler-Larsen, 1997; Hernes, 1997; Kramer, 1991).

Also the change of the company's name and logo (or only the thought of a potential change) seemed to be a problem for many people. Usually neither of the two merger partners wanted to give up their own company name in favour for the partner organization's name. A good and acceptable solution for both parties was a combination of the two names. Examples of successful combinations – despite initial resistance – were 'Zumtobel Staff' and 'Prinoth by Leitner Snow'.

According to social identity theory, individuals have a positive self-esteem from everything that is related to their own company and thus more positive emotions (pride and joy). With one exception, no interviewee mentioned disadvantages of their own pre-merger company, while many mentioned 'negative' sides of the partner company and/or of the merged company as a whole. 'The other's' products and organizational culture are not respected as much as their own pre-merger identity: 'Whatever the others do is perceived negatively and is judged as "bullshit" – if I may use this term' (I–3, §83). There is an interesting case which illustrates that negative topics were more likely to be attributed to the partner company: while co-workers from their own pre-merger company were perceived as very committed and as high 'identifiers' with the pre-merger organization, members of the partner company were classified as low 'identifiers' and as less committed towards their pre-merger organization.

We have seen that such an ingroup favouritism is connected with negative emotions towards the outgroup. Negative emotions like scepticism and mistrust, fear of exploitation and fear of contamination, and envy or jealousy towards the partner company hinder the creation of a common superordinate identity. However the lack of emotional involvement also seems to be an obstacle to the creation of a common identity. There were clear indications in the interviews that a rational approval was not enough for identification and commitment.

> But to be honest, I don't have the feeling they belong to us. (I–14, §88)

> I can't say which feelings I have for it [the merger]. This is just a big and important story which we have to continue. And this implies shaking up the company. But I don't feel really good about it, perhaps because I just don't feel touched by it. For me it is simply one of those issues everybody keeps taking about. Actually, it is somewhat alien to me; I can't really say I feel strongly about it . . . it is like an alien element, to which I have almost no reference points. (I–14, §91)

Furthermore language barriers, geographical distance and different national as well as organizational cultures also presented impediments to a smooth and fast integration.

> That's for sure, people strongly identify with the company Leitner, but not with the whole merged company Leitner–Poma. The case with Prinoth was different: their headquarters is next to our company building and some of the offices are next to each other. Therefore we are continuosly in contact with each other and we feel like one company. Next to the culture aspect – because we are from the same country – it is for sure also a question of geographical proximity. Neither

is given in the case of Poma. Most of our staff had no contact with Poma members. Well, it might be that some have met them at a trade fair or at an opening ceremony . . . (I–1, §33)

A few interviewees thought that the best post-merger strategy was to continue with separate corporate cultures, with separate brands, and with old company names. Others promoted a common way. They considered joint projects and products as a good way of achieving a strong identification with the merger partner. Although it might be difficult to develop common products, it might also be very rewarding because people tend to identify with what they have created. Leitner and Poma continued to use different brand strategies and reduced their synergies to the sharing of markets. Prinoth was bought by Leitner more or less at the same time as Poma. However, in the Prinoth case, the common product development and production started immediately after the announcement. Also the name changed ('Prinoth by Leitner Snow'), and the Prinoth offices were translocated next to Leitner's. This helped to develop a 'we' identification quickly.

The interview data showed that the objectives of and reasons for the merger or the acquisition should be understandable to employees, in order to gain their trust and commitment. If there is no comprehensible reason for a managerial action, employees tend to boycott or at least not commit themselves to the newly merged company. For Schwarzkopf people, for example, it was not clear why Henkel had made an effort to buy all the highly profitable Schwarzkopf works and then closed all of them down within two years. It did not count whether Henkel had 'good' reasons or not to do this. As long as people do not understand the purpose and do not feel that the new owner cares about them, they will react with negative emotions and oppose the managerial decisions forcefully.

10.2   EMPLOYEES' JOB SATISFACTION

'From the moment of the announcement, job satisfaction tremendously diminished' (I–6, §217). The reasons for the decrease in job satisfaction were several. People often could not cope with the pressure and stress due to an increased work load and to high levels of uncertainty. 'Others could not cope with the pressure and said: "No, I can't stand this any longer. I prefer to voluntarily leave the company!"' (I–14, §67).

Another important factor that influenced job satisfaction was perceived fairness or injustice. If employees thought that managerial decisions were unfair, they reacted with anger, envy, disillusionment, frustration and demotivation. People were, for example, disappointed about their new position or asked questions such as 'Why do I have to leave the company and not my colleague?' Job satisfaction varied among employees of the same company. For employees who had been happy with the pre-merger company and had felt highly committed, it was more difficult to keep that level of job satisfaction in the newly merged company. The changes were perceived negatively because they were associated with the loss of something loved.

While most of the members of Schwarzkopf had felt happy, committed and satisfied in their pre-merger company, there were also a few individuals who had perceived Schwarzkopf as too fragmented, too hierarchical, ignorant, conservative, narrow-minded, slow in decision making, characterized by power games and full of 'grey eminences'. These individuals felt that their innovative and opposing ideas had not been welcome within this system. They were unsatisfied with Schwarzkopf and looking forward to the changes through the Henkel management. The changes due to the acquisition were thus perceived as positive and challenging. Otherwise it appears that employees' job satisfaction is often reversed through a merger or an acquisition: employees who demonstrated high satisfaction in the pre-merger stages develop into unsatisfied employees, and unsatisfied members' job satisfaction seems to increase through the M&A changes.

> There was a lack of readiness and willingness to make decisions. There were of course struggles for power, and everybody wanted to be the number one somewhere. The grey eminences with the lowest management skills prevailed. Thus everybody who was active and wanted to do more than just the ordinary office work had his/her problems – myself included. (I–8, §15)

> Lastly, when the project started at Henkel, I was asked to help. This was incredibly interesting and it was a huge challenge. (. . .) As I said, this was fascinating, and I started to realize that there are also other opportunities outside Schwarzkopf – and then several opportunities arose. (I–8, §34)

In a similar way, the following example illustrates the influence of management style on employees' job satisfaction:

> We had a manager at one of the former Hervis subsidiaries whose team was not behind him. His attitude was very authoritarian, almost like a dictator. The team was demotivated, criticized and moaned about everything, complained about Sportler and about everything Sportler did, while everything from the former Hervis was perceived positively. When this guy left, a new manager came. And within a few weeks, the crew had developed into a Sportler-team! He is a sunny-boy, but he really lived the Sportler philosophy, he started with enthusiasm and with eagerness to work, and he managed to immediately create a good atmosphere. I was impressed how fast this can go. Today, this is a successful subsidiary with completely satisfied people who say: 'This is great! I never realized in what a hell we had been before . . . ' You can see now that a group has developed that really knows what it is all about. (I–9, §95)

Also external factors (such as economic downward trend) or internal 'hard' facts (like the change of company size) can change employees' job satisfaction and commitment. In the case of Sportler, for example, the acquisition of the Hervis outlets was perceived as a too rapid and 'unhealthy' growth. It was not only a big change for the former Hervis employees. The employees of the buying company also suffered from the shock due to the rapid change in their organizational identity. There is a price to pay for lower job satisfaction:

> Nowadays we have the huge problem of thefts committed by staff members. In the growing company the bond with a person [with the proprietor] is not as strong any more and invites incorrect behaviour. These employees are not aware that the stock, for example, is also their good from which they live. They think they can get rich at others' expense. The way they treat the products – whether they look after them or whether they just throw them in a corner – is another indication that they just don't care . . . Such damages do sometimes cost more then a theft. The sense of responsibility decreased a lot. The geographical distance is a problem too in this respect. (I–9, §§102–3)

In addition to theft as a coping mechanism of unsatisfied employees, rumours also increased. Work ethic and productivity suffered. Employees chatted for hours during worktime and took every opportunity to express their frustrations.

> The dissatisfaction was also reflected in the working morale. The secretary from the floor above came every morning into our office – instead of directly going to hers – in order to chat for about an hour and in order to get rid of her frustration. (I–6, §27)

Previous interview citations have already demonstrated that staff members were looking for new jobs and signing contracts without informing their superiors. These were just other forms of coping with low job satisfaction. Also increasing absenteeism rates became a problem. Summarizing we can say that decreased job satisfaction had serious consequences for motivation, commitment, relationships and performance.

10.3   RELATIONSHIPS

10.3.1   Relationships between Co-workers

Relationships between company members are influenced by culture and management style. For example, people from French Poma felt more power distance, conformed to hierarchical report structures and liked clear

instructions, while employees of South Tyrolean Leitner were more independent (from a Leitner perspective). This was also reflected in communication and in the way people addressed their superiors. Schwarzkopf
members who identified highly with their company perceived Henkel's hierarchy structure as more rigid than their own. While Schwarzkopf employees were sitting together with their superiors at the lunch table, in Henkel's
canteen employees were separated from management. It is interesting that
this perception was not shared by all Schwarzkopf members. Those who
identified less with the pre-merger organization perceived Henkel as more
open and cooperative than the rigid Schwarzkopf management style.

When two quite different organizational cultures merge, culture clashes
may occur which make relationship building between members of the
two partner organizations more difficult. However within the pre-merger
companies relationships also often change as a result of the merger.
Relationships between employees deteriorate because of *fears* of losing
their job or a good position. Individuals become *jealous* and, using different
methods, fight for attention in order to be privileged. Power games,
intrigues and harassment are the undesirable consequences which result in
high fluctuation rates.

> We were simply unable to take on more people. There were of course intense
> emotions: feelings of impotence, helplessness, compassion. Especially power-
> lessness. People were offended, and said things like: 'You are in a good position!'
> and 'Why does this happen to us?' There were feelings of injustice, and people
> who were completely unrelated to the matter were accused of wrong-doing, like
> 'I have been in the company for 15 or 18, 20 years, she has only been here for two
> or three years. Why is she allowed to stay and I not?' Further, it was also difficult
> to find a new company for these people. (I–7, §149)

> As indicated, there were formations of groups. Former friendships deteriorated
> into more distant relationships because nobody really knew who would be left
> in the company. In this situation everybody tries to look at his or her own inter-
> ests, of course. You could feel this. I felt it with extreme intensity because I
> worked for [name of merger partner] and against [name of own company]. Of
> course there were *aggressions* against me. (I–8, §132)

The interviews confirm Appelbaum and his colleagues' (2000a, 2000b) findings regarding the difficult position of 'survivors' of the merger. They feel
sad because of loosing working colleagues and they are aware of their powerlessness to change their colleagues' situation. Their grief is not accepted
by those who know they will have to leave, and so they often also have to deal
with the envy, aggression and accusations of their dismissed co-workers.
The ones who can stay in the company often feel compassion for those who
have to leave. They want to help, but they are dominated by a sense of help-
lessness, powerlessness and often also by guilt. They are frustrated by the

bad atmosphere and angry with the company. Relationships deteriorate among colleagues. This creates further psychological stress, and job satisfaction becomes less.

> Somehow I had the feeling that they didn't take my attempt to support and console them seriously. Then I felt even more helpless and excluded from the whole situation. It wasn't that bad that we wouldn't have talked to each other any more, but whenever a topic about the future came up, there was always a kind of reproach on us, like 'You can't imagine what this is like and how we feel!' And then you just feel bad about it. (I–6, §84)

> Yes, it is a feeling of . . . I would say, a feeling of sheer helplessness. Some people openly said what they thought, others didn't. Both groups were involved in infights and group conflict. Some were coming up with statements such as 'You can have an easy laugh, because you are not affected and can stay!' There were also arguments and quarrels. This is an extremely disagreeable situation! Really stupid. Some people in lower management positions said: 'I feel really sorry, but I can't change anything . . .' If you are on a lower hierarchical level you just don't have the chance and the power to find jobs for other people. (I–7, §147)

10.3.2   Relationships between Superiors and Employees

Not only relationships among employees are affected by M&As. The relationship between superiors and employees can change dramatically too. Managers themselves feel high levels of uncertainty, and are often under pressure and stress. In such situations they have less time to cultivate relationships or they do not know how to deal with their own insecurities. Therefore they are frequently perceived as more distant and unapproachable by employees. The relationship becomes cooler. Some employees start to toady up to management and to speak ill of their co-workers. This is something that affects negatively the relationship among colleagues.

> In such situations it also happens that people start to talk bad about each other, in order that someone else may be hit by the downsizing and not they themselves. I think this doesn't happen consciously, more unconsciously. (. . .) Also free-rider behaviours start and toadying up to people and those things . . . Some couldn't stop toadying until today [Interviewee laughs]. (I–14, §64)

One of the big challenges which middle managers especially have to deal with is the fact that employees do not necessarily identify with the new strategy they have to implement. Middle managers experience this situation as a dilemma:

> The technical director gets to feel it most intensely: 'Why do we have to accept this! Our product is better! This doesn't make sense! We have only problems with

their damn product . . . ', and so on. All this comes back to the technical director. And since he has to bring the project to its end, there often happen to be problems also between such superiors and their employees, because the managers get instructions from the top with which the employees don't identify. This is the point. (I–3, §93)

However there are also positive examples. In some cases relationships among co-workers and between superiors and employees improve in the post-merger situation. This happens in cases where employees do not have to worry about their future because they are either sure to keep the job or they already have a new job in prospect. They feel secure and help each other on a small scale as much as possible in order to better deal with the increased work load.

The relationship between management and their employees can remain intact, even though those employees have to be dismissed. Where those dismissed feel that the company cares about them and expresses appreciation and gratitude through a nice farewell party, for example, it is more probable that the relationship between those dismissed and management will be well-functioning. A warm treatment of those dismissed is also a positive signal for the 'survivors' because they realize that their company is caring about its members.

> In one specific situation, the branch manager was quite relieved to see one particular co-worker leave the firm. However, even against this background, a farewell party was organized and colleagues were arranging for a good atmosphere. It is nice for me to see if there is still a positive relationship, and if such a former employee three years after still says, 'We had a good time together!' This would be my desire. But of course this is not always the case. (I–9, §101)

Celebrations in general can help to bring people together and to improve relationships: 'Shared enjoyment and joint celebrations help to build bonds. If this does not happen, important values are missing' (I–9, §135).

10.4 PERCEIVED PERFORMANCE

The interviews demonstrated that often neither employees nor middle managers knew precisely how well their pre-merger company had performed compared to the post-merger organization. For this reason it was more revealing to ask the interview partners about the 'perceived' performance instead of the 'real' performance. Indeed it is the perception of success or failure of the M&A that determines whether or not employees feel proud or frustrated and whether or not they stay with the firm.

Employees found it difficult to deal with all the changes. They were particularly affected by a high turnover rate of their superiors. Every new CEO or manager had a different personality, a different style, and a tendency to change 'everything'. Many want to seem busy and do things only for the sake of doing them. The strategic orientation is difficult to maintain, and productivity declines:

> They pushed us back and forth (. . .) and nobody really knew her/his place. Doing serious work is extremely difficult in these situations. When again and again, new managers come along with the ambition to remodel everything from the ground up, this inevitably leads to heightened operational activity, lacking any good strategy. This cannot be good. (I–14, §14)

Also the long coffee breaks and talks with colleagues which employees seem to need in order to digest all their negative emotions have an impact on performance. Frightened, frustrated and/or angry employees often reduce their work input to a minimum. The absenteeism rate grows and therefore unsatisfied workers are extremely expensive.

> A project was started in order to help the company regain profits. It was clear that an increase in productivity by 10 per cent was only realistic if we managed to win confidence and support from staff. Perhaps we could gain even more – it is not easily measurable in numbers because also other factors play a role. But it is true that an unsatisfied crew, that is adopting a wait-and-see position, can ruin the company. Only if the company makes enormously high profits will it be able to compensate for unsatisfied employees. (I–15, §90)

It seems that negative emotions, like anger at management, anxieties or frustration, lead to a perception of the M&A as a mistake. One interview partner of Schwarzkopf who was irritated about and frustrated with the acquisition said: 'Economically, there was no need to close down our company. The finances were all right. Henkel made a mistake' (I–7, §47). On the other hand, positive feelings, like pride in working for an attractive and big company, motivated employees. They saw the merger or the acquisition as a positive challenge and as a good decision. Therefore they were confident that the merged company would perform well. One interview partner of Schwarzkopf expressed his *happiness* when the company was bought by Henkel and felt that this was a *positive challenge*. The perception of the acquisition and the buying company therefore differed substantially from the former interview partner: 'Within Schwarzkopf everything was out of date and antiquated. In contrast, Henkel has developed a modern and successful management culture' (I–8, §92). It is a necessary prerequisite for M&A integration success to build on the confidence of the staff members so that success is feasible.

PART III

Conclusions

11. Discussions

A boom in merger activities has characterized the world economic scene in recent decades. This picture was dominated by cheerful and hyped-up messages regarding strategic and operational benefits of newer and bigger organizations. However the analysis becomes somewhat gloomy when considering the high degrees of merger failure and the negative implications for those affected by the M&A. The traditional literature is mostly concerned with organizations as rather logical and rational entities, failing to appreciate that highly emotional events such as M&As interfere with logic and rationalism. This book calls for an increasing awareness of emotions and of appropriate forms of managerial communication to deal with organizational changes.

The present work highlights the significance of managerial communication and management behaviour towards their employees in a comprehensive conceptual framework. The combined impact of these dimensions on employees' emotions is stressed for periods of significant organizational change. Five outcome dimensions, employee identification and employee commitment to the newly merged organization, job satisfaction, the development of relationships and perceived performance, were investigated in a qualitative study involving four companies. The results provided support for the framework. The development of this conceptual framework can be seen as a major contribution of this study. Furthermore the development of an instrument that is suitable for a survey of emotions in the M&A context is considered unique.

11.1 RECAPTURING EMOTIONS IN M&As

11.1.1 Cross-sectional versus Longitudinal Study

The literature recommends investigating M&A phenomena relatively soon after the announcement. It came as a surprise that the present study could not confirm this: the empirical findings show that people remember M&A-related episodes in detail over a long time. Brain researchers and psychologists could give an explanation for this phenomenon when they assert that, in the human brain, an event is always stored together with the emotions this event evoked (Harris, 1995; Penfield, 1952). In consequence an event can only be recalled in connection with the emotions involved at that time. The interviews and the analysis of the 'temperature curves' proved that people experienced M&As as rather emotionally challenging periods. They also remember emotions related to the merger over a long time. In this sense there were no differences between interview partners who only recently had gone through a merger (for example, Leitner members) or who had experienced the big changes several years prior to the time of the interview (for example, Schwarzkopf members). In both cases, respondents could easily recall the emotional intensity and express which kinds of emotions emerged.

For this reason there was not seen the need to do a longitudinal study: a cross-sectional investigation with retrospect questions was seen as sufficient. One could argue that emotions at the corresponding times might have been different from the respondents' memory of the emotions experienced. However, following a sense-making perspective (for example, Vaara, 2003; Weick, 1995), it does not matter. It is not the fact per se which counts. More important for future perceptions (and emotions) is how the individual consciously or unconsciously 'interpreted' the experience had in the past.

11.1.2   Differences in Information according to Hierarchical Layer

Although the interview questions were basically identical or adapted to the interviewee, the amount and quality of information obtained from top management was very different from the information gained from middle management and from employees. Interestingly, answers from persons in similar positions, but different organizations, were in certain aspects more similar compared to the answers from interviewees of the same company but holding diverse positions.

For comprehensible reasons, top managers and/or company owners know more about the history of the merger, strategies, financial backgrounds and numbers. Therefore these interview partners tended to lead the conversation in these directions. Questions regarding 'soft' factors, employees' perceptions of the M&A, and emotions were sometimes either completely misunderstood (despite our broaching the subject again) or not answered to the same extent as by middle managers and employees.

Interviews and open conversations with middle management were the most interesting regarding our objectives. These executives are in an intermediate position between decision makers and affected dependants. Middle managers are basically those most affected by the organizational change. This is also confirmed by the literature (for example, Cartwright and

Cooper, 2000): they are responsible for the implementation of the owners' or top management's decision. They are subject to decision makers' expectations, to uncertainty due to the lack of top-down information and are exposed to employees' irritations, fears and questions. Middle managers are also regularly in contact with colleagues (middle managers) from the partner company, but generally on a more informal level than top managers are. Therefore they get more insights and confront more problems. Consequently middle managers often define M&As as extremely demanding and stressful events.

In parallel with the merger or acquisition, some organizations offer special supporting seminars for improving, for instance, communication and teamworking skills. The purpose of those seminars and workshops is to prepare middle managers for the organizational changes. These companies' efforts are welcome and highly appreciated by those who had the chance to attend the training. People in leading positions who were less prepared for the big changes had to learn by 'trial and error'. These individuals report more frequently the challenging situations they would confront in a different way, next time.

The responses of employees without leading function within the company were only of limited interest for the present study. In general, most of the employees were not well enough informed about the merger. Also, some of these interview partners were reluctant to answer questions from an external interviewer (except in the case of closer acquaintance). A further explanation derives from the impression that employees (that is, workers met in the canteen) are not used to being interviewed, to expressing their opinions and especially not ready to express their emotions and thoughts to someone from outside. The last and probably best explanation for the less informative employee interviews is simply the fact that some jobs are not affected by the merger. Employees for whom nothing changes thus feel quite indifferent to the M&A.

The few affected employees ready to answer, however, indicated that they were happy to have had the chance to talk about those highly emotional events, because just to talk about them had a kind of 'therapeutical' effect.

All this said, it is evident that the position of the interviewee within the company is a crucial factor as regards the findings that can be obtained. Nevertheless there are huge differences from M&A situation to M&A situation as well. The differences are not only due to the commonly known influencing factors such as company size, M&A type, industry branch, nationalities involved or organizational culture. The dissimilarities in terms of employees' emotional reactions between the companies analysed were in first place because of different managerial behaviour and communication style.

11.1.3 Managerial Communication and Behaviour

Most of the M&A literature emphasizes the importance of good top-down communication. The announcement of the merger or acquisition appears to be one of the most important moments, therefore it has to be well prepared and to be announced to all staff members at the same moment in order to avoid uncertainties and rumours. It is also suggested that the announcement should be made by the top management or by the company owner. If possible, it is suggested that the M&A be announced in a big company meeting which allows time for questions (for example, Appelbaum *et al.*, 2000a; Cartwright and Cooper, 2000). The findings of the present study do not confirm this procedure. In the big announcement meetings people are often overwhelmed by their feelings of excitement or shock. Usually they do not dare to ask the questions that really make them afraid. According to the findings of the present study, line managers have a more important role in the post-merger integration process than the literature recognizes. The fact that the whole company has to change its identity often leads to high degrees of insecurity, fears, disappointment, grief and anger among employees. It is all the more important that they have a superior whom they know well, whom they trust and who prepares them for the changes. Especially in big organizations, top managers and owners are often considered as too distant from employees. People do not dare to ask top managers about issues that bother them. They need a confidant(e) with whom to discuss their concerns. This person of trust should also be the one who has the courage to tell bad news. In the case of small family businesses with a special relationship to the owner, he or she will have this function. The important role of informal networks in organizations in general has been recognized by Krackhardt and Hanson (1993). The present findings fully confirm this and lead to the assumption that the informal leaders might be even more important during periods of major changes, as in the post-merger integration stage.

Generally speaking, the more employees felt themselves to be informed honestly, openly and frequently, and the more consistent all the visible managerial signals were, the higher was the chance for employees to experience positive emotions. Poor top-down communication, on the other hand, led to feelings of uncertainty and rumours and to negative emotions such as trust, fear, anger, frustration or aggression.

11.1.4 Emotions in M&As

The findings of the empirical study confirm the statements that M&A situations are indeed highly emotional phenomena for all those affected (for example, Appelbaum *et al.*, 2000b; Cartwright and Cooper, 2000; Marks, 1999). Interview partners recalled a whole range of experienced emotions and mentioned them unaided. While in the literature mostly negative (unpleasant) affects are mentioned (Appelbaum *et al.*, 2000b; Dixon and Marks, 1999; Marks and Mirvis, 1986) and studied (Empson, 2001; Fugate *et al.*, 2002; Kiefer, 2002b), it was surprising to find that a whole range of positive emotions exists as well (see Table 7.1). However it has to be pointed out that negative emotions or cognitive related affect terms were predominant.

The intensity of emotions varied according to the event that triggered them and according to the perceived likelihood that the event might affect the individual. The announcement of the merger, the first meeting(s) with the staff of the partner organization, and the period when the strategies were implemented and the changes started to affect the working life, were identified as the most intense times for the majority of the interviewees. In the case where top management decided not to implement the integration strategies immediately, but to start slowly and to take advantage of potential synergy effects only later, the real problems and emotional turmoil arise at that postponed moment. In cases where managers waited too long to take action employees' insecurities increased and their emotions became more painful. All unpleasant information or change seems to be more welcome to those affected than too long periods of uncertainty. How intense and painful it was considered depended on the position of the individuals in the company and on their interpretation of the situation. Uncertainties regarding dismissals are amongst the most dreadful aspects of post-merger stages, if not *the* most frightening issue. In order to reduce these periods of uncertainty with all its undesirable consequences, the literature (for example, Cartwright and Cooper, 2000) suggests that management should plan in advance and announce immediately and to all how many in total will be dismissed and who those persons will be. The findings of this study can confirm this.

11.1.5 Identification and Commitment

In theory, identification and commitment can be considered as two separate concepts. In the interviews, however, identification was most of the time expressed through commitment.

According to social identity theory, individuals have a positive self-esteem in everything that is related to their own ingroup, connected with positive emotions. Indeed it could be seen that people experience positive emotions (pride and joy) towards their own pre-merger company. They strongly identify with their company's products, organizational culture, name and logo, and with the company's successes. Most of the interviewees were more critical and/or negative about issues related to the partner company. Furthermore most of them did not express 'we' identifications when talking about the whole merged organization. It often takes years before a real 'we' feeling related to the merged organization can be established.

In some cases, employees identify first of all with their group or department and not with the (pre-merger) company as a whole. This corresponds to the hypothesis of social identity theorists that members often identify with the group of most interaction (Dahler-Larsen, 1997; Hernes, 1997; Kramer, 1991). The commitment is based on a personal relationship.

11.1.6   Job Satisfaction

While most of the interviewees were happy with their pre-merger company, their job satisfaction fell soon after the announcement. Reasons for dissatisfaction can be external factors (for example, economic downward trend) or internal 'hard' facts (for example, change of company size). However, most of the time, dissatisfaction was a consequence of managerial behaviour and communication style which triggered negative emotions. Perceived injustice, as well as high levels of stress and perceived pressure, were the most obvious sources of employees' decreased job satisfaction and lack of commitment. This is in line with assertions in the stress literature (Campbell Quick *et al.*, 2000; Cooper and Cartwright, 1994; Kirkcaldy and Cooper, 1992; McTigue Bruner and Cooper, 1991; Siu *et al.*, 1997).

Unsatisfied staff members can become an expensive element. In addition to theft as a coping mechanism of unsatisfied employees, people worry instead of working. Rumours increase. Employees are not able to work efficiently any more and chat for hours with their colleagues (during working hours) in order to let off their frustration. Another coping mechanism of unsatisfied individuals is to look for a new job and to leave the company voluntarily. Also increasing absenteeism rates become a problem. These findings are confirmed by authors who described these phenomena in the context of the 'merger syndrome' (Appelbaum *et al.*, 2000b; Bruckman and Peters, 1987; Dickmann, 2000; Marks, 1999; Marks and Mirvis, 1986; Schlieper-Damrich, 2000).

The findings show that decreased job satisfaction has serious consequences for motivation, commitment, relationships and performance.

11.1.7   Relationships

Relationships between co-workers and between superiors and employees often deteriorate during post-merger periods. Uncertainty about the future, competition in keeping or getting a position, fears, jealousy and envy, and anger can result in conflicts. Often the 'survivors' also suffer from the changes. They feel guilty and sad because they are aware of their powerlessness to change the situation of their colleagues. Furthermore they have to deal with the accusations of their dismissed colleagues. Joint farewell parties, as suggested in the literature (Appelbaum *et al.*, 2000a; Cartwright and Cooper, 2000) are often a good way of overcoming these problems and conflicts. A warm treatment of those dismissed is also a positive signal for the 'survivors' because they realize that their company is caring about its members.

11.1.8 Perceived Performance

From the interviews it seems that negative emotions such as anger at management, anxieties and frustration lead to a perception of the M&A as a mistake. On the other hand, positive feelings like pride in working for an attractive and important company, excitement at being challenged or happiness because of a promotion, motivate employees. They see the merger or the acquisition as a positive challenge and as a good decision. They are therefore confident that the merged company will perform successfully. Thus the perception of the partner company, of the M&A and of its success differed substantially between interview partners who predominantly experienced positive emotions and those who predominantly suffered from unpleasant emotions.

Several interview partners did not know how well the merged company performed compared to the two pre-merger companies. However, success materializes out of staff members' belief that success is possible.

11.1.9 Individual Realities

The findings imply that emotions are both individual and a collective phenomenon. People within the same department or team are exposed to similar realities and to a similar information system. They therefore tend to experience events in a similar way and experience similar emotions. However this is not necessarily true for the whole company because employees in different departments might be in a different situation (for example, no dismissals compared to other departments). Since superiors have a big influence on employees' emotions and since line managers from different departments are likely to communicate and behave differently in periods of major organizational changes, employees' emotions vary from group to group. Furthermore every single employee – the perceiver of the managerial 'stimuli' – has his or her own experiences and mental predispositions and, consequently, interprets events in a unique way. This means that to a certain extent everybody lives in an individual reality concerning an M&A event.

Interestingly this is not only true for emotions and for 'soft' factors like job satisfaction, commitment and so on. Also the so-called 'hard facts' are often not that 'hard' and unambiguous. Analysis of the 'temperature curves' showed that people in the same organization may experience the same merger process as a completely different event. For example, even the date of announcement was perceived differently by the interview partners and varied in one case by up to nine months (in one of the companies the date of the official announcement was given as the summer of a certain year, while others indicated February of the following year). This also shows that what seems to be an obviously communicated announcement to the communicator does not necessarily mean that the recipients perceived this information as a merger announcement. It can happen that the first announcement via e-mail was simply misunderstood, ignored or deleted by the receiver. If such patterns of misunderstanding arise, there may be significant differences between the official and perceived announcement for individuals within the company. This argues in favour of the adopted qualitative methods. Following a positivistic approach and conducting a quantitative study would not have allowed such findings.

To conclude the discussion of the findings, it can be maintained that the empirical study supports the conceptual framework (Figure 4.5). The findings revealed that managerial communication and behaviour influence employees' emotions. There are also obvious relations between employees' emotions and (a) their identification with the merged company, (b) their commitment, (c) their job satisfaction, (d) relationships within the company, and (e) perceived performance.

11.2   LIMITATIONS OF THE STUDY

Despite all efforts, certain limitations apply to this study. They will be discussed and explained subsequently and transformed into suggestions for future research.

First, it is difficult to separate emotions from other states such as moods or enduring emotional states arising from temper (anxiety; for example, see Herriot, 2001). This leads to terminological ambiguities and consequently the categorization of 'emotions' in the analysis of the interviews might be criticized. The expression 'cognition-related affect terms' (for example, see Table 7.1) was thus used in order to broaden the view and to allow for reporting not only 'classical' emotions but emotion-related experiences as well.

Second, scholars (for example, Vanman and Miller, 1993) have argued that emotions are difficult to measure. This sets limits to the theoretical questions that can be addressed. Indeed most of the emotion measures come from appraisal and biosocial theorists and are studied in laboratories. Psychophysiological measurement methods – such as decoding of visual expression through careful video analysis, measurement of covert facial muscle activity via electromyography (EMG) or measurements of the arousal of the autonomic nervous system (ANS) via electrodermal activity (EDA) – are not applicable for retrospect studies or for studies of naturalistic inter-group interactions. Although it is proposed to use a set of methods for measuring the same emotional experience in order to increase reliability and validity (Tomiuk, 2000), the only applicable emotion measurement methods in the present study are self-reports through in-depth interviews and through questionnaire techniques. Usually rating scales and checklists are used to measure emotions. Instead, here, a projective technique ('temperature curve') was used alongside verbal statements. The purpose was, first, not to influence interview partners by presenting potential answers, and second, to assess the intensity of emotions over a longer period of time. This technique is considered suitable for the purposes of this study. However, since the 'temperature curve' has not been applied by other emotion researchers, this method might be challenged.

Third, considering the confidentiality problems before the official M&A announcement, it is difficult to gain access to companies in the pre-merger or during-the-merger stage. Therefore a retrospective study of emotions appeared to be the closest we could get. We assumed that very strong emotions can be recalled with ease even after a long time. However one has to be aware that people always 'make sense' out of their experiences (Weick, 1995, 2001). Therefore emotions can be seen either in a more positive or in a more negative way than they were at the time of the event, depending on the person's predispositions. This might be seen as a limitation of the emotion study in retrospect. On the other hand, following a constructivist and a cognitive appraisal perspective, it does not really matter what exactly happened. Only perceptions are important. However, in order to prove this assumption, a longitudinal study during and after the M&A might be interesting for future research.

Fourth, the study of employees' emotions and managerial communication and behaviour in the post-merger stage calls for a consideration of both perspectives. The combination of both managerial perceptions and employees' perceptions could provide a valid picture of the phenomenon investigated. However, except for one case, it was impossible to negotiate access to both employees and their respective line managers successfully. This was a consequence of the sensitivity of the topic and/or managers' lack of time.

However, in order to overcome this problem and in order to gather a broader picture, the dyadic approach (Denzin and Lincoln, 1994a; Fetterman, 1998; Maxwell, 1998; Yin, 1998) was further extended, and *three* hierarchy levels were sampled: top managers or company owners, middle managers and employees without leading function. This methodology is considered appropriate to reducing potential biases and overcoming potential critique pertaining.

11.3   IMPLICATIONS FOR FUTURE STUDIES

Literature about change management tends to put emotions on a level with resistance. In order to avoid or reduce resistance, it is suggested that company members be openly and rationally informed about the reasons for the merger or the acquisition. It is supposed that people have to realize the logic behind it, and they will then agree and contribute to the implementation of the M&A. Implicitly there is the hope that no emotions would arise, and if there were any, that they would soon disappear. Despite all communication and implementation strategies, this often remains wishful thinking.

Psychologists consider emotions as an expression of individual experiences. Therefore there are no 'negative' emotions which have to be avoided. Emotions have a signalling function. A sensitive eye for emotions and careful interpretations can lead to new understandings of situations and to less painful coping mechanisms. A trend towards higher awareness of emotions has been apparent for a few years. However there are still lots of opportunities for future research to contribute to this awareness.

The findings imply that emotions are both an individual and a collective phenomenon. This supports the decision to rely on both cognitive appraisal theory and social identity theory to explore emotions in the present study.

To see emotions as an individual phenomenon is in line with one of the current waves of research which recognizes that leadership has a vast influence on employees' emotions. The notion of emotional contagion is useful for explaining negative changes in employees' emotions as a consequence of negative emotional displays from leaders. Lewis (2000), for example, found that managers' negative emotional display had a significant and negative main effect on participant assessment of leader effectiveness compared to a more neutral emotional display. Additionally, the concept of emotional intelligence has influenced discussions in recent years (Ashkanasy *et al.*, 2002; Bar-On and Parker, 2000; Cooper, 1997; Goleman, 1995; Goleman *et al.*, 2002a). Emotionally intelligent leaders are supposed to influence their teams in a positive way and to be more efficient and successful. These leaders rely on and cope with emotions by bringing them to the surface; they understand how emotions affect the group's work and they behave in a way that builds relationships inside and outside the team, and thus strengthen the team's ability to face challenges and organizational changes (Urch Druskat and Wolff, 2001). Emotional intelligence has therefore become a vogue concept which has triggered many publications. However it has not been applied to mergers and acquisitions yet. Further research is suggested to follow this track.

Considering emotions as a collective phenomenon is supported by another stream of current emotion research. Scholars of this line of thought focus on an interaction model of individuals in organizations. They draw on psychological schools of emotion research and on the nature of social life to assume that an individual's emotions (physiological and psychological responses) occur in a world that is primarily socially influenced and symbolic (Rafaeli and Worline, 2001). Ambiguity in the causes and interpretations of physiological and psychological responses makes room for cultures, groups and symbolic contexts to influence people's emotions (Ashforth and Humphrey, 1995; Ashkanasy *et al.*, 2000; Fineman, 2000). Main topics of interest in this culture-related context are, for instance, identity and commitment, two dimensions of the present study.

Both directions, individual psychological as well as social constructivist perspectives, will have numerous opportunities for further research. Emotions in organizations, and especially in M&As, are not extensively studied as yet, but emotion is what connects people to one another, and to organizations. Emotional bonds are what produce organizations, rather than legal, financial or geographical bonds (Rafaeli, 1996). In this sense, the management of the future will primarily be concerned with managing their own emotions, and with managing the emotions of employees, customers, competitors and other stakeholders. This implies emotionally intelligent leaders. Considering that emotions also have a spillover effect from private life to job life and the other way around, from organizations into family life, future research will have to deal with this emotional complexity.

Future M&A research on emotions should aim to win support from companies for a longitudinal study and address employees and their direct line managers. This would have merit both conceptually and methodologically, allowing for comparisons of employee perceptions and their respective line managers'. However, because of the complex nature and the difficulties of getting organizational support to such an extent, this approach might possibly remain wishful thinking. Furthermore, in case a longitudinal study is intended to be done quantitatively, one has to be aware that the questionnaires cannot be conducted anonymously because the researcher has to know which employee is 'linked' to which manager. Therefore this route might only be viable for qualitative research with supportive companies but not for a quantitative survey.

Should a quantitative study be chosen for further research, it is suggested that only 'employees' be addressed. This implies that every single company member who is embedded in a hierarchy below at least one layer of management can be the target of a questionnaire; that is, middle managers and employees. The indication of which hierarchical level the respondent is on within the company would allow for an analysis of emotions and perceptions within and between different organizational 'layers'.

Depicting the 'temperature curve' quantitatively might be difficult since the interviews showed that people do not recall emotions in isolation but always in association with certain other events. In a quantitative study with emotion rating scales it is therefore interesting to see how similar and how intense emotions in certain situations are among people. It does not matter whether they think of the same date of announcement: it is more important how they felt at the moment of the perceived announcement of the merger. Consequently a way to employ quantitative methodologies successfully in the study of the post-merger process is to filter out the main events (announcement, first contact with the partner organization, raising questions about one's own career, first joint projects and so on) and to ask about the personal emotional intensity of each individual experience. Since the interviews revealed that negative emotions tend to be attributed to others and not to the particular person, it is recommended that a quantitative survey project these emotions onto other persons.

Another suggestion for future research is to ask both companies involved in the M&A. In the present study this was not important because every dimension of the conceptual framework could be analysed without the perspective of the partner company. However, when analysing cultural dimensions or relationships across the borders of the pre-merger companies, it is crucial to take into consideration the views of both organizations.

It might also be interesting to explore the differences between national and cross-boarder mergers and acquisitions and their impact on employees' emotions. Although in this project both cases were considered in the choice of the companies (however, international M&As were predominant), it is difficult to make clear statements on the implications a national merger has for employees' emotions compared to an international one. The interviews only demonstrated that language differences and geographical distance have an impact on personal relationships and on identification with the new organization as a whole.

11.4   IMPLICATIONS FOR MANAGEMENT

Nowadays decision makers are aware of the importance of including a culture-fit check in the due-diligence process prior to signing an M&A contract. Whether they base their decision on cultural compatibility or not is another issue. However literature claiming its importance has at least achieved awareness among top managers.

Emotional aspects, however, are still neglected by M&A decision makers. Since the M&A literature neglects emotions too, this does not come as a surprise. This project illustrated that managers have a strong impact on employees' emotions during periods of major organizational changes. Considering this responsibility, it is important for leaders to be aware of their role as managers, not only of tasks and strategies, but also of people and their emotions. Some managers do this naturally, some do not. Those who ignore their responsibility to lead emotions have to manage the damage which results from disappointed, unsatisfied, uncommitted and departing employees.

It is therefore useful to know that positive M&A-related emotions facilitate M&A success. The study showed that employees who experience positive emotions related to the merger or the acquisition are more likely to accept the managerial decision, to identify with the merged organization and to commit themselves. Furthermore they are able to see the M&A as a positive challenge instead of a devastating life event, their job satisfaction is higher and they are more motivated to contribute. A well managed and positively experienced merger can also prevent relationships among co-workers and between employees and superiors from deteriorating. Positive emotions also lead to a better perceived performance of the M&A, which is a prerequisite for further motivation, commitment and thus 'real' performance.

11.4.1   The Importance of a Vision

In line with literature promoting the human factor in M&As, the empirical study demonstrated that people need to be convinced in order to accept the major organizational change with all its challenging consequences and in order to be ready to contribute to its success. Employees are more likely to be committed and satisfied with the outcome of a merger if they understand its benefits for all those affected. It is therefore crucial that managers have a clear vision and that they are ready and able to communicate it. The clearer the picture employees have in mind about the upcoming changes, and the more sense this picture makes to them, the more motivated they are to work jointly towards the common purpose. A clear orientation and an appealing picture of the company's future are prerequisites to trigger positive emotions. Since emotions per definition imply a certain action readiness, it is easier to convince people to make their contribution to the implementation of the merger.

11.4.2 Managerial Communication

Managerial communication is most effective when it is open and honest. Bad news is considered better and less harmful for all those involved than no news and uncertainty. In periods of great changes such as a post-merger situation, employees need frequent and regular information in order to feel secure. Since uncertainty leads to negative emotions, to stress, rumours, inefficiency, high absenteeism rates and disloyal employees, it is worth keeping employees informed and involving them as much as possible. Managers cannot overcommunicate in these stages. The messages must be consistent and should be supported by tangible signs if they are to attain high credibility. It is not enough to proclaim changes if no clear sign of implementation follows. People need to see that something changes in the declared direction. This creates a sense of security, credibility and trust in management.

This clearly demonstrates, firstly, that you cannot overcommunicate. Even simple sentences like 'I also do not know more at the moment, but I will keep you informed' can be reassuring and help to set people's minds at rest. Secondly, it demonstrates that the impression of what is 'enough' information and 'frequent' communication is only a subjective and individual perception and not an objective fact. This said, it does not matter how much, how intensively and how openly superiors really communicate with their dependants. Due to the fact that perceptions create realities, all that matters is what is perceived by the receiver.

The role of informal networks and the important role of line managers should get more attention in post-merger integration processes. In periods of major organizational changes and high degrees of uncertainty, as pointed out earlier, it is crucial for employees to have a superior whom they know well, whom they trust and who prepares them for the changes; and who also informs them about negative implications of the changes. In the post-merger context, the role of line managers is more important than the literature recognizes. This is especially the case with big organizations, where top managers and owners are considered too distant from employees. Employees need a person who they can trust, liaise with on a tutor/mentor-like level and discuss their concerns. In the case of small family businesses the owner may have this function if there is a special relationship of trust between him/her and the employees.

11.4.3 Managerial Behaviour

Excellent top-down communication does not help if non-verbal communication and managers' behaviour speak another language. People will notice discrepancies and react with negative emotions and either resistance or withdrawal. Consistency in the long run is only attainable if the words pronounced are open and honest.

Strong leaders are what employees want in the post-merger process. The findings of the empirical project clearly reveal a call for managerial action. It seems that it is less the decision itself than the reduction of unbearable uncertainty that counts. Therefore implementation should happen fast. In the case of inevitable dismissals, for example, it is preferable to announce immediately how many and who will be dismissed, instead of leaving employees in uncertainty and (existential) fears for months or even years. This is in line with findings of other authors (for example, Cartwright and Cooper, 2000).

Relationships among employees deteriorate if they feel the pressure of competition for their jobs. The 'necessity' to display that they are 'better' than their colleagues leads to undesirable and harmful bullying behaviour. In such cases superiors have to interfere immediately, otherwise the situation only gets worse.

For dismissed employees as well as for 'survivors', it is essential to know that the company respects them and cares about them. It is therefore highly appreciated if management supports those who have to leave the company in finding a new job, with training for future jobs and/or with financial support. It is actually more the sign that 'the company cares about us' which leads to positive emotions than the kind or amount of support. As long as employees notice the honest attempt to support them, they will appreciate it. For the same reason farewell parties for those dismissed, a thank you and a few kind words have a tremendous positive effect, for those affected as well as for 'survivors'.

Some acquiring companies try to keep employees for a certain period of time after giving them notice, in order to garner employees' knowledge. Companies promise tempting remunerations on the condition that employees will not voluntarily leave the company before the company wants them to go. This semi-forced way of keeping employees works. However it would be more desirable for all parties to have committed employees who feel happy and proud to work for a caring company and who do not consider voluntarily leaving the organization. In this sense, immediate announcement of all dismissals, support systems and farewell parties are not only a precious thing for those who have to leave the company: they are also very powerful signals for 'survivors', showing them that they are working for a company 'with heart'. According to the literature (for example, Appelbaum *et al.*, 2000a), this will lead to survivors' acceptance of the M&A decision and to a higher commitment towards the newly merged company. Furthermore it will improve future relationships between superiors and employees as well as between those dismissed and the company, given that dismissed employees also contribute strongly to the organization's public image.

Not only unpleasant issues have to be implemented soon. Company members need to know and to see that the hassle of the M&A makes sense. Successes help to convince people. Everybody likes to be identified with successes, and is proud, more committed and more motivated when the first successes prove that it was a wise decision to merge or at least not a disadvantage to be taken over. Management can purposefully achieve quick successes by initiating small joint projects.

The literature provides evidence of the efficacy of corporate identity as a strategic management tool (for example, Alessandri, 2001). Although some practitioners argue that maintaining separated (brand/corporate) strategies is easier, there is evidence that (in the long run) it is recommendable to create a common identity. Joint projects with cross-organizational project teams are a real opportunity to bring people together and to create a common identity. The joint development of products, for example, can be useful to generate identification with the common 'baby'.

Parties and celebrations have the capacity to bring people together. They offer people the opportunity to socialize and to get to know each other from another perspective in a more relaxed atmosphere. Social events enjoyed with the members of the partner organization are therefore a supportive initiative in building a common identity.

11.4.4 Key Factor Esteem

It might sound simple, but the key factor for successful people management in the post-merger integration process seems to be appreciation. The common ground of most of the suggestions mentioned in this work is respect and the acknowledgment of the individual employee as a valuable person. Everybody seems to need recognition and to feel important and precious. It is interesting that all interviewees who reported their scepticism about the M&A or their resistance to it claimed that their ideas were not heard, that they were not involved, that they did not get as much information as co-workers, that superiors did not tell them the whole truth or that managers did not care about their concerns and sorrows. If this was the situation in the pre-merger organization, they were looking forward to great opportunities through the M&A. If they experienced adequate appreciation in the newly merged organization, they felt motivated again, highly committed, and they perceived the partner organization and the merger as very successful. If this perceived lack of esteem appeared in the post-merger organization, these members coped with their negative emotions by looking for alternative jobs in other organizations and by spreading negative rumours about their own (post-merger) company.

Managers are therefore advised to be aware of this need and to respect employees and their emotions. This implies the following determinations:

- not to leave employees in suspense, but to communicate honestly, openly and continuously what is going on,
- to demonstrate to employees that they are crucial to success,
- to involve people,
- to take time to explain the sense of the decisions and to prepare employees to confront the new challenges (training can help to accelerate the change process and to avoid long periods of painful experience),
- to give orientation to people by creating pictures of a common identity in their minds,
- to be consistent in communication and in behaviour,
- not to behave arrogantly but to listen to and respect others' opinions and ways of doing things,
- not to raise unrealistic hopes among employees, but to straightforwardly tell the truth,
- to educate employees regarding personal responsibilities,
- to fix the general framework, but to let people act with personal responsibility,
- to employ in-house trainers who help to develop communication, team working, conflict management and other skills,
- to plan the merger well in advance, allowing for immediate implementations and rapid small successes.

11.4.5 Leader Personality

The interviews have shown that the personality of the leader has a huge impact on employees' emotions. Superiors who are aware of themselves and their emotions, who are sensitive to people and their emotions, and who know how to react, are called emotionally intelligent leaders.

It was not the purpose of this work to study and measure emotional intelligence, but, interestingly, the findings point in this direction. The interviews imply that managers who communicate and behave according to the 'guidelines' in emotional intelligence literature are more successful in terms of the dimensions chosen in this project.

To the knowledge of the authors, the connection between emotionally intelligent leadership and M&A success has not explicitly been studied yet. However several authors have described leader qualities and behaviour required for successful M&A integration (for example, Cartwright and Cooper, 2000; Haspeslagh and Jemison, 1991; Marks and Mirvis, 2001; Picot, 2002). Picot (2002), for example, recommends that leaders aim at giving strategic orientation and establish a general framework. Developing and discussing a common vision within the 'crash barriers' by involving people creates personal and emotional identification and trust (Goleman *et al.*, 2002b; Haspeslagh and Jemison, 1991; Picot, 2002). The creation of internal and external information and communication processes allows informing employees in time, consistently and openly, about changes. This creates transparency and thus a sense of integrity and trustworthiness (Goleman *et al.*, 2002a; Marks and Mirvis, 1992). The call for guaranteeing current and future business activities during a merger or an acquisition in order not to irritate and lose clients (Picot, 2002) corresponds to the emotional intelligence competence 'service orientation'. The harmonization and union of the existing organizational cultures in order to create a commonly acceptable organizational culture require the managerial ability to create bonds, to communicate, to cooperate and to build teams.

Literature about change management often refers to transformative leadership (Ashkanasy and Tse, 2000; Channer and Hope, 2001; Covin *et al.*, 1997; Humphrey, 2002; Mossholder *et al.*, 2000). The characteristics and behaviour of transformative leaders are very similar to the leader qualities described by the emotional intelligence literature. Since mergers and acquisitions are big organizational changes, transformative leaders – with emotional intelligence competencies – are required. The logical consequence is that emotional intelligence matters for M&A success.

M&As necessarily involve unpleasant decisions. However our findings revealed that employees' reaction mainly depends on the way bad news is communicated and how individuals are treated by the management. Purely 'logical' and 'rational' communication of the motives for merging is not always sufficiently convincing for employees. Avoidance or attempts to reduce the intensity of emotions does not help. Management needs to accept that emotions play a critical role in M&As. Managers have to develop an awareness of their own emotions and learn to cope with employees' emotions. This will help to turn post-merger integration processes into a successful and relatively positive experience for all those affected.

Bibliography

Abraham, Rebecca (1999), 'Emotional Intelligence in Organizations: A Conceptualization', *Genetic Social and General Psychology Monographs*, 125 (2), 209–24.

Abrams, Dominic and Michael Hogg (1990), *Social Identity Theory: Constructive and Critical Advances*, London: Harvester Wheatsheaf.

AK-Wien (2000), 'Beiträge zur Wirtschaftspolitik Nr. 6', in Wien: Arbeiterkammer Wien.

Alessandri, Sue Westcott (2001), 'Modeling Corporate Identity: A Concept Explication and Theoretical Explanation', *Corporate Communications*, 6 (4), 173–82.

Allport, Gordon W. (1954), *The Nature of Prejudice*, Cambridge: Addison-Wesley.

Alvesson, Mats (2000), 'Social Identity and the Problem of Loyalty in Knowledge-Intensive Companies', *The Journal of Management Studies*, 37 (8), 1101–23.

Anastasio, P., B. Bachmann, S. Gaertner, and J. Dovidio (1997), 'Categorization, Recategorization and Common Intergroup Identity', in Russell Spears (Ed.), *The Social Psychology of Stereotyping and Group Life*, Oxford: Blackwell, pp. 236–56.

Andersen, Peter A. and Laura K. Guerrero (1998), 'Handbook of Communication and Emotion: Research, Theory, Applications, and Contexts', *Reference Reviews Incorporating ASLIB Book Guide*, 12 (3), 6.

Antonacopoulou, Elena P. and Yiannis Gabriel (2001), 'Emotion, Learning and Organizational Change: Towards an Integration of Psychoanalytic and Other Perspectives', *Journal of Organizational Change Management*, 14 (5), 435–51.

Appelbaum, Steven H., Joy Gandell, Barbara Shapiro, Pierre Belisle, and Eugene Hoeven (2000a), 'Anatomy of a Merger: Behavior of Organizational Factors and Processes throughout the Pre- During- Post-Stages (part 2)', *Management Decision*, 38 (10), 674–84.

Appelbaum, Steven H., Joy Gandell, Harry Yortis, Shay Proper, and Francois Jobin (2000b), 'Anatomy of a Merger: Behavior of Organizational Factors and Processes throughout the Pre- During- Post-Stages (part 1)', *Management Decision*, 38 (9), 649–62.

Ashforth, Blake E. and Ronald H. Humphrey (1995), 'Emotion in the Workplace: A Reappraisal', *Human Relations*, 48 (2), 97–125.

Ashforth, Blake E. and Fred A. Mael (1996), 'Organizational Identity and Strategy as a Context for the Individual', *Advances in Strategic Management*, 13, 17–62.

Ashkanasy, Neal M. and B. Tse (2000), 'Transformational Leadership as Management of Emotions: A Conceptual View', in Neal M. Ashkanasy, Charmine E.J. Härtel, and Wilfred J. Zerbe (Eds), *Emotions in the Workplace: Research, Theory, and Practice*, Westport: Quorum Books, pp. 221–35.

Ashkanasy, Neal M., Charmine E.J. Härtel, and Wilfred J. Zerbe (Eds) (2000), *Emotions in the Workplace: Research, Theory, and Practice*, Westport: Quorum Books.

Ashkanasy, Neal M., Wilfred J. Zerbe, and Charmine E.J. Härtel (Eds) (2002), *Managing Emotions in the Workplace*, New York: M.E. Sharp.

Averill, James R. (1980), 'A Constructivist View of Emotion', in Robert Plutchik and Henry Kellerman (Eds), *Emotion: Theory, Research and Experience*, New York: Academic Press, pp. 134–99.

Averill, James R. (1982), *Anger and Aggression: An Essay on Emotion*, New York: Springer-Verlag.

Averill, James R. (1986), 'The Acquisition of Emotions during Adulthood', in Rom Harré (Ed.), *The Social Construction of Emotions*, New York: Basil Blackwell, pp. 98–119.

Axtell, Carolyn, Toby Wall, Chris Stride, Kathryn Pepper, Chris Clegg, Peter Gardner, and Richard Bolden (2002), 'Familiarity Breeds Content: The Impact of Exposure to Change on Employee Openness and Well-Being', *Journal of Occupational & Organizational Psychology*, 75 (2), 217–31.

Bagozzi, Richard P., Mahesh Gopinath, and Prashanth U. Nyer (1999), 'The Role of Emotions in Marketing', *Journal of the Academy of Marketing Science*, 27 (2), 184–206.

Bar-On, Reuven and James D.A. Parker (2000), *The Handbook of Emotional Intelligence: Theory, Development, Assessment, and Application at Home, School and in the Workplace*, San Francisco: Jossey-Bass/Wiley.

Bartel, Caroline A. and Richard Saavedra (2000), 'The Collective Construction of Work Group Moods', *Administrative Science Quarterly*, 45 (2), 197–231.

Baruch, Yehuda and Sally Woodward (1998), 'Stressful Situations? The Case of Management Buyout/Buyins', *Management Decision*, 36 (10), 641–8.

Bettencourt, B.A., Marilynn B. Brewer, M.R. Croak, and Norman Miller (1992), 'Cooperation and the Reduction of Intergroup Bias: The Role of

Reward Structure and Social Orientation', *Journal of Experimental Social Psychology*, 28, 301–19.

Bettencourt, B.A., K. Charlton, and C. Kernahan (1997), 'Numerical Representation of Groups in Cooperative Settings: Social Orientation Effects on Ingroup Bias', *Journal of Experimental Social Psychology*, 33, 630–59.

Bijlsma-Frankema, Katinka (2001), 'On Managing Cultural Integration and Cultural Change Processes in Mergers and Acquisitions', *Journal of European Industrial Training*, 25 (2/3/4), 192–207.

Birch, William J. (1983), 'A Human Resources Perspective on Mergers', *Personnel Journal*, 62 (3), 244–6.

Bourantas, Dimitris and Irene I. Nicandrou (1998), 'Modelling Post-Acquisition Employee Behavior: Typology and Determining Factors', *Employee Relations*, 20 (1), 73.

Brewer, Marilynn B. (1999), 'The Psychology of Prejudice: Ingroup Love or Outgroup Hate?', *Journal of Social Issues*, 55, 429–44.

Brewer, Marilynn B. and Norman Miller (1984), 'Beyond the Contact Hypothesis: Theoretical Perspectives on Desegregation', in Norman Miller and Marilynn B. Brewer (Eds), *Groups in Contact: The Psychology of Desegregation*, Orlando: Academic Press.

Brief, Arthur P. (1998), *Attitudes in and around Organizations*, Thousand Oaks, CA: Sage Publications.

Brief, Arthur P. and Loriann Roberson (1989), 'Job Attitude Organization: An Exploratory Study', *Journal of Applied Social Psychology*, 19, 717–27.

British Institute of Management (1986), 'The Management of Acquisitions and Mergers', Discussion Paper No. 8, Economics Department.

Brooks, Ian and Jillian Dawes (1999), 'Merger as a Trigger for Cultural Change in the Retail Financial Services Sector', *The Service Industries Journal*, 19 (1), 194–206.

Brown, Rupert (1984), 'The Effect of Intergroup Similarity and Co-operative vs. Competitive Orientation on Intergroup Discrimination', *British Journal of Social Psychology*, 23, 21–33.

Brown, Rupert (2000), 'Social Identity Theory: Past Achievements, Current Problems and Future Challenges', *European Journal of Social Psychology*, 30, 745–78.

Brown, Rupert and Dominic Abrams (1986), 'The Effects of Intergroup Similarity and Goal Interdependence on Intergroup Attitudes and Task Performance', *Journal of Experimental Social Psychology*, 22, 78–92.

Brown, Rupert and Gillian Wade (1987), 'Superordinate Goals and Intergroup Behaviour: The Effect of Role Ambiguity and Status on

Intergroup Attitudes and Task Performance', *European Journal of Social Psychology*, 17, 131–42.

Bruckman, John C. and Scott C. Peters (1987), 'Mergers and Acquisitions: The Human Equation', *Employment Relations Today*, 14 (1), 55–63.

Buck, Ross, Erika Anderson, Arjun Chaudhuri, and Ipshita Ray (2004), 'Emotion and Reason in Persuasion: Applying the ARI Model and the CASC Scale', *Journal of Business Research*, 57 (6), 647–56.

Buckley, Peter J. and Pervez N. Ghauri (Eds) (2002), *International Mergers & Acquisitions*, London: International Thomson Business Press.

Buono, Anthony F. and James L. Bowditch (1989), *The Human Side of Mergers and Acquisitions: Managing Collisions between People, Cultures, and Organizations*, 1st edn, San Francisco: Jossey-Bass Publishers.

Buono, Anthony F., James L. Bowditch, and John W. Lewis, III (1985), 'When Cultures Collide: The Anatomy of a Merger', *Human Relations*, 38 (5), 477–500.

Buono, Anthony F., James L. Bowditch, and John W. Lewis, III (2002), 'When Cultures Collide: The Anatomy of a Merger', in Peter J. Buckley and Pervez N. Ghauri (Eds), *International Mergers & Acquisitions*, London: International Thomson Business Press, pp. 307–24.

Burkitt, Ian (1997), 'Social Relationships and Emotions', *Sociology*, 31 (1), 37–57.

Byrne, Donn (1971), *The Attraction Paradigm*, New York: Academic Press.

Cacioppo, John T. and W.L. Gradner (1999), 'Emotion', *Annual Review of Psychology*, 50, 191–214.

Callahan, Jamie L. and Eric E. McCollum (2002), 'Conceptualizations of Emotion Research in Organizational Contexts', *Advances in Developing Human Resources*, 4 (1), 4–21.

Campbell Quick, James, Joanne H. Gavin, Cary L. Cooper, Jonathan D. Quick, and Robert E. Gilbert (2000), 'Executive Health: Building Strength, Managing Risks', Executive Commentary, *The Academy of Management Executive*, 14 (2), 34–46.

Carr, Adrian (2001), 'Understanding Emotion and Emotionality in a Process of Change', *Journal of Organizational Change Management*, 14 (5), 421–34.

Cartwright, Sue and Cary L. Cooper (1990), 'The Impact of Mergers and Acquisitions on People at Work: Existing Research and Issues', *British Journal of Management*, 1, 65–76.

Cartwright, Sue and Cary L. Cooper (1992), *Mergers and Acquisitions: The Human Factor*, Oxford: Butterworth Heinemann.

Cartwright, Sue and Cary L. Cooper (1993a), 'The Psychological Impact of Merger and Acquisition on the Individual: A Study of Building Society Managers', *Human Relations*, 46 (3), 327.

Cartwright, Sue and Cary L. Cooper (1993b), 'The Role of Culture Compatibility in Successful Organizational Marriage', *The Academy of Management Executive*, 7 (2), 57.

Cartwright, Sue and Cary L. Cooper (1994), 'The Human Effects of Mergers and Acquisitions', *Journal of Organizational Behavior*, 1 (Trends in Organizational Behavior), 47–61.

Cartwright, Sue and Cary L. Cooper (1995), 'Organizational Marriage: "Hard" versus "Soft" Issues?', *Personnel Review*, 24 (3), 32–42.

Cartwright, Sue and Cary L. Cooper (1996), *Managing Mergers, Acquisitions and Strategic Alliances: Integrating People and Cultures*, Oxford: Butterworth Heinemann.

Cartwright, Sue and Cary L. Cooper (2000), *HR Know-How in Mergers and Acquisitions*, London: Institute of Personnel and Development.

Caspi, Avshalom (1984), 'Contact Hypothesis and Inter-Age Attitudes: A Field Study of Cross-Age Contact', *Social Psychology Quarterly*, 47, 74–80.

Channer, Philip and Tina Hope (2001), *Emotional Impact: Passionate Leaders and Corporate Transformation*, New York: Palgrave.

Cherniss, Cary and Daniel Goleman (2001), *The Emotionally Intelligent Workplace: How to Select for, Measure, and Improve Emotional Intelligence in Individuals, Groups, and Organizations*, 1st edn, San Francisco: Jossey-Bass.

Ciompi, Luc (1999), *Die emotionalen Grundlagen des Denkens: Entwurf einer fraktalen Affektlogik,* 2nd edn, Göttingen: Vandenhoeck & Ruprecht.

Clark, Arthur J. (1995), 'Projective Techniques in the Counselling Process', *Journal of Counselling and Development*, 73 (3), 311.

Collier, Mary Jane (1994), 'Cultural Identity and Intercultural Communication', in Larry A. Samovar and Richard E. Porter (Eds), *Intercultural Communication: A Reader*, 7th edn, Belmont, CA: Wadsworth, pp. 36–45.

Cooper, Cary L. and Sue Cartwright (1994), 'Healthy Mind; Healthy Organization – A Proactive Approach to Occupational Stress', *Human Relations*, 47 (4), 455.

Cooper, Cary L. and Sue Cartwright (1996), *Managing Mergers, Acquisitions and Strategic Alliances: Integrating People and Cultures*, Oxford: Butterworth Heinemann.

Cooper, Cary L. and Sydney Finkelstein (2004), *Advances in Mergers and Acquisitions*, London & New York: Elsevier JAI.

Cooper, Cary L. and Alan Gregory (2003), *Advances in Mergers and Acquisitions*, London & New York: JAI Press.

Cooper, Robert K. (1997), 'Applying Emotional Intelligence in the Workplace', *Training & Development*, 51 (12), 31–8.

Cornelius, Randolph R. (1996), *The Science of Emotion: Research and Tradition in the Psychology of Emotions*, Upper Saddle River, NJ: Prentice Hall.

Covin, Teresa Joyce, Thomas A. Kolenko, Kevin W. Sightler, and R. Keith Tudor (1997), 'Leadership Style and Post-Merger Satisfaction', *The Journal of Management Development*, 16 (1), 22–33.

Covin, Teresa Joyce, Kevin W. Sightler, Thomas A. Kolenko, and R. Keith Tudor (1996), 'An Investigation of Post-Acquisition Satisfaction with the Merger', *The Journal of Applied Behavioral Science*, 32 (2), 125.

Crain, Robert L. and Rita E. Mahard (1982), 'The Consequences of Controversy Accompanying Institutional Change: The Case of School Desegration', *American Sociological Review*, 47, 697–708.

Dahler-Larsen, Peter (1997), 'Organizational Identity as a Crowded Category: A Case of Multiple and Quickly Shifting "We" Typifications', in Sonja Sackmann (Ed.), *Cultural Complexity in Organizations: Inherent Contrasts and Contradictions*, Thousand Oaks, CA: Sage Publications.

Damasio, Antonio R. (1994), *Descartes's Error: Emotion, Reason, and the Human Brain*, New York: Avon Books.

Dannemiller Tyson, Associates (2000), *Whole-Scale Change: Unleashing the Magic in Organizations*, San Francisco, CA: Berrett-Koehler.

Darwin, Charles (1872), *The Expression of the Emotions in Man and Animals*, London: J. Murray.

Dasborough, Marie T. and Neal M. Ashkanasy (2002), 'Emotion and Attribution of Intentionality in Leader-Member Relationships', *The Leadership Quarterly*, 13 (5), 615–34.

Datta, Deepak K. and G. Puia (1995), 'Cross-Border Acquisitions: An Examination of the Influence of Relatedness and Cultural Fit on Shareholder Value Creation in U.S. Acquiring Firms', *Management International Review*, 35 (4), 337–59.

Davy, Jeanette A., Angelo Kinicki, Christine Scheck, and John Kilroy (1989), 'Acquisitions Make Employees Worry', *Personnel Administrator*, 34 (8), 84–90.

Dawson, Geraldine (1994), 'Frontal Electroencephalographic Correlates of Individual Differences in Emotion Expression in Infants: A Brain Systems Perspective on Emotion', *Monographs of the Society for Research in Child Development*, 59 (2–3), 135–51, 250–83.

De Sousa, Ronald (1987), *The Rationality of Emotion*, Cambridge: MIT Press.

Denzin, Norman K. (1978), *The Research Act: A Theoretical Introduction to Sociological Methods*, 2nd edn, New York: McGraw-Hill.

Denzin, Norman K. and Yvonna S. Lincoln (1994a), 'Entering Qualitative Research', in Norman K. Denzin and Yvonna S. Lincoln (Eds), *Handbook of Qualitative Research*, Thousand Oaks, CA: Sage Publications, pp. 1–17.

Denzin, Norman K. and Yvonna S. Lincoln (Eds) (1994b), *Handbook of Qualitative Research*, Thousand Oaks, CA: Sage Publications.

Desforges, D.M., C.G. Lord, and M.A. Pugh (1997), 'Role of Group Representativeness in the Generalization Part of the Contact Hypothesis', *Basic and Applied Psychology*, 19, 183–204.

Desforges, D.M., C.G. Lord, S.L. Ramsey, J.A. Mason, M.D. Van Leeuwen, S.C. West, and M.R. Lepper (1991), 'Effects of Structured Cooperative Contact on Changing Negative Attitudes towards Stigmatized Social Groups', *Journal of Personality and Social Psychology*, 60, 531–44.

Deshpande, Rohit, John U. Farley, and Frederick E. Webster (1993), 'Corporate Culture, Customer Orientation, and Innovativeness', *Journal of Marketing*, 57 (1), 23.

Dickmann, Michael (2002), 'Mergers & Acquisitions: Wogen der Emotionen glätten – eine HR Aufgabe', *Personalführung*, 6, 124–30.

Diehl, M. (1988), 'Social Identity and Minimal Groups: The Effects of Interpersonal and Intergroup Attitudinal Similarity on Intergroup Discrimination', *British Journal of Management*, 27, 289–300.

Diener, Ed, Eunkook M. Suh, Richard E. Lucas, and Heidi L. Smith (1999), 'Subjective Well-Being: Three Decades of Progress', *Psychological Bulletin*, 125 (2), 276–302.

Dimberg, Ulf (1988), 'Facial Electromyography and the Experience of Emotion', *Journal of Psychophysiology*, 2 (4), 277–82.

Dixon, Diane and Mitchell Lee Marks (1999), 'Making Mergers, Acquisitions & Alliances Work', *Health Forum Journal*, 42 (6), 30–33.

Doherty, R. William (1998), 'Emotional Contagion and Social Judgment', *Motivation & Emotion*, 22 (3), 187–209.

Doosje, Bertjan, Nyla R. Branscombe, Russell Spears, and Antony S.R. Manstead (1998), 'Guilty by Association: When One's Group Has a Negative History', *Journal of Personality and Social Psychology*, 75 (4), 872–86.

Doosje, Bertjan, Russell Spears, and Naomi Ellemers (2002), 'Social Identity as Both Cause and Effect: The Development of Group Identification in Response to Anticipated and Actual Changes in the Intergroup Status Hierarchy', *British Journal of Social Psychology*, 41 (1), 57–76.

Dovidio, John F. and Samuel L. Gaertner (1986), 'Prejudice, Discrimination, and Racism: Historical Trends and Contemporary Approaches', in John F. Dovidio and Samuel L. Gaertner (Eds), *Prejudice, Discrimination, and Racism*, Orlando: Academic Press, pp. 1–34.

Dovidio, John F., Samuel L. Gaertner, A. Validzic, K. Matoka, B. Johnson, and S. Frazier (1997), 'Extending the Benefits of Recategorizations: Evaluations, Self-Disclosure, and Helping', *Journal of Experimental Social Psychology*, 33, 401–20.

Edvardsson, Bo and Inger Roos (2001), 'Critical Incident Techniques: Towards a Framework for Analysing the Criticality of Critical Incidents', *International Journal of Service Industry Management*, 12 (3/4), 251–68.

Edvardsson, Bo and Tore Strandvik (2000), 'Is a Critical Incident Critical for a Customer Relationship?', *Managing Service Quality*, 10 (2), 82–91.

Ekman, Paul (1982), *Emotion in the Human Face*, Cambridge: Cambridge University Press.

Ekman, Paul (1984), 'Expression and Nature of Emotion', in Klaus Rainer Scherer and Paul Ekman (Eds), *Approaches to Emotion*, Hillsdale, NJ: L. Erlbaum Associates, pp. 319–43.

Ekman, Paul and Wallace V. Friesen (1971), 'Constants across Cultures in the Face and Emotion', *Journal of Personality and Social Psychology*, 17 (2), 124–9.

Ekman, Paul and Wallace V. Friesen (1975), *Unmasking the Face: A Guide to Recognizing Emotions from Facial Clues*, Englewood Cliffs, NJ: Prentice-Hall.

Ellemers, Naomi, Russell Spears, and Bertjan Doosje (2002), 'Self and Social Identity', *Annual Review of Psychology*, 53, 161–86.

Ellsworth, Phoebe C. and Craig A. Smith (1988), 'From Appraisal to Emotion: Differences among Unpleasant Feelings', *Motivation & Emotion*, 12 (3), 271–302.

Elster, Jon (1999), *Alchemies of the Mind: Rationality and the Emotions*, Cambridge: Cambridge University Press.

Empson, Laura (2000), 'Merging Professional Service Firms', *Business Strategy Review*, 11 (2), 39–46.

Empson, Laura (2001), 'Fear of Exploitation and Fear of Contamination: Impediments to Knowledge Transfer in Mergers between Professional Service Firms', *Human Relations*, 54 (7), 839–62.

Fairburn, James and Paul A. Geroski (1989), 'The Empirical Analysis of Market Structure and Performance', in James Fairburn and John A. Kay (Eds), *Mergers and Merger Policy*, New York: Oxford University Press.

Festinger, Leon (1954), 'A Theory of Social Comparison Processes', *Human Relations*, 7, 117–40.

Fetterman, David M. (1998), 'Ethnography', in Leonard Bickman and

Debra J. Rog (Eds), *Handbook of Applied Social Research Methods*, Thousand Oaks, CA: Sage Publications, pp. 473–504.

Fiedler, Klaus and Herbert Bless (2000), 'The Formation of Beliefs at the Interface of Affective and Cognitive Processes', in Nico H. Frijda, Antony S.R. Manstead, and Sacha Bem (Eds), *Emotions and Beliefs: How Feelings Influence Thoughts*, Paris: Editions de la Maison des Sciences de l'Homme, pp. 144–70.

Fineman, Stephen (1999), 'Emotion and Organizing', in Stewart Clegg, Cynthia Hardy, and Walter R. Nord (Eds), *Studying Organizations*, London: Sage Publications.

Fineman, Stephen (2000), *Emotion in Organizations*, London: Sage 2000.

Fishbein, Martin and Icek Ajzen (1975), *Belief, Attitude, Intention, and Behavior: An Introduction to Theory and Research*, Reading, MA, London: Addison-Wesley.

Fisher, Anne B. (1994), 'How to Make a Merger Work', *Fortune*, 129 (2), 66.

Fisher, Vardis E. and Joseph V. Hanna (1931), *The Dissatisfied Worker*, New York: Macmillan.

Fiske, Susan T., Jun Xu, Amy C. Cuddy, and Peter Glick (1999), '(Dis)respecting versus (Dis)liking: Status and Interdependence Predict Ambivalent Stereotypes of Competence and Warmth', *Journal of Social Issues*, 55 (3), 473–89.

Fotinatos-Ventouratos, Ritsa and Cary L. Cooper (1998), 'Social Class Differences and Occupational Stress', *International Journal of Stress Management*, 5 (4), 211–22.

Fox, Shaul, Yair Amichai-Hamburger, and Edward A. Evans (2001), 'The Power of Emotional Appeals in Promoting Organizational Change Programs', *The Academy of Management Executive*, 15 (4), 84–95.

Fram, Eugene H. and Elaine Cibotti (1991), 'The Shopping List Studies and Projective Techniques: A 40-Year View', *Marketing Research*, 3 (4), 14.

Franks, David D. (1994), 'The Etymology of Emotion', in Catherine G. Valentine and Steve Derné (Eds), *Sociology of Emotions*, Washington: American Sociological Association, pp. 38–41.

Freud, Sigmund (2001), 'Introductory Lectures on Psycho-Analysis', in James Strachey (Ed.), *The Standard Edition of the Complete Psychological Works of Sigmund Freud,* Vol, 15–16, London: Vintage.

Frijda, Nico H. (1986), *The Emotions*, Cambridge: Cambridge University Press.

Frijda, Nico H. (1993), *Appraisal and Beyond: The Issue of Cognitive Determinants of Emotion*, Hove, Sussex, UK: Lawrence Erlbaum Associates.

Frijda, Nico H., Antony S.R. Manstead, and Sacha Bem (2000), *Emotions and Beliefs: How Feelings Influence Thoughts*, New York: Cambridge University Press.

Fugate, Mel, Angelo J. Kinicki, and Christine L. Scheck (2002), 'Coping with an Organizational Merger over Four Stages', *Personnel Psychology*, 55 (4), 905–28.

Gabler-Verlag (Ed.) (1993), *Gabler Wirtschaftslexikon*, Wiesbaden: Gabler-Verlag.

Gaertner, Samuel L., John F. Dovidio, and Betty A. Bachman (1996), 'Revisiting the Contact Hypothesis: The Induction of a Common Ingroup Identity', *International Journal of Intercultural Relations*, 20 (3–4), 271–90.

Gaertner, Samuel L., J.A. Mann, A.J. Murrell, and John F. Dovidio (1989), 'Reducing Intergroup Bias: The Benefits of Recategorization', *Journal of Personality and Social Psychology*, 57, 239–49.

Gaertner, Samuel L., J.A. Mann, John F. Dovidio, A.J. Murrell, and M. Pomare (1990), 'How Does Cooperation Reduce Intergroup Bias?', *Journal of Personality and Social Psychology*, 59, 692–704.

Gaertner, Samuel L., John F. Dovidio, Jason A. Nier, Brenda S. Banker, Christine M. Ward, Melissa Houlette, and Stephenie Loux (2000), 'The Common Ingroup Identity Model for Reducing Intergroup Bias: Progress and Challenges', in Dora Capozza and Rupert Brown (Eds), *Social Identity Processes: Trends in Theory and Research*, London: Sage Publications, pp. 133–48.

Gardham, Karen and Rupert Brown (2001), 'Two Forms of Intergroup Discrimination with Positive and Negative Outcomes: Explaining the Positive-Negative Asymmetry Effect', *British Journal of Social Psychology*, 40 (1), 23–34.

George, Jennifer M. (1990), 'Personality, Affect, and Behavior in Groups', *Journal of Applied Psychology*, 75 (2), 107–16.

Gerpott, Torsten J. (1993), *Integrationsgestaltung und Erfolg von Unternehmensakquisitionen*, Stuttgart: Schäffer-Poeschel.

Gertsen, Martine Cardel and Anne-Marie Søderberg (1998), 'Foreign Acquisitions in Denmark: Cultural and Communicative Dimensions', in Anne-Marie Søderberg, Martine C. Gertsen, and Jens Erik Torp (Eds), *Cultural Dimensions of International Mergers and Acquisitions*, Berlin/New York: Walter de Gruyter.

Geuens, Maggie and Patrick De Pelsmacker (1999), 'Affect Intensity Revisited: Individual Differences and the Communication Effects of Emotional Stimuli', *Psychology & Marketing*, 16 (3), 195–209.

Goleman, Daniel (1995), *Emotional Intelligence*, New York: Bantam Books.

Goleman, Daniel (1998a), 'What Makes a Leader?', *Harvard Business Review*, 76 (6), 92–102.

Goleman, Daniel (1998b), *Working with Emotional Intelligence*, New York: Bantam Books.

Goleman, Daniel, Richard E. Boyatzis, and Annie McKee (2002a), *The New Leaders: Transforming the Art of Leadership into the Science of Results*, London: Little, Brown.

Goleman, Daniel, Richard E. Boyatzis, and Annie McKee (2002b), *Primal Leadership: Realizing the Power of Emotional Intelligence*, Boston: Harvard Business School Press.

Greenland, Katy and Rupert Brown (2000), 'Categorization and Intergroup Anxiety in Intergroup Contact', in Dora Capozza and Rupert Brown (Eds), *Social Identity Processes: Trends in Theory and Research*, London: Sage Publications, pp. 167–83.

Grier, Sonya A. and Rohit Deshpande (2001), 'Social Dimensions of Consumer Distinctiveness: The Influence of Social Status on Group Identity and Advertising Persuasion', *Journal of Marketing Research*, 38 (2), 216–24.

Grossman, Michele and Wendy Wood (1993), 'Sex Differences in Intensity of Emotional Experience: A Social Role Interpretation', *Journal of Personality and Social Psychology*, 65 (5), 1010–22.

Gutknecht, John E. and J. Bernard Keys (1993), 'Mergers, Acquisitions and Takeovers: Maintaining Morale of Survivors and Protecting Employees', *The Academy of Management Executive*, 7 (3), 26.

Hall, Peter D. and David Norburn (1987), 'The Management Factor in Acquisition Performance', *Leadership & Organization Development Journal*, 8 (3), 23–30.

Halpern, Paul and J. Fred Weston (1983), 'Corporate Acquisitions: A Theory of Special Cases? A Review of Event Studies Applied to Acquisitions/Discussion', *The Journal of Finance*, 38 (2), 297–317.

Harlos, Karen P. and Craig C. Pinder (2000), 'Emotion and Injustice in the Workplace', in Stephen Fineman (Ed.), *Emotion in Organizations*, London: Sage, pp. 255–76.

Harris, Thomas A. (1995), *I'm OK - You're OK*, London: Arrow Books.

Harrison, Roger (1972), 'How to Describe your Organization', *Harvard Business Review*, 5 (1), 119–28.

Haslam, S. Alexander (2001), *Psychology in Organizations: The Social Identity Approach*, London: Sage.

Haspeslagh, Philippe C. and David B. Jemison (1991), *Managing Acquisitions: Creating Value through Corporate Renewal*, New York: Free Press.

Hazlett, Richard L. and Sasha Yassky Hazlett (1999), 'Emotional Response to Television Commercials: Facial EMG vs. Self Report', *Journal of Advertising Research*, 39 (2), 7–23.

Hernes, Helge (1997), 'Cross-Cultural Identifications in Organizations', in Sonja Sackmann (Ed.), *Cultural Complexity in Organizations: Inherent Contrasts and Contradictions*, Thousand Oaks, CA: Sage Publications, pp. 343–66.

Herriot, Peter (2001), 'Future Work and its Emotional Implications', in Roy Payne and Cary L. Cooper (Eds), *Emotions at Work: Theory, Research and Applications in Management*, New York: Wiley, pp 307–25.

Hersey, Rexford Brammer (1932), *Workers' Emotions in Shop and Home: A Study of Individual Workers from the Psychological and Physiological Standpoint*, Philadelphia: University of Pennsylvania Press.

Herzberg, Frederick, Bernard Mausner, and Barbara Snyderman (1959), *The Motivation to Work*, 2nd edn, New York: Wiley.

Hewstone, Miles and Rupert Brown (1986), *Contact and Conflict in Intergroup Encounters*, Oxford: Basil Blackwell.

Hinkle, Steve and Rupert Brown (1990), 'Intergroup Comparison and Social Identity: Some Links and Lacunae', in Dominic Abrams and Michael Hogg (Eds), *Social Identity Theory: Constructive and Critical Advances*, London: Harvester Wheatsheaf, pp. 48–70.

Hochschild, Arlie Russell (1983), *The Managed Heart: Commercialization of Human Feeling*, trans. Ernst Kardorff, Berkeley: University of California Press.

Hofstede, Geert (1980), 'Culture and Organizations', *International Studies of Management & Organization*, 10 (4), 15–42.

Hogg, Michael and Dominic Abrams (1988), *Social Identifications: A Social Psychology of Intergroup Relations and Group Processes*, London: Routledge.

Hogg, Michael A. and Deborah J. Terry (2003), 'Social Identity and Self-Categorization Processes in Organizational Contexts', *Academy of Management Review*, 25 (1), 121–40.

Hogg, Michael, Deborah J. Terry, and K.M. White (1995), 'A Tale of Two Theories: A Critical Comparison of Identity Theory with Social Identity Theory', *Social Psychology Quarterly*, 58 (4), 255–60.

Holbrook, Morris B. and Meryl P. Gardner (2000), 'Illustrating a Dynamic Model of the Mood-Updating Process in Consumer Behavior', *Psychology & Marketing*, 17 (3), 165–94.

Hollander, Sharon L. (1988), 'Projective Techniques Uncover Real Consumer Attitudes', *Marketing News*, 22 (1), 34.

Hörnig, Bodo (1985), *Beteiligungs- und Fusionsvorhaben: Eine entscheidungs- und investitionstheoretische Untersuchung*, Berlin: Duncker & Humbolt.

House, Robert J. and Lawrence A. Wigdor (1967), 'Herzberg's Dual-Factor Theory of Job Satisfaction and Motivation: A Review of the Evidence and a Criticism', *Personnel Psychology*, 20 (4), 369–89.

Howard, Nigel (1993), 'The Role of the Emotions in Multi-Organizational Decision-Making', *The Journal of the Operational Research Society*, 44 (6), 613.

Hubbard, Nancy and John Purcell (2001), 'Managing Employee Expectations during Acquisitions', *Human Resource Management Journal*, 11 (2), 17–33.

Hughes, Jeffrey P. and William F. Wolff (1987), 'Financing Mergers and Acquisitions', *The Bankers Magazine*, 170 (2), 7.

Humber, Todd (2002), 'Emotional Intelligence', *Canadian HR Reporter*, 15 (16), G1–G2.

Humphrey, Ronald H. (2002), 'The Many Faces of Emotional Leadership', *The Leadership Quarterly*, 13 (5), 493–504.

Hunt, J.W. (1988), 'Managing the Successful Acquisition: A People Question', *London Business School Journal*, 2–15.

Hussey, Michael and Nicola Duncombe (1999), 'Projecting the Right Image: Using Projective Techniques to Measure Brand Image', *Qualitative Market Research*, 2 (1), 22–30.

Huy, Quy Nguyen (1999), 'Emotional Capability, Emotional Intelligence, and Radical Change', *Academy of Management Review*, 24 (2), 325–45.

Huy, Quy Nguyen (2002), 'Emotional Balancing of Organizational Continuity and Radical Change: The Contribution of Middle Managers', *Administrative Science Quarterly*, 47 (1), 31–69.

Irrmann, Olivier (2002), 'Organizational Culture and Identity Strategies in International Management: An Interdisciplinary Review,' Competitive Paper, 28th EIBA Conference, Athens, 8–10 December.

Isen, Alice M. and Reuven Bar-On (1991), 'Positive Affect as a Factor in Organizational Behaviour', in Barry M. Staw and Larry L. Cummings (Eds), *Research Organizational Behavior*, Greenwich, CT: JAI Press.

Ivancevich, John M., David M. Schweiger, and Frank R. Power (1987), 'Strategies for Managing Human Resources During Mergers and Acquisitions', *Human Resource Planning*, 10 (1), 19–35.

Izard, Carroll E. (1971), *The Face of Emotion*, New York: Appleton-Century-Crofts.

Izard, Carroll E. (1977), *Human Emotions*, New York: Plenum Press.

Izard, Carroll E. (1990), 'Facial Expressions and the Regulation of Emotions', *Journal of Personality and Social Psychology*, 58 (3), 487–98.

James, William (1890), 'What is an Emotion?', *Mind*, 9, 188–205.

James, William and Carl Georg Lange (1922), *The Emotions*, Baltimore: Williams & Wilkins Company.

Jansen, S.A. (2001), *Mergers & Acquisitions, Unternehmensakquisitionen und - kooperationen*, 4th edn, Wiesbaden: Gabler.

Jansen, S.A. and K. Körner (2000), 'Szenen einiger Unternehmens-Ehen: Vier Hochzeiten und drei Todesfälle', *Frankfurter Allgemeine Zeitung,* 8 November, 49.

Jansen, S.A. and N. Pohlmann (2000), 'Anforderungen und Zumutungen: Das HR Management bei Fusionen', *Personalführung,* 2, 30–39.

Jemison, David B. and Sim B. Sitkin (1986), 'Corporate Acquisitions: A Process Perspective', *Academy of Management Review,* 11 (1), 145.

Johnson, Lesley (2002), 'Using the Critical Incident Technique to Assess Gaming Customer Satisfaction', *UNLV Gaming Research & Review Journal,* 6 (2), 1–12.

Johnston, Lucy and Miles Hewstone (1990), 'Intergroup Contact: Social Identity and Social Cognition', in Dominic Abrams and Michael Hogg (Eds), *Social Identity Theory: Constructive and Critical Advances,* London: Harvester Wheatsheaf, pp. 185–210.

Judge, Timothy A. and Randy J. Larsen (2001), 'Dispositional Affect and Job Satisfaction: A Review and Theoretical Extension', *Organizational Behavior and Human Decision Processes,* 86 (1), 67–98.

Judge, Timothy A., Edwin A. Locke, Cathy C. Durham, and Avraham N. Kluger (1998), 'Dispositional Effects on Job and Life Satisfaction: The Role of Core Evaluations', *Journal of Applied Psychology,* 83 (1), 17–34.

Katzell, Raymond A. (1964), 'Personal Values, Job Satisfaction and Job Behavior', in Henry Borow (Ed.), *Man in a World at Work,* Boston: Houghton Mifflin, pp. xvii, 606.

Kelly, Janice R. and Sigal G. Barsade (2001), 'Mood and Emotions in Small Groups and Work Teams', *Organizational Behavior and Human Decision Processes,* 86 (1), 99–130.

Kiefer, Tina (2002a), 'Analysing Emotions for a Better Understanding of Organizational Change: Fear, Joy and Anger during a Merger', in Neal M. Ashkanasy, Wilfred J. Zerbe, and Charmine E.J. Härtel (Eds), *Managing Emotions in the Workplace,* Armonk, NY: M.E. Sharpe, pp. 45–69.

Kiefer, Tina (2002b), 'Understanding the Emotional Experience of Organizational Change: Evidence from a Merger', *Advances in Developing Human Resources,* 4 (1), 39–61.

Kiefer, Tina and Sabine Eicken (1999), 'Das Erleben der UBS-Fusion. Warum das Ereignis mehr als nur Angst ausgelöst hat', *Psychoscope,* 7 (20), 9–12.

Kiefer, Tina and Sabine Eicken (2002), 'Das emotionale Erleben einer Großfusion: Eine explorative Studie', *Wirtschaftspsychologie,* 9 (3), 27–32.

King, Nathan (1970), 'Clarification and Evaluation of the Two-Factor Theory of Job Satisfaction', *Psychological Bulletin,* 74 (1), 18–31.

Kirkcaldy, B.D. and Cary L. Cooper (1992), 'Cross-cultural Differences in Occupational Stress among British and German Managers', *Work & Stress*, 6 (2), 177–90.

Kleppestø, S. (1998), 'A Quest of Social Identity – The Pragmatics of Communication in Mergers and Acquisitions', in Anne-Marie Søderberg, Cardel Gertsen Martine, and Erik Torp Jens (Eds), *Cultural Dimensions of International Mergers and Acquisitions*, Berlin: Walter de Gruyter, pp. 145–66.

Kluger, Avraham N. and Anat Rafaeli (2000), 'Affective Reactions to Physical Appearance', in Neal M. Ashkanasy, Charmine E.J. Härtel, and Wilfred J. Zerbe (Eds), *Emotions in the Workplace: Research, Theory, and Practice*, Westport: Quorum Books, pp. 141–55.

Krackhardt, David and Jeffrey R. Hanson (1993), 'Informal Networks: The Company Behind the Chart', *Harvard Business Review*, 71 (4), 104–11.

Kramer, R.M. (1991), 'Intergroup Relations and Organizational Dilemmas: The Role of Categorization Processes', *Research in Organizational Behaviour*, 13, 191–228.

Kraut, Robert E. and Robert E. Johnson (1979), 'Social and Emotional Messages of Smiling: An Ethological Approach', *Journal of Personality and Social Psychology*, 37, 1539–53.

Krell, Gertraude and Richard Weiskopf (2001), 'Leidenschaften in Organisationsproblem', in Georg Schreyögg and Jörg Sydow (Eds), *Emotionen und Management*, Wiesbaden: Gabler, pp. 1–46.

Kunin, Theodore (1955), 'The Construction of a New Type of Attitude Measure', *Personnel Psychology*, 8, 65–78.

Langer, Ellen J., Richard S. Bashner, and Benzion Chanowitz (1985), 'Decreasing Prejudice by Increasing Discrimination', *Journal of Personality and Social Psychology*, 49 (1), 113–20.

Latack, Janina C. and Stephen J. Havlovic (1992), 'Coping with Job Stress: A Conceptual Evaluation Framework for Coping Measures', *Journal of Organizational Behavior*, 13 (5), 479–508.

Lazarus, Richard S. (1991), *Emotion and Adaptation*, New York: Oxford University Press.

Lazarus, Richard S. (1995), 'Emotions Express a Social Relationship, But It Is an Individual Mind That Creates Them', *Psychological Inquiry*, 6 (3), 253–65.

Lazarus, Richard S. and Yochi Cohen-Charash (2001), 'Discrete Emotions in Organizational Life', in Roy Payne and Cary L. Cooper (Eds), *Emotions at Work: Theory, Research and Applications in Management*, New York: Wiley, pp. 46–81.

Lazarus, Richard S., James R. Averill, and Edward M. Opton (1970),

'Toward a Cognitive Theory of Emotions', in Magda B. Arnold (Ed.), *Feelings and Emotions*, New York: Academic Press, pp. 207–32.

LeDoux, Joseph E. (1996), *The Emotional Brain: The Mysterious Underpinnings of Emotional Life*, New York: Simon & Schuster.

LeDoux, Joseph E. (1998), *Das Netz der Gefühle: Wie Emotionen entstehen*, London: Weidenfeld & Nicolson.

Levenson, Robert W., Paul Ekman, Karl Heider, and Wallace V. Friesen (1992), 'Emotion and Autonomic Nervous System Activity in the Minangkabau of West Sumatra', *Journal of Personality and Social Psychology*, 62 (6), 972–88.

Leventhal, Howard (1984), 'A Perceptual Motor Theory of Emotion', in Klaus Rainer Scherer and Paul Ekman (Eds), *Approaches to Emotion*, Hillsdale, NJ: L. Erlbaum Associates, pp. 271–91.

Lewis, Kristi M. (2000), 'When Leaders Display Emotion: How Followers Respond to Negative Emotional Expression of Male and Female Leaders', *Journal of Organizational Behavior*, 21 (2), 221–34.

Leyens, Jacques-Philippe, Paola M. Paladino, Ramon Rodriguez-Torres, Jeroen Vaes, Stephanie Demoulin, Armando Rodriguez-Perez, and Ruth Gaunt (2000), 'The Emotional Side of Prejudice: The Attribution of Secondary Emotions to Ingroups and Outgroups', *Personality and Social Psychology Review*, 4 (2), 186–97.

Lindsley, Dana H., Daniel J. Brass, and James B. Thomas (1995), 'Efficacy-Performance Spirals: A Multilevel Perspective', *Academy of Management Review*, 20 (3), 645–78.

Locke, Edwin A. (1969), 'What is Job Satisfaction?', *Organizational Behavior and Human Decision Processes*, 4 (4), 309–36.

Lofquist, Lloyd H. and Renâe V. Dawis (1969), *Adjustment to Work: A Psychological View of Man's Problems in a Work-Oriented Society*, New York: Appleton-Century-Crofts Educational Division.

Luomala, Harri T. and Martti Laaksonen (2000), 'Contributions from Mood Research', *Psychology & Marketing*, 17 (3), 195–233.

Mackie, Diane, Thierry Devos, and Eliot R. Smith (2000), 'Intergroup Emotions: Explaining Offensive Action Tendencies in an Intergroup Context', *Journal of Personality and Social Psychology*, 79 (4), 602–16.

Mandler, George (1975), *Mind and Emotion*, New York: Wiley.

Mandler, George (1980), 'The Generation of Emotion: A Psychological Theory', in Robert Plutchik and Henry Kellerman (Eds), *Emotion: Theory Research and Experience*, New York: Academic Press.

Mandler, George (1984), *Mind and Body: Psychology of Emotion and Stress*, New York: Norton.

Marks, Mitchell Lee (1988), 'The Merger Syndrome: The Human Side of Corporate Combinations', *Journal of Buyouts & Acquisitions*, 18–23.

Marks, Mitchell Lee (1997), 'Consulting in Mergers and Acquisitions Interventions Spawned by Recent Trends', *Journal of Organizational Change Management*, 10 (3), 267–79.

Marks, Mitchell Lee (1999), 'Surviving a Merger', *Electric Perspectives*, 24 (6), 26–35.

Marks, Mitchell Lee and Philip H. Mirvis (1985), 'Merger Syndrome: Stress and Uncertainty (Part 1)', *Mergers and Acquisitions*, 20 (2), 50.

Marks, Mitchell Lee and Philip H. Mirvis (1992), 'Rebuilding After the Merger: Dealing with "Survivor Sickness"', *Organizational Dynamics*, 21 (2), 18.

Marks, Mitchell Lee and Philip H. Mirvis (1997a), 'Revisiting the Merger Syndrome: Crisis Management (Part 2)', *Mergers and Acquisitions*, 32 (1), 34–40.

Marks, Mitchell Lee and Philip H. Mirvis (1997b), 'Revisiting the Merger Syndrome: Dealing With Stress', *Mergers and Acquisitions*, 31 (6), 21–7.

Marks, Mitchell Lee and Philip H. Mirvis (2001), 'Making Mergers and Acquisitions Work: Strategic and Psychological Preparation', *The Academy of Management Executive*, 15 (2), 80–94.

Marks, Mitchell Lee and Philip Harold Mirvis (1986), 'The Merger Syndrome', *Psychology Today*, 20 (10), 36.

Marques, José M. (1990), 'The Black-Sheep Effect: Out-Group Homogeneity in Social Comparison Settings', in Dominic Abrams and Michael Hogg (Eds), *Social Identity Theory: Constructive and Critical Advances*, London: Harvester Wheatsheaf, pp. 131–51.

Martin, Albert (1998), *Affekt, Kommunikation und Rationalität in Entscheidungsprozessen: Ergebnisse einer Studie über den Einfluss von Gruppenstrukturen auf das Problemlösungsverhalten*, München: Rainer Hampp Verlag.

Martin, Patricia Y. and Barry A. Turner (1986), 'Grounded Theory and Organizational Research', *Journal of Applied Behavioral Science*, 22 (2), 141–57.

Maxwell, Joseph A. (1998), 'Designing a Qualitative Study', in Leonard Bickman and Debra J. Rog (Eds), *Handbook of Applied Social Research Methods*, Thousand Oaks, CA: Sage Publications, pp. 69–100.

Mayer, John D. and Peter Salovey (1993), 'The Intelligence of Emotional Intelligence', *Intelligence*, 17, 433–42.

McGuire, William J. (1984), 'Search for the Self: Going Beyond Self-Esteem and the Reactive Self', in Robert A. Zucker, A.I. Rabin, and Joel Aronoff (Eds), *Personality and the Prediction of Behaviour*, New York: Academic Press.

McKinsey & Associates (1988), Michael L. McManus and Michael Lee

Hergert (Eds), *Surviving Merger and Acquisition*, Glenview, IL.: Scott, Foresman & Co.

McTigue Bruner, Barbara and Cary L. Cooper (1991), 'Corporate Financial Performance and Occupational Stress', *Work & Stress*, 5 (4), 267–87.

Mead, M. (1975), 'Review of Darwin and Facial Expression', *Journal of Communication*, 25, 209–13.

Mergers&Acquisitions (2003), C.M. Picot Finance GbR; available at www.mergers-and-acquisitions.de.

Meschi, Pierre-Xavier (1997), 'Longevity and Cultural Differences of International Joint Ventures: Toward Time-Based Cultural Management', *Human Relations*, 50 (2), 211–28.

Meyer, Wulf-Uwe, Achim Schützwohl, and Rainer Reisenzein (1993), *Einführung in die Emotionspsychologie*, Bern: Verlag Hans Huber.

Miller, Norman, Marilynn B. Brewer, and K. Edwards (1985), 'Cooperative Interaction in Desegrated Settings: A Laboratory Analogue', *Journal of Social Issues*, 41, 63–79.

Moats Kennedy, Marilyn (1997), 'So How'm I Doing?', *Across the Board*, 34 (6), 53–4.

Morgan, Robert M. and Shelby D. Hunt (1994), 'The Commitment-Trust Theory of Relationship Marketing', *Journal of Marketing*, 58 (3), 20–38.

Morosini, Piero (1998), *Managing Cultural Differences: Effective Strategy and Execution across Cultures in Global Corporate Alliances*, 1st edn, Oxford: Pergamon.

Mossholder, Kevin W., Randall P. Settoon, Achilles A. Armenakis, and Stanley G. Harris (2000), 'Emotion during Organizational Transformations: An Interactive Model of Survivor Reactions', *Group & Organization Management*, 25 (3), 220–43.

Nahavandi, Afsaneh and Ali R. Malekzadeh (1988), 'Acculturation in Mergers and Acquisitions', *Academy of Management Review*, 13 (1), 79–90.

Nahavandi, Afsaneh and Ali R. Malekzadeh (1993), *Organizational Culture in the Management of Mergers*, Westport, CT: Quorum Books.

Napier, Nancy K. (1989), 'Mergers and Acquisitions, Human Resource Issues and Outcomes: A Review and Suggested Typology', *The Journal of Management Studies*, 26 (3), 271–87.

Nehme, Michel G. (1995), 'Identity and Fear: A Survey Study of the Arab East', *Studies in Comparative International Development*, 30 (4), 3.

Nelson, Adrian, Cary L. Cooper, and Paul R. Jackson (1995), 'Uncertainty amidst Change: The Impact of Privatization on Employee Job Satisfaction and Well-Being', *Journal of Occupational and Organizational Psychology*, 68 (1), 57–71.

Nesdale, Drew and Debbie Flesser (2001), 'Social Identity and the Development of Children's Group Attitudes', *Child Development*, 72 (2), 506–17.

Nippa, Michael (2001), 'Intuition und Emotion in der Entscheidungsfindung', in Georg Schreyögg and Jörg Sydow (Eds), *Emotionen und Management*, Wiesbaden: Gabler, pp. 213–48.

Oehlrich, Marcus (1999), *Strategische Analyse von Unternehmensakquisitionen: Das Beispiel der Pharmazeutischen Industrie*, Wiesbaden: Deutscher Universitätsverlag.

Öhman, Arne (1986), 'Face the Beast and Fear the Face: Animal and Social Fears as Prototypes for Evolutionary Analyses of Emotion', *Psychophysiology*, 23 (2), 123–45.

Olie, René (1990), 'Culture and Integration Problems in International Mergers and Acquisitions', *European Management Journal*, 8 (2), 206–15.

Ortmann, Günther (2001), 'Emotion und Entscheidung', in Georg Schreyögg and Jörg Sydow (Eds), *Emotionen und Management*, Wiesbaden: Gabler, pp. 277–312.

Ortony, Andrew, Gerald L. Clore, and Allan Collins (1988), *The Cognitive Structure of Emotions*, Cambridge: Cambridge University Press.

Ostroff, Cheri (1992), 'The Relationship between Satisfaction, Attitudes, and Performance: An Organizational Level Analysis', *Journal of Applied Psychology*, 77 (6), 963–74.

Parkinson, Brian (1996), *Changing Moods: The Psychology of Mood and Mood Regulation*, London: Longman.

Parkinson, Brian (1997), 'Untangling the Appraisal-Emotion Connection', *Personality and Social Psychology Review*, 1 (1), 62–79.

Parrott, W. Gerrod and Rom Harré (1996), 'Some Complexities in the Study of Emotions', in Rom Harré and W. Gerrod Parrott (Eds), *The Emotions: Social, Cultural and Biological Dimensions*, London: Sage Publications.

Paterson, Janice M. and Jane Cary (2002), 'Organizational Justice, Change Anxiety, and Acceptance of Downsizing: Preliminary Tests of an AET-Based Model', *Motivation & Emotion*, 26 (1), 83–103.

Payne, Roy (2001), 'Measuring Emotions at Work', in Roy Payne and Cary L. Cooper (Eds), *Emotions at Work: Theory, Research and Applications in Management*, New York: Wiley, pp. 107–29.

Penfield, W. (1952), 'Memory Mechanisms', *American Medical Association*, 67, 178–98.

Pescosolido, Anthony T. (2002), 'Emergent Leaders as Managers of Group Emotion', *The Leadership Quarterly*, 13 (5), 583–99.

Pettigrew, Andrew M. (1979), 'On Studying Organizational Cultures', *Administrative Science Quarterly*, 24 (4), 570.

Picot, Gerhard (2002), *Handbook of International Mergers and Acquisitions: Preparation, Implementation, and Integration*, Houndmills: Palgrave/ Macmillan.

Piirto, Rebecca (1990), 'Measuring Minds in the 1990s', *American Demographics*, 12 (12), 30.

Pilegge, Anthony J. and Rolf Holtz (1997), 'The Effects of Social Identity on the Self-Set Goals and Task Performance of High and Low Self-Esteem Individuals', *Organizational Behavior & Human Decision Processes*, 70 (1), 17–26.

Pinder, Craig C. (1998), *Work Motivation in Organizational Behavior*, Upper Saddle River, NJ: Prentice Hall.

Piontkowski, Ursula, Arnd Florack, Paul Hoelker, and Peter Obdrzalek (2000), 'Predicting Acculturation Attitudes of Dominant and Non-Dominant Groups', *International Journal of Intercultural Relations*, 24 (1), 1–26.

Planes, Virginia Carrero, Daniel Pinazo Calatayud, and Miguel Angel Gimeno (2002), 'Identifying the Manager Role and its Influence on Managers' Self-Perceived Performance', *Psicothema*, 14 (2), 191–8.

Plutchik, Robert (1980), *Emotion: A Psychoevolutionary Synthesis*, New York: Harper & Row.

Plutchik, Robert (1984), 'Emotion: A General Psychoevolutionary Theory', in Klaus Rainer Scherer and Paul Ekman (Eds), *Approaches to Emotion*, Hillsdale, NJ: L. Erlbaum Associates, pp. 197–219.

Porter, L.W. (1961), 'A Study of Perceived Need Satisfactions in Bottom and Middle Management Jobs', *Journal of Applied Psychology*, 45, 1–10.

Probst, Tahira M. (2002), 'The Impact of Job Insecurity on Employee Work Attitudes, Job Adaptation, and Organizational Withdrawal Behaviors', in Jeanne M. Brett and Fritz Drasgow (Eds), *The Psychology of Work: Theoretically based Empirical Research*, Mahwah, NJ: Lawrence Erlbaum Associates, pp. 141–68.

Probst, Tahira M. (2003), 'Exploring Employee Outcomes of Organizational Restructuring: A Solomon Four-Group Study', *Group & Organization Management*, 28 (3), 416–39.

Rafaeli, Anat (1996), 'What is an Organisation? Who are the Members?' in Cary L. Cooper and Susan E. Jackson (Eds), *Creating Tomorrow's Organizations: A Handbook for Future Research in Organizational Behavior*, New York: John Wiley & Sons, pp. 121–39.

Rafaeli, Anat and Monica C. Worline (2001), 'Individual Emotion in Work Organizations', *Social Science Information*, 40 (1), 95–125.

Reisenzein, Rainer, Wulf-Uwe Meyer, and Achim Schützwohl (2003), *Kognitive Emotionstheorien*, Bern: Huber.

Rhoades, Stephen A. (1983), *Power, Empire Building, and Mergers*, Lexington: Lexington Books.

Richards, Lyn (1999), *Using NVivo in Qualitative Research*, London: Sage Publications.

Risberg, Anette (1997), 'Ambiguity and Communication in Cross-Cultural Acquisitions: Towards a Conceptual Framework', *Leadership & Organization Development Journal*, 18 (5), 257–66.

Rockness, Joanne W., Howard O. Rockness, and Susan H. Ivancevich (2001), 'The M&A Game Changes', *Financial Executive*, 17 (7), 22–5.

Rokeach, Milton, P.W. Smith, and R.I. Evans (1960), 'Two Kinds of Prejudice or One?' in Milton Rokeach (Ed.), *The Open and Closed Mind: Investigations into the Nature of Belief Systems and Personality Systems*, New York: Basic Books Inc.

Rolls, E.T. (1990), 'A Theory of Emotion, and its Application to Understanding the Neural Basis of Emotion', *Cognition and Emotion*, 4, 161–90.

Roos, Inger (2002), 'Methods of Investigating Critical Incidents: A Comparative Review', *Journal of Service Research*, 4 (3), 193–204.

Roseman, Ira J. (1984), 'Cognitive Determinants of Emotion: A Structural Theory', *Review of Personality and Social Psychology*, 5, 11–36.

Rozin, Paul and Edward B. Royzman (2001), 'Negativity Bias, Negativity Dominance, and Contagion', *Personality and Social Psychology Review*, 5 (4), 296–320.

Russell, James A. (1989), 'Measures of Emotion', in Robert Plutchik and Henry Kellerman (Eds), *Emotion: Theory, Research, and Experience*, Vol. 4, San Diego: Academic Press, pp. 83–111.

Ryan, Ann Marie, Mark J. Schmit, and Raymond Johnson (1996), 'Attitudes and Effectiveness: Examining Relations at an Organizational Level', *Personnel Psychology*, 49 (4), 853–82.

Sackmann, Sonja A. (1992), 'Culture and Subcultures: An Analysis of Organizational Knowledge', *Administrative Science Quarterly*, 37 (1), 140–61.

Salk, Jane E. and Oded Shenkar (2001), 'Social Identities in an International Joint Venture: An Exploratory Case Study', *Organization Science*, 12 (2), 161–78.

Salovey, Peter and John D. Mayer (1990), 'Emotional Intelligence', *Imagination, Cognition and Personality*, 9 (3), 185–211.

Schachter, Stanley (1964), 'Interaction of Cognitive and Physiological Determinants of Emotional States', in L. Berkovitz (Ed.), *Advances in Experimental Social Psychology*, Vol. 1, New York: Academic Press, pp. 49–80.

Schachter, Stanley and Jerome Singer (1962), 'Cognitive, Social, and

Physiological Determinants of Emotional State', *Psychological Review*, 69 (5), 379–99.

Schaudwet, C., K. Greene, and M. Dunkel (2002), 'Integration: Kontrolliertes Schwitzen', *Wirtschaftswoche*.

Schein, Edgar H. (1983), 'The Role of the Founder in Creating Organizational Culture', *Organizational Dynamics*, 12 (1), 13.

Schein, Edgar H. (1985), *Organizational Culture and Leadership*, 1st edn, San Francisco: Jossey-Bass.

Scherer, Klaus R. (1988), *Facets of Emotion: Recent Research*, Hillsdale: Erlbaum.

Scherer, Klaus R. (1993), 'Studying the Emotion-Antecedent Appraisal Process: An Expert System Approach', *Cognition and Emotion*, 7 (3–4), 325–55.

Scherer, Klaus R. and Harald G. Wallbott (1994), 'Evidence for Universality and Cultural Variation of Differential Emotion Response Patterning', *Journal of Personality and Social Psychology*, 66 (2), 310–28.

Schlieper-Damrich, Ralph (2000), 'Integration verlangt Führung – Thesen zur Merger-Fähigkeit', *Personalführung*, 2, 40–46.

Schmader, Toni (2002), 'Gender Identification Moderates Stereotype Threat Effects on Women's Math Performance', *Journal of Experimental Social Psychology*, 38 (2), 194–201.

Schuler, Randall and Susan Jackson (2001), 'HR Issues and Activities in Mergers and Acquisitions', *European Management Journal*, 19 (3), 239–53.

Searby, Frederick W. (1969), 'Control of Post-Merger Change', *Harvard Business Review*, 47 (5), 4–13.

Seneca, Lucius Annaeus (reprinted 1981), *De Ira*, Pisa: Giardini.

Shaver, Phillip, Judith Schwartz, Donald Kirson, and Cary O'Conner (1987), 'Emotion Knowledge: Further Exploration of a Prototype Approach', *Journal of Personality & Social Psychology*, 52 (6), 1061–86.

Sherif, Muzafer (1967), *Group Conflict and Co-operation: Their Social Psychology*, London: Routledge & Kegan Paul.

Shih, Margaret, Todd L. Pittinsky, and Nalini Ambady (1999), 'Stereotype Susceptibility: Identity Salience and Shifts in Quantitative Performance', *Psychological Science*, 10 (1), 80–83.

Sinetar, Marsha (1981), 'Mergers, Morale and Productivity', *Personnel Journal*, 60 (11), 863–7.

Sinkovics, Rudolf R., Elfriede Penz, and Pervez N. Ghauri (2005), 'Analysing Textual Data in International Marketing Research', *Qualitative Market Research – An International Journal*, 8 (1), (accepted for publication).

Siu, Oi-Ling, Cary L. Cooper, and Ian Donald (1997), 'Occupational

Stress, Job Satisfaction and Mental Health among Employees of an Acquired TV Company in Hong Kong', *Stress Medicine*, 13 (2), 99–107.

Smith, Craig A. (1989), 'Dimensions of Appraisal and Psychological Response in Emotion', *Journal of Personality & Social Psychology*, 56 (3), 339–53.

Smith, Craig A. and Phoebe C. Ellsworth (1985), 'Patterns of Cognitive Appraisal in Emotion', *Journal of Personality & Social Psychology*, 48 (4), 813–38.

Smith, Craig A. and Phoebe C. Ellsworth (1987), 'Patterns of Appraisal and Emotion Related to Taking an Exam', *Journal of Personality & Social Psychology*, 52 (3), 475–88.

Smith, Craig A. and Richard S. Lazarus (1993), 'Appraisal Components, Core Relational Themes, and the Emotions', *Cognition and Emotion*, 7 (3–4), 233–69.

Smith, Eliot R. (1993), 'Social Identity and Social Emotions: Towards New Conceptualizations of Prejudice', in Diane Mackie and David L. Hamilton (Eds), *Affect, Cognition, and Stereotyping: Interactive Processes in Group Perception*, San Diego: Academic Press, pp. 297–315.

Smith, Eliot R., Julie Murphy, and Susan Coats (1999), 'Attachment to Groups: Theory and Measurement', *Journal of Personality and Social Psychology*, 77 (1), 94–110.

Smith, Patricia Cain, Lorne M. Kendall, and Charles L. Hulin (1969), *The Measurement of Satisfaction in Work and Retirement: A Strategy for the Study of Attitudes*, Chicago: Rand McNally.

Søderberg, Anne-Marie, Martine C. Gertsen, and Jens Erik Torp (Eds) (1998), *Cultural Dimensions of International Mergers and Acquisitions*, Berlin/New York: Walter de Gruyter.

Sparks, Kate, Cary L. Cooper, Yitzhak Fried, and Arie Shirom (1997), 'The Effects of Hours of Work on Health: A Meta-Analytic Review', *Journal of Occupational and Organizational Psychology*, 70 (4), 391–408.

Stanley, Robb O. and Graham Burrows (2001), 'Varieties and Functions of Human Emotion', in Roy Payne and Cary L. Cooper (Eds), *Emotions at Work: Theory, Research and Applications in Management*, New York: Wiley, pp. 3–19.

Stauss, Bernd and Paul Mang (1999), ' "Culture Shocks" in Inter-Cultural Service Encounters?', *The Journal of Services Marketing*, 13 (4/5), 329–46.

Staw, Barry M. and Jerry Ross (1985), 'Stability in the Midst of Change: A Dispositional Approach to Job Attitudes', *Journal of Applied Psychology*, 70 (3), 469–80.

Staw, Barry M., Nancy E. Bell, and John A. Clausen (1986), 'The Dispositional Approach to Job Attitudes: A Lifetime Longitudinal Test', *Administrative Science Quarterly*, 31 (1), 56–77.

Stephan, Walter G. and David Rosenfield (1978), 'Effects of Desegregation on Racial Attitudes', *Journal of Personality and Social Psychology*, 36 (8), 795–804.

Stephan, Walter G. and Cookie W. Stephan (1985), 'Intergroup Anxiety', *Journal of Social Issues*, 41 (3), 157–75.

Strauss, Anselm L. and Juliet M. Corbin (1990), *Basics of Qualitative Research: Grounded Theory Procedures and Techniques*, Newbury Park, CA: Sage Publications.

Strauss, Anselm L. and Juliet M. Corbin (1994), 'Grounded Theory Methodology', in Norman K. Denzin and Yvonna S. Lincoln (Eds), *Handbook of Qualitative Research*, Thousand Oaks, CA: Sage Publications, pp. 273–85.

Tajfel, Henri (1972), 'Experiments in a Vacuum', in Joachim Israel and Henri Tajfel (Eds), *The Context of Social Psychology: A Critical Assessment*, London: Academic Press.

Tajfel, Henri (1978a), 'Interindividual Behaviour and Intergroup Behaviour', in Henri Tajfel (Ed.), *Differentiation between Social Groups: Studies in the Social Psychology of Intergroup Relations*, London: Academic Press, pp. 27–60.

Tajfel, Henri (1978b), 'Social Categorization, Social Identity and Social Comparison', in Henri Tajfel (Ed.), *Differentiation Between Social Groups: Studies in the Social Psychology of Intergroup Relations*, London: Academic Press, pp. 61–76.

Tajfel, Henri (1982), *Social Identity and Intergroup Relations*, Cambridge: Cambridge University Press.

Tajfel, Henri and John C. Turner (1979), 'An Integrative Theory of Intergroup Conflict', in William G. Austin and Stephen Worchel (Eds), *The Social Psychology of Intergroup Relations*, Monterey, CA: Brooks/ Cole Pub. Co.

Tajfel, Henri and John C. Turner (1986), 'The Social Identity Theory of Intergroup Behaviour', in William G. Austin and Stephen Worchel (Eds), *Psychology of Intergroup Relations*, 2nd edn, Chicago: Nelson-Hall Publishers.

Tarrant, Mark, Adrian C. North, Mark D. Edridge, Laura E. Kirk, Elizabeth A. Smith, and Roisin E. Turner (2001), 'Social Identity in Adolescence', *Journal of Adolescence*, 24 (5), 597–609.

Tassinary, Louis G. and John T. Cacioppo (1992), 'Unobservable Facial Actions and Emotion', *Psychological Science*, 3 (1), 28–33.

Terry, Deborah, Victor J. Callan, and Geoffrey Sartori (1996), 'Employee Adjustment to an Organizational Merger: Stress, Coping and Intergroup Differences', *Stress Medicine*, 12 (2), 105–22.

Terry, Deborah J., Craig J. Carey, and Victor J. Callan (2001), 'Employee

Adjustment to an Organizational Merger: An Intergroup Perspective', *Personality and Social Psychological Bulletin*, 27 (3), 267–80.

ThomsonFinancial (2002), *Worldwide and US Announced Press Release - 4Q02*. Available:http://www.thomson.com/financial/investbank/fi_invest bank_league_tablearchiv e_mergers.jsp 20.7.2003].

ThomsonFinancial (2004), *Thomson Financial Worldwide M&A: Mergers Unleashed*. Available:http://www.thomson.com/cms/assets/pdfs/financial/ league_table/mergers_andacquisitions/1Q2004/press_releases/1Q04_ MA_PR_Worldwide_US_Finl_Adv.pdf15.09.2004].

Tomiuk, Marc Alexandre (2000), 'The Impact of Service Providers' Emotional Displays on Service Evaluation: Evidence of Emotional Contagion', Ph D Dissertation, Montrèal: Concordia University.

Tomkins, Silvan S. (1962), *Affect, Imagery, Consciousness*, New York: Springer.

Ulich, Dieter and Philipp Mayring (1992), *Psychologie der Emotionen*, Stuttgart: W. Kohlhammer.

UNCTAD (2000), *World Investment Report 2000*, New York and Geneva: UNCTAD.

Unger, H. (1986), 'The People Trauma of Major Mergers', *Journal of Industrial Management*, 10–17.

Urch Druskat, Vanessa and Steven B. Wolff (2001), 'Building the Emotional Intelligence of Groups', *Harvard Business Review*, 79 (3), 80–90.

Uttal, Bro and Jaclyn Fierman (1983), 'The Corporate Culture Vultures', *Fortune*, 108 (8), 66–72.

Vaara, Eero (2002), 'On the Discursive Construction of Success/Failure in Narratives of Post-Merger Integration', *Organization Studies*, 23 (2), 211–48.

Vaara, Eero (2003), 'Post-Acquisition Integration as Sensemaking: Glimpses of Ambiguity, Confusion, Hypocrisy, and Politicization', 40, 4, 859–94.

van Knippenberg, Daan (2000), 'Work Motivation and Performance: A Social Identity Perspective', *Applied Psychology: An International Review*, 49 (3), 357–71.

van Knippenberg, Daan, Barbara van Knippenberg, Laura Monden, and Fleur de Lima (2002), 'Organizational Identification after a Merger: A Social Identity Perspective', *British Journal of Social Psychology*, 41 (2), 233–52.

Van Oudenhoven, Jan Pieter, Jan Tjeerd Groenewoud, and Miles Hewstone (1996), 'Cooperation, Ethnic Salience and Generalization of Interethnic Attitudes', *European Journal of Social Psychology*, 26 (4), 649–61.

Vanman, Eric J. and Norman Miller (1993), 'Applications of Emotion Theory and Research to Stereotyping and Intergroup Relations', in Diane Mackie and David L. Hamilton (Eds), *Affect, Cognition, and*

Stereotyping: Interactive Processes in Group Perception, San Diego: Academic Press, pp. 213–38.

Verbeke, Willem (1997), 'Individual Differences in Emotional Contagion of Salespersons: Its Effect on Performance and Burnout', *Psychology & Marketing*, 14 (6), 617–36.

Vroom, Victor Harold (1964), *Work and Motivation*, New York: Wiley.

Walsh, James P. (1988), 'Top Management Turnover Following Mergers and Acquisitions', *Strategic Management Journal*, 9, 173–83.

Walter, Gordon A. (1985), 'Culture Collisions in Mergers and Acquisitions', in Peter J. Frost, Lary F. Moore, Meryl R. Louis, Craig C. Lundberg, and Joanne Martin (Eds), *Organizational Culture*, Beverly Hills, CA: Sage Publications, pp. 301–14.

Wann, Daniel L. and Nyla R. Branscombe (1995), 'Influence of Level of Identification with a Group and Physiological Arousal on Perceived Intergroup Complexity', *British Journal of Social Psychology*, 34 (3), 223–35.

Warr, Peter B. (1994), 'A Conceptual Framework for the Study of Work and Mental Health', *Work & Stress*, 8 (2), 84–97.

Wasserman, Varda, Anat Rafaeli, and Avraham N. Kluger (2000), 'Aesthetic Symbols as Emotional Cues', in Stephen Fineman (Ed.), *Emotion in Organizations*, London: Sage, pp. 140–66.

Weick, Karl E. (1995), *Sensemaking in Organizations*, Thousand Oaks, CA: Sage Publications.

Weick, Karl E. (2001), *Making Sense of the Organization*, Oxford: Blackwell Publishers.

Weiner, Bernard (1985), 'An Attributional Theory of Achievement, Motivation, and Emotion', *Psychological Review*, 92 (4), 548–73.

Weiss, Howard M. and Arthur P. Brief (2001), 'Affect at Work: A Historical Perspective', in Roy Payne and Cary L. Cooper (Eds), *Emotions at Work: Theory, Research and Applications in Management*, New York: Wiley, pp. 133–71.

Weiss, Howard M. and Russell Cropanzano (1996), 'Affective Events Theory: A Theoretical Discussion of the Structure, Causes and Consequences of Affective Experiences at Work', in Barry M. Staw and Larry L. Cummings (Eds), *Research in Organizational Behavior: An Annual Series of Analytical Essays and Critical Reviews*, Greenwich, CT: JAI Press.

Weiss, Howard M., Jeffrey P. Nicholas, and Catherine S. Daus (1999), 'An Examination of the Joint Effects of Affective Experiences and Job Beliefs on Job Satisfaction and Variations in Affective Experiences over Time', *Organizational Behavior and Human Decision Processes*, 78 (1), 1–24.

Wenger, M.A., F.N. Jones, and M.H. Jones (1962), 'Emotional Behaviour', in Douglas K. Candland (Ed.), *Emotion: Bodily Change, an Enduring Problem in Psychology*, Princeton, NJ: Van Nostrand, p. 263.

Werner, M. (1999), 'Post-Merger-Integration – Problemfelder und Lösungsansätze', *zfo*, 6, 332–7.

Widerszal-Bazyl, Maria, Cary L. Cooper, Kate Sparks, and Paul E. Spector (2000), 'Managerial Stress in Private and State Organisations in Poland', *Stress Medicine*, 16 (5), 299–314.

Wilder, David A. (1978), 'Reduction of Intergroup Discrimination through Individuation of the Outgroup', *Journal of Personality and Social Psychology*, 36, 1361–74.

Wilder, David A. (1984), 'Intergroup Contact: The Typical Member and the Exception to the Rule', *Journal of Experimental Social Psychology*, 20, 177–94.

Wilder, David A. and P.N. Shapiro (1989), 'Role of Competition Induced Anxiety in Limiting the Beneficial Impact of Positive Behaviour by an Outgroup Member', *Journal of Personality and Social Psychology*, 56 (1), 60–69.

Williams, Simon J. (2001), *Emotion and Social Theory: Corporeal Reflections on the (Ir)rational*, London: Sage Publications.

Witt, S. (1998), *Unternehmenserwerb und Mikropolitik*, Hamburg: Steuer- und Wirtschaftsverlag.

Wolff, Steven B., Anthony T. Pescosolido, and Vanessa Urch Druskat (2002), 'Emotional Intelligence as the Basis of Leadership Emergence in Self-Managing Teams', *The Leadership Quarterly*, 13 (5), 505–22.

Wong, Chi-Sum and Kenneth S. Law (2002), 'The Effects of Leader and Follower Emotional Intelligence on Performance and Attitude: An Exploratory Study', *Leadership Quarterly*, 13 (3), 243–74.

Yin, Robert K. (1998), 'The Abridged Version of Case Study Research: Design and Method', in Leonard Bickman and Debra J. Rog (Eds), *Handbook of Applied Social Research Methods*, Thousand Oaks, CA: Sage Publications, pp. 229–60.

Zanna, Mark P. and John K. Rempel (1988), 'Attitudes: A New Look at an Old Concept', in Daniel Bar-Tal and Arie W. Kruglanski (Eds), *The Social Psychology of Knowledge*, Cambridge: Cambridge University Press, pp. 315–34.

Index